KASHI SATSANGH

Invocation

Om Bhuur Bhuvah Svah
Tat Savitur Varennyam
Bhargo Devasya Dhimahi
Dhiyo Yo Nah Prachodayaat

OM - That Divine Illumination
Which Pervades the Bhu Loka - Physical Plane,
Consciousness of the Physical Plane
Bhuvar Loka- Antariksha or Intermediate Space
Consciousness of the Prana
Swar Loka – Swarga - Heaven
Consciousness of the Divine Mind
On that Savitur - Divine Illumination
Which is the Most Adorable - Varenyam
Which is of the nature of Divine Effulgence - Bhargo Devasya

I MEDITATE
May that Divine Intelligence – Dhiyah
Awaken- Pracodyat our Spiritual Consciousness.

~~~~~
~~~~~

KASHI SATSANGH

HINDU PRAYERS AND HYMNS

Guidance For Bhakti Yog
Spiritual Awakening
&

Sadhana

Pandit Nar Chowbey
Spiritual Leader – Vishwa Bhavan Mandir

MOTILAL BANARSIDASS PUBLISHERS
PRIVATE LIMITED • DELHI

First Edition : Delhi, 2019

ISBN : 978 81 208 4261 8

Also available at
MOTILAL BANARSIDASS
41 U.A. Bungalow Road, Jawahar Nagar, Delhi 110 007
1 B, Jyoti Studio Compound, Kennedy Bridge, Nana Chowk, Mumbai 400 007
203 Royapettah High Road, Mylapore, Chennai 600 004
236, 9th Main III Block, Jayanagar, Bengaluru 560 011
8 Camac Street, Kolkata 700 017
Ashok Rajpath, Patna 800 004
Chowk, Varanasi 221001

MLBD Cataloging-in-Publication Data
Kashi Satsangh: Hindu Prayers And Hymns
by PANDIT NAR CHOWBEY
ISBN : 978 81 208 4261 8
Includes Glossary, Bibliography and Index

Published by
Motilal Banarsidass Publishers Private Limited
www.mlbd.com • mlbd@mlbd.com
Printed by Imprint Books, New Delhi - 110085

Dedicated To My Parents

Mr & Mrs Heeralall & Violet Chowbey
Maatru Devo Bhava, Pitru Devo Bhava
Aachaarya Devo Bhava, Atithi Devo Bhava
Mother, Father, Guru and Guests
Are All Forms Of God
My Humble Respects To Them

Contents

OM SHANTI SHANTI SHANTI

PREFACE

Some of us are born with the intent to pursue our passion, while some of us are born with the intent on sacrificing so our children can pursue their passion. I was lucky enough to be one of those children who has never had to sacrifice. I have always been told I can do whatever I feel is right for me, whatever I feel is challenging or comfortable. I have always been able to take advantage of each opportunity that came my way from the help and support of my parents. They have always made sure I had everything I needed and more, all the while teaching me values and morals that will take me far in living an honest and fulfilling life. Our family dynamic has grown tremendously as Ravi and I have matured. Our family unit is a form of support, love and guidance and it is something to never be questioned, something that will always remain, no matter where we live, who enters our lives, or where our lives, opportunities, and sacrifices take us.

My father has been speaking about studying in India all my life. He has been speaking about studying music, writing a book, and experiencing the way of life there. This is a man who came to the United States with nothing, built a life for himself and his family, worked the the graveyard shifts in the beginning of his career around the time I was born, and continues to always do his part and more in philanthropic measures. Here he was going on and on about his dreams, while I am out here living mine because of him. There was no question in my mind that he needed to go. I am personally excited to have a book of his, featuring his interpretations of Sanatan

Dharma to keep forever, from a time in his life where he got to fulfil his lifelong dream.

I am so proud that my father was able to do this. I am so proud that our family is able to take part in all of these opportunities and I can only thank my parents, grand-parents, and ancestors for instilling in us a strong sense ofself and love for our family. My father has taught us throughout our whole life, from taking notes during presidential debates when we were 10 and being quizzed on them to writing essays on why we wanted to study abroad, but the one thing that has resonated within me is that throughout all of my family's accomplishments, my father always instilled in us the quote by Mahatma Gandhi, "Simple Living, High Thinking," and I think it was immensely symbolic that he gave up his life in his home to study his passion for Sanatan Dharma, while making sure his wife and children continued to enjoy the comfortable spoils of his success.

To my father, thank you for everything! I know your time in India was well worth it and I am so glad you were able to accomplish this in this lifetime. I cannot wait for you to come home!

With my deepest gratitude and love,

Nargis Chowbey

ACKNOWLEDGEMENTS

KASHI SATSANGH — Hindu Prayers and Hymns is a collection of Mantras, Stotrams, Chaalisas, Aartis and Bhajans. This collection was assembled during my studies in Kashi – India. My inspiration to do this came from many sources during my lifetime and also mostly inspired during my time in India.

There is no claim to originality in this work. The words and information within this book are all available in ancient and modern scriptural work. To all the authors, creators, known and unknown, I owe a deep debt of gratitude to all of them.

My hope is that this book will allow seekers, practitioners, followers and inquisitive minds to learn, practice, and sing the praises of God through any of the mediums listed. Mantras become a part of our minds, Stotrams sing the mighty praises of God, Aartis allow us to perform worship to God, Chaalisas reminds us of the many actions performed by God, and Bhajans allow us to rejoice and be connected with God.

Although this book has been reviewed and edited by many Hindu and Sankrit Scholars in Kashi, I am certain that you will find many mistakes within. For that, I beg your forgiveness in advance.

My biological and spiritual influence certainly came from my paternal grandfather – Pandit Daulat Ram Chowbey who was the first Dharma Aacharya of Guyana. His entire life was dedicated to Sanatan Dharma where he served Hindus in Guyana and in the Caribbean. Within his Gurukul in Golden Grove, he spent countless hours teaching Karma Khand to numerous young and upcoming Pandits and provided spiritual guidance to a host of Shishyas. It was always a pleasure to be in his company during Satsanghs, Kathas and Yagnas. He is someone that provided my spiritual inspiration, influence, and motivation for Satsangh. I am truly indebted to him, my Guru, my parents, and my ancestors.

My undying respect to the lotus-like feet of my parents, Heeralall and Violet Chowbey, whose unconditional love for me has allowed me to grow and succeed regardless of challenges and impediments. I feel their blessings in my life wherever my journey takes me and I will forever be grateful to them for the sacrifices they made to ensure my ultimate happiness. I owe a debt of gratitude to both of them.

My humble respects at the feet of my Guru – Pandit Reepu Daman Persaud. The founder and leader of the Guyana Hindu Dharmic Sabha. My humble respect at the feet of Pandit Arjun Doobay who spent considerable time with me from a very young age during my of my children. My humble respects at the feet of my brother, Pandit Shri Prakash Gossai, the founder of the Buvaneshwar Mandir NY, who shared much of his precious time with me during Satsanghs, Kathas and

Yagnas. I had the pleasure of sharing numerous spiritual and life experiences with him. The impact of my inspiration from him will always drive me to sing the praises and glorify God in all his majesty.

My Humble respects to Pandit Satrohan Sharma of Los Angeles, Pandit Rajin Balgobind – Founder of Shri Krishna Mandir – Guyana, Pandit Chunelall Narine – Founder of Shri Trimurti Bhavan – New York, Pundit Munelall Maharaj – Trinidad & Tobago, who have all influenced my spiritual journey in God Realisation and Love for All.

My love, thanks and appreciation for the support and encouragement from the devotees of the Beautiful Vishwa Bhavan Mandir- Atlanta Georgia and the Los Angeles Satsangh Group during my time there.

My Love to my Dharampatni Kumari Chowbey and my children, Nargis and Ravi Chowbey. Thanks for your support, encouragement and allowing me to spend this time in India away from all of you. I know it's a huge sacrifice for all of you to allow me to be gone for such a long time and for that I am very grateful.

My love and respect to all.

KASHI SATSANGH

Hindu Prayers And Hymns

Om Shree Ganeshaaya Namah
Om Shree Sarasawatyai Namah
Om Shree Guru Bhyo Namah

HAR HAR MAHADEV JAI JAI GANGE

PRAYERS

SADHANA

Sadhana is the practice of devotion or Bhakti Yog.
Mantras, Stotrams, Chaalisas, Aartis and Bhajans lead
Our spiritual practice to spiritual knowledge and
Ultimately purification of our heart and
Becoming one with God.

MANTRAS

Mantras are especially crafted incantations that hold
Immense power. They have boundless spiritual energy
That helps in concentrating on the almighty.

PURIFICATION

Om Apavitrah Pavitro Vaa
Sarva Avasthaam Gatopi Vaa
Yah Smaret Punnddarii Kaakssam
Sa Baahya bhyantarah Shucih

OM - If one is Apavitra - impure or Pavitra – pure or
Even in all other conditions He who remembers
Pundarikaksha - Another name of Sri Vishnu
Literally meaning with lotus-like eyes
He becomes pure outwardly as well as inwardly.

~~~~~
~~~~~

KASHI SATSANGH

Om, let my speech be established in my mind
Let my mind be established in my speech
Let the knowledge of the self - manifest
Atman grow in me
Let my mind and Speech be the support
To experience the knowledge of the Vedas,
Let what is heard by me from the
Vedas be not a mere appearance
What is gained by studying day and night be retained
I speak about the divine truth, I speak about the
Absolute truth, may that protect me,
May that protect the preceptor
May that protect the preceptor
Om Peace, Peace, Peace.

Om Bhuur Bhuvah Svah
Tat Savitur Varennyam
Bhargo Devasya Dhiimahi
Dhiyo Yo Nah Prachodayaat

OM - That divine Illumination which pervades
The Bhu Loka - physical plane,
Consciousness of the physical plane Bhuvar Loka -
Antariksha or intermediate space
Consciousness of the Prana
And Swar Loka – Swarga - Heaven
Consciousness of the divine mind
On that savitur - divine illumination
Which is the most adorable - varenyam
Which is of the nature of divine
Effulgence - Bhargo Devasya
I meditate
May that divine intelligence – Dhiyah
Awaken - Pracodyat our spiritual consciousness.

Karaagre Vasate Lakssmih
Karamadhye Sarasvati
Karamuule Tu Govindah
Prabhaate Karadarshanam

At the top of the hand - Palm, dwell Devi Lakshmi And
At the middle of the Hand dwell, Devi Saraswati
At the base of the Hand dwell, Sri Govinda.

Shaanta Aakaaram Bhujaga Shayanam
Padma-Naabham Suresham
Vishva Aadhaaram Gagana Sadrisham
Megha Varnam Shubhanggam
Lakshmi Kaantam Kamala Nayanam
Yogibhir Dhyaana-Gamyam
Vande Vishnum Bhava Bhaya Haranam
Sarva Lokaika Naatham

Salutations to Sri Vishnu, Who has a serene
Appearance
Who rests on a Serpent - Adisesha,
Who has a Lotus on his navel
Who is the Lord of the Devas
Who sustains the Universe, Who is boundless
Infinite like the Sky, Whose colour is like
The cloud- Bluish
Who has a beautiful and auspicious body
Who is the Husband of Devi Lakshmi,
Whose eyes are like Lotus, Who is attainable to the
Yogis by meditation salutations to that Vishnu Who
Removes the fear of worldly existence and
Who is the Lord of all the Lokas.

Twameva Maataa Cha Pitaa Twameva
Twameva Bandhush Cha Sakhaa Twameva
Twameva Vidhyaa Dravinnam Twameva
Twameva Sarvam Mama Deva Deva

You truly are my Mother and You truly are my Father
You truly are my Relative and You truly are my Friend
You truly are my Knowledge and
You truly are my wealth
You truly are my All, My God of Gods.

Om Prithvi Twayaa Dhritaa Lokaa

Devi Twam Vishnunaa Dhritaa
Twam Cha Dhaaraya Maam Devi
Pavitram Kuru Chaasanam

OM - O Prithivi Devi, by You are borne the entire Loka-World and Devi, You in turn are borne by Sri Vishnu Please hold me on Your lap, O Devi, and make this Asana - seat of the worshipper, pure.

Gurur Brahmaa Gurur Vishnu
Gururdevo Maheshvarah
Gurur Sakshat Param Brahma
Tasmai Shrii Gurave Namah

The Guru is Brahma, the Guru is Vishnu
The Guru deva is maheswara - Shiva
The Guru is Verily the Para - Brahman –
Supreme Brahman salutations to that Guru.

Om Asato Maa Sad Gamaya
Tamaso Maa Jyotir Gamaya
Mrityor Maa Amritam Gamaya
Om Shaantih Shaantih Shaantih

OM - O Lord keep me not in the unreality of the Bondage of the phenomenal world, but lead me Towards the reality of the eternal self.
O Lord Keep me not in the darkness of ignorance, but Lead me towards the light of spiritual knowledge
O Lord keep me not in the fear of death due to the Bondage of the mortal world, but lead me towards The immortality gained by the knowledge of the Immortal self beyond death.
OM - May there be Peace, Peace, Peace
At the three levels

Adidaivika, Adibhautika and Adhyatmika.

Om Bhadram Karnnebhih Shrinnuyaama Devaah
Bhadram Pashyema Akshabhir Yajatraah
Sthirair Anggais Tussttuvaa Gung Sastanuu Bhir
Vyashema Devahitam Yadayuhu

OM - O Devas, May we hear with our ears
What is auspicious
May we see with our eyes what is
Auspicious and Adorable
May we be prayerful in life with steadiness in
Our bodies and Minds
May we offer our lifespan allotted by the
Devas for the service of God.

Swasti Na Indro Vriddha Shravaaha
Swasti Naha Pushaa Vishva Vedaaha
Swasti Nas Taarkshyo Arishtta Nemihi
Svasti No Vrihaspatir Dadhaatu
Om Shaantih Shaantih Shaantih

May Indra of Vedas with great Wisdom and
Glory grant us well - being by bestowing wisdom
May pushan - The Sun God, The Nourisher of great
Knowledge grant us well - being by nourishing us and
Granting knowledge May Tarksya - A mythical
Bird of great protective power and
A thunderbolt to misfortunes, grant us well being by
Protecting us from misfortunes and May Brihaspati
The Guru of the Devas, grant us well being at the
Adibhautika, Adidaivika and Adhyatmika levels.
Om, Peace, Peace, Peace.

Vakratunda Mahakaya Suryakoti Samaprabha Nirvighnam
Kuru Me Deva Sarva Kaaryeshu Sarvada.

O God Ganesha, Radiant as millions of Suns
Please, remove obstacles in all of my tasks, always.

Gajaananam Bhuuta Ganaadi Sevitam
Kapittha Jambuuphala Chaaru Bhakshnam
Umaasutam Shoka VinaashakaaraNam
Namaami Vighneshwara Paadapankajam

I bow to Lord Ganesha who has an elephant head
Who is attended by the band of his followers
Who eats his favorite wood-apple and rose-apple Fruits
Who is the son of Goddess Uma – Parvati
Who is the cause of destruction of all sorrow
I salute to his feet which are like lotus.

Ya Devi Sarva Bhutesu Maatri Rupena Samsthita
Ya Devi Sarva Bhutesu Shakti Rupena Samsthita
Ya Devi Sarva Bhutesu Buddhi Rupena Samsthita
Ya Devi Sarva Bhutesu Laxmi Rupena Samsthita
Namastasyai Namastasyai Namastasyai Namo Namah

To the Divine Goddess who resides in all existence
In the form of Universal Mother
To the Divine Goddess who resides in all existence
In the form of Energy
To the Divine Goddess who resides in all existence
In the form of intellegence
To the Divine Goddess who resides in all existence
In the form of true wealth
We bow to her, we bow to her,
Continually we bow to her

~~~

~~~

KASTURITILAKAM

Kasturitilakam Lalaat Patale Vakshasthale Kaustubham
Nasagre Varmauktikam Kartale Venu Kare Kankanam
Sarvange Harichandanam Sulalitam Kanthe Cha Muktawali
Gopastri Pariveshtito Vijayate Gopala Chudamani

Salutations to Gopala Who is adorned with the
Sacred marks of Kasturi - Musk on His forehead
And Kaustubha jewel on His chest
His nose is decorated with a shining pearl
The palms of his hands are gently holding a Flute
The Hands themselves are beautifully decorated with
Bracelets His whole body is smeared with sandal paste
As if playfully anointed
His neck is decorated with a necklace of pearls
Surrounded by the cowherd Women
Gopala is shining in the middle in
Celebration like a jewel on the head

Om Sham No Mitrah
Sham Varunnah
Sham No Bhawatwaryamaa
Sham No Indro Brihaspatih
Sham No Vishnnur Urukramah

OM - May mitra be propitious with us
May Varuna be propitious with us
May the Honorable Aryama be propitious with us

May Indra and Brihaspati be propitious with us
May Vishnu with long strides be propitious with us.

Om Sarveshaam Swastir Bhavatu
Sarveshaam Shaantir Bhavatu
Sarveshaam Purnnam Bhavatu
Sarveshaam Manggalam Bhavatu
Om Shaantih Shaantih Shaantih

May there be well-being in Aall
May there be peace in all, May there be fulfilment in all
May there be auspiciousness in all
Om Peace, Peace, Peace.

Om Sarve Bhavantu Sukhinah
Sarve Santu Nir Aamayaah
Sarve Bhadraanni Pashyantu
Maa Kashchid Duhkha Bhaag Bhavet
Om Shaantih Shaantih Shaantih

OM - May all become happy, May all be free from
Illness May all see what is auspicious,
May no one suffer.
Om Peace, Peace, Peace.

Om Saha Naav Avatu
Saha Nau Bhunaktu
Saha Viiryam Karavaavahai
Tejasvi Naawa Dhiitam Astu
Maa Vidvishaavahai
Om Shaantih Shaantih Shaantih
Om Purna Madaha
Purnam Idam
Purnaat Purnam Udachyate
Purnasya Purnam Aadaaya
Purnam Eva Vashissyate
Om Shaantih Shaantih Shaantih

OM - That Outer World is Purna - full with Divine
Consciousness this inner world is also Purna - full with

Divine consciousness from Purna comes Purna
From the fullness of Divine consciousness the world is
Manifested taking Purna from Purna, Purna indeed
Remains because Divine consciousness is
Non-Dual and Infinite.
Om Peace, Peace, Peace.

Om Dyauh Shaantih, Antarikshagung Shaantih
Prithivii Shaantih, Aapah Shaantih
Oshadhayah Shaantih, Vanaspatayah Shaantih
Vishve Devaah Shaantih, Brahma Shaantih
Sarvagung Shaantih, Shaantiheva Shaantih Saa Maa,
Shaantih-Edhi
Om Shaantih Shaantih Shaantih

OM, May there be Peace in Heaven,
May there be Peace in the Sky, May there be Peace in
The Earth, May There be Peace in the Water,
May there be Peace in the plants, May there be Peace
in the Trees, May there Be Peace in the Gods,
May there be peace in the various Worlds, May there be
Peace in Brahman, May there be Peace in All,
May there be Peace indeed Within Peace,
Giving Me the Peace which Grows within Me
Om, Peace, Peace, Peace.

~~~

~~~

SRI GANESHA MANTRAS

Muussika Vaahana Modaka Hasta
Chaamara Karnna Vilambita Suutra
Vaamana Ruupa Mahesvara Putra
Vighna Vinaayaka Paada Namaste

Salutations to Sri Vighna Vinayaka, Whose vehicle is
The Mouse, Who has the Modaka in His hand, Whose
Large ears are like fans, Who wears a long sacred
Thread, Who is short in stature and is the Son of
Sri Maheswara - Lord Shiva
Prostrations at the feet of Sri Vighna Vinayaka
The remover of the Obstacles of His Devotees.

Om Gannaanaam Tvaa Ganna Patim Hava Amahe
Kavim Kaviinaam Upama Shravas Tamam
Jyessttha Raajam Brahmannaam Brahmannas Pata
Aa Nah Shrnnvan Nuutibhih Siida Saadanam
Om Mahaa-Ganna Adhipataye Namah

OM - O Ganapati, To You Who are the Lord of the
Ganas - Celestial attendants or followers,
We offer our sacrificial oblation You are the wisdom of
The wise and the uppermost in Glory
You are the Eldest Lord, Ever Unborn and is of the
Nature of Brahman - Absolute Consciousness
You are the Embodiment of the Sacred Pranava - Om
Please come to us by listening to our prayers and be

Present in the seat of this sacred sacrificial altar.
OM - Our prostrations to the Maha Ganadhipati
The Great Lord of the Ganas.

Shukla Ambara Dharam Vishnnum
Shashi Varnnam Chatur Bhujam
Prasanna Vadanam Dhyaayet
Sarva Vighno Pashaantaye

We meditate on Sri Ganesha,
Who is wearing white clothes
Who is All - Pervading, Who is bright in appearance
Like the Moon and Who is having four hands
Who is having a compassionate and gracious face
Let us meditate on Him to ward of all obstacles.

Vakra Tunndda Maha-Kaaya
Suurya Koti Samaprabha
Nirvighnam Kuru Me Deva
Sarva Kaaryeshu Sarvadaa

I meditate on Sri Ganesha, Who has a curved trunk,
Large Body, Who has the Brilliance of a million Suns
O Lord, please make all my works
Free of obstacles, always.

~~~

~~~

SHRI GANESHA GAYATRI

Om Ekadantaaya Vidmahe
Vakratunddaaya Dhiimahi
Tanno Dantiih Prachodayaat
Svasti Shrii Ganna Naayakam Gaja
Mukham Moreshvaram Siddhidam
Ballaallam Murudde Vinaayakam
Aham Cintaamannim Thevare
Lennyaadrau Girijaatmajam
Suvaradam Vighneshvaram Ojhare
Graame Raanjanna Naamake
Gannapatim Kuryaat Sadaa Manggalam

May wellbeing, come to those who remember
Sri Vinayaka
May Swasti - well-being come to those who remember
Sri Gananayaka - Leader of
The Ganas or celestial attendants
Who has the auspicious face of an Elephant
Who abides as Moreshwara at Morgaon
Who abides as Siddhida - Giver of Siddhis at Siddhatek
Who abides as Sri Ballala - at Pali, Who abides as

Vinayaka - Remover of obstacles at Muruda - Mahad
Who abides as Chintamani - Chintamani,
A wish-fulfilling Gem at Thevara - Thevur or Theur
Who abides as Girijatmaja - Son of Devi Girija or Parvati
At Lenyadri Who abides as Vigneshwara at Ojhara - Ozar
Where He is the giver of abundant Boons
Who abides as Ganapati in the village named
Raanjana - Ranjangaon
May He always bestow His auspicious grace on us.

~ ~ ~

GANAPATI STUTI

Om shree riddhi sidhhi sahitam
Shree ganapatayaiya namah
Vighnesham nardev dukh harnam sansar sandaranam
Anandam pragdati mangal yutam labhpradam sidhidam
Om gang ganapatye namah
Loksya aatap harnam matipatim prerna dam prabhum
Vande shailsutasutam ganpatim mangalaya
Devam priyam
Om shree riddhi siddhi sahitam
Sri ganpatye namo namah

~ ~ ~

SHRI GANESH ATHARVASHIRISHA

Shri Ganeshaya Namaha

Om Bhadramkarne Bishnunayama Devaha
Bhadram Pashyemak-shyabhirya Jatrah
Sthirai Rangai Stuvasa Stanumbihi
Vyashema Devahitam Yadayuh
Svastina Indro Vruddhashravah
Svastina Pusha Vishvavedaha
Svastinastakshyo Arishta Nemih
Svastino Brihaspatir-Dadhatu

Om Shanti Shanti Shantihi

Atha Ganesh Atharvashirsham Vyakhya Syamaha

Om Namste Ganpataye
Tvameva Pratyaksham Tatvamasi
Tvamev Kevalam Kartasi
Tvamev Kevalam Dhartasi
Tvamev Kevlam Hartasi
Tvamev Sarvam Khalvidam Bramhasi
Tvam Sakshadatmasi Nityam
Hritam Vachmi
Satyam Vachmi
Ava Tvam Mam
Ava Vaktaram

Ava Shrotaram
Ava Dataram
Ava Dhataram
Avanuchanamava Shishyam
Ava Paschatat
Ava Purastat
Avo Uttaratat
Ava Dakshinatat
Ava Chordhvatat
Ava Dharatat
Sarvatomam Pahi Pahi Samantat
Tvam Vangmayastvam Chinmaya
Tvam Anandmayastvam Bramhamaya
Tvam Sachitananda Dvitiyosi
Tvam Pratyaksham Bramhasi
Tvam Jynanmayo Vijyanamayosi

Sarvam Jagadidam Tatvo Jayate
Sarvam Jagadidam Tatvastishtati
Sarvam Jagadidam Tvay Layameshyati
Sarvam Jagadidam Tvayi Pratyeti
Tvam Bhumi Rapo Nalo Nilo Nabha
Tvam Chatvarim Vak Padani

Tvam Gunatraya Atitaha
Tvam Dehatraya Atitaha
Tvam Kalatraya Atitaha
Tvam Muladharastitiyosi Nityam
Tvam Shaktitrayaat Akaha
Tvam Yogino Dhayayanti Nityam
Tvam Bramhastvan, Vishnustvam
Rudrastvam, Indrastvam Agnistvam
Vayustvam, Suryastvam, Chandramastvam
Bramhabhur Bhuvasvorom

Ganadim Purvamuccharaya Varnadim Tadanantaram
Anusvaara Parataraha
Ardhendu Lasitam
Taaren Hruddam
Etatva Manusva Rupam

Gakarah Purva Rupam
Akaro Madhyama Rupam
Anusvaras Chantya Rupam
Binduruttara Rupam
Nadah Sandhanam
Saishitaa Sandihi
Saisha Ganeshvidhya
Ganak Rishi;
Nichrud Gayatri Chandah
Ganpatir Devata
Om 'GANG' Ganpataye Namah

Ek Dantaya Vid Mahe
Vakratundaya Dhimahi
Tanno Danti Prachodayat

Ek Dantam Chatur Hastam
Pashmam Kusha Dharinam
Radanch Vardam Hastair
Bhibhraanum Mushaka-dhvajam
Raktam Lambodaram Shoorpakarnakam
Rakta Vasasamam
Rakta Gandhanu Liptangam
Rakta Pushpaihi Supujitam
Bhaktanu Kampinam Devam
Jagat Kaarana Machutam
Avir Bhutamcha Shrustyado
Prakrute Purushatparam
Evam Dhayayati Yo Nityam
Sa Yogi Yoginam Varah
Namo Vrat Pataye, Namo Ganapataye
Namah Pramatha Patye,
Namste Astulambodaraya Ekdantaaya
Vighna Nashine Shiv Sutaya
Shri Varad Murtiye Namah

SRI GANESHA AARTI

Jay Ganesh, Jay Ganesh, Jay Ganesh Devaa
Maataa Jaakii Paarvatii, Pitaa Mahaadevaa

Victory to You, O Lord Ganesha, Victory to You, O Lord Ganesha, Victory to You, O Lord Ganesha Deva.
You are born of Mother Parvati and
Lord Shiva is your father.

Ek Danta Dayaavanta, Chaar Bhujaadhaarii
Maathe Par Tilak Sohe, Muuse Kii Savaarii

You have a single tusk, You are filled with compassion
And You have four hands.
You have a beautiful vermillion mark on Your forehead,
And You ride on Your Vahana - vehicle which is in the Form of a mouse.

Paan Caddhe, Phuul Caddhe Aur Caddhe Mewaa
Ladduan Ka Bhog Lage, Santa Karen Sevaa

Devotees offer you paan (betel leaves), flowers,
Mewa (dry fruits), and sweets in the form of laddus;
Saints offer devotional services to You.

Andhan Ko Aankh Deta, Koddhin Ko Kaayaa
Baanjhan Ko Putra Deta, Nirdhan Ko Maayaa

You bestow vision to the blind, and heal the leper.
You bestow children to the barren woman,
And wealth to the destitute.

Suura Shyaama Shaarann Aae Saphal Kiije Sevaa
Maataa Jaakii Paarvatii, Pitaa Mahaadevaa

We pray to you day and night. Please bestow
Success on us.
You are born of Mother Parvati and
Lord Shiva is your father.

Jay Ganesh, Jay Ganesh, Jay Ganesh Devaa

Victory to You, O Lord Ganesha, Victory to You, O Lord Ganesha, Victory to You, O Lord Ganesha Deva.

GURU DEVA

Dhyaana Muulam Gurur Muurtih
Puujaa Muulam Guru Padam
Mantra Muulam Gurur Vaakyam
Moksha Muulam Guru Kripaa

The Root of Meditation is the Form of the Guru
The Root of Worship is the Feet of the Guru
The Root of Mantra is the Word of the Guru
The Root of Liberation is the Grace of the Guru.

Kaayena Vaachaa Manase Indriyairvaa
Buddhy Aatmanaa Vaa Prakrteh Svabhaavaat
Karomi Yad Yat Sakalam Parasmai
Naraayanayeti Samarpayaami

Whatever I do with my body, speech, mind or sense
Organs whatever I do using my intellect, feelings of
Heart or unconsciously through the natural
Tendencies of my mind whatever I do, I do all for
Others, without the sense of attachment to the results
I surrender them all at the Lotus Feet of
The Supreme Guru.

Gurur Brahmaa Gurur Vishnnu
Gururdevo Maheshvarah
Gurur Sakshat Param Brahma
Tasmai Shrii Gurave Namah

The Guru is Brahma, the Guru is Vishnu
The Guru Deva is Maheswara - Shiva
The Guru is Verily the Para - Brahman - Supreme
Brahman. Salutations to that Guru.

Akhanda Mandala Akaaram
Vyaaptam Yena Chara Acharam
Tat Padam Darshitam Yena
Tasmai Shrii Gurave Namah

Salutations to the Guru Whose Form is an Indivisible
Whole of Presence by whom is Pervaded the Moving
And The Non - Moving Being by Whom is Revealed
Out of Grace Those Feet of Indivisible Presence
Salutations to that Guru.

~~~

GURU GAYATRI

Om Gurudevaaya Vidmahe
Parabrahmaaya Dhiimahi
Tanno Guruh Prachodayaat

~~~

GURU PADUKA STOTRAM

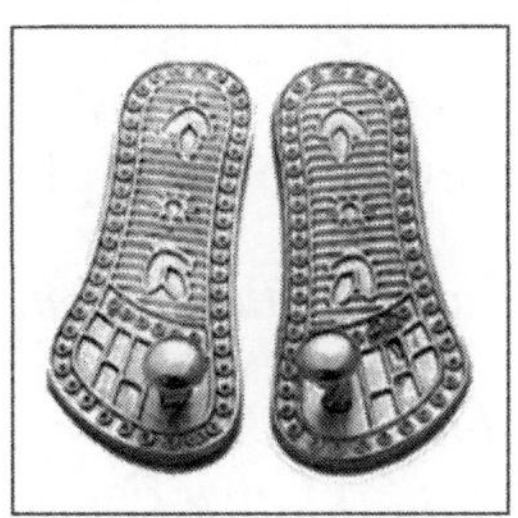

Anantha Samsara Samudhra Thara Naukayithabhyam
Guru Bhakthithabhyam
Vairagya Samrajyadha Poojanabhyam,
Namo Nama Sri Guru Padukhabyam.

Salutations and salutations to the sandals of my Guru,
Which is a boat, which helps me,
Cross the endless ocean of life,
Which endows me, with the sense of
Devotion to my Guru, and by worship of which,
I attain the dominion of renunciation.

Kavithva Varasini Sagarabhyam, Dourbhagya Davambudha
Malikabhyam,
Dhoorikrutha Namra Vipathithabhyam,
Namo Nama Sri Guru Padukhabyam.

Salutations and salutations to the sandals of my Guru,
Which is the ocean of knowledge,
Resembling the full Moon,
Which is the water, which puts out the fire of
misfortunes, And which removes distresses of those
Who prostrate before it.

Natha Yayo Sripatitam Samiyu Kadachidapyasu
Daridra Varya,
Mookascha Vachaspathitham Hi Thabhyam,

Namo Nama Sri Guru Padukhabyam.

Salutations and Salutations to the sandals of my Guru,
Which make those who prostrate before it,
Possessors of great wealth, even if they are very poor,
And which makes even dumb people into great orators.

Naleeka Neekasa Pada Hrithabhyam, Nana Vimohadhi Nivarikabyam
Nama Janabheeshtathathi Pradhabhyam,
Namo Nama Sri Guru Padukhabyam.

Salutations and salutations to the sandals of my Guru,
Which attracts us, to lotus like feet of our Guru,
Which cures us, of the unwanted desires,
And which helps to fulfill the desires of
Those who salute.

Nrupali Mouleebraja Rathna Kanthi Sariddha Raja Jjashakanyakabhyam
Nrupadvadhabhyam Nathaloka Pankhthe
Namo Nama Sri Guru Padukhabyam.

Salutations and salutations to the sandals of my Guru,
Which shine like gems on the crown of a king,
Which Shine like a maid in the crocodile infested stream,
And which make the devotees attain the status of a king.

Papandhakara Arka Paramparabhyam Thapathryaheendra Khageswarabhyam
Jadyadhi Samsoshana Vadaveebhyam
Namo Nama Sri Guru Padukhabyam.

Salutations and salutations to the sandals of my Guru,
Which is like a series of Suns, driving away the dark sins,
Which is like the king of eagles,
Driving away the cobra of miseries,
And which is like a terrific fire drying away
The ocean of ignorance.

Shamadhi Shatka Pradha Vaibhavabhyam,
Samadhi Dhana Vratha Deeksithabhyam,
Ramadhavadeegra Sthirha Bhakthidabhyam,
Namo Nama Sri Guru Padukhabyam.

Salutations and Salutations to the sandals of my Guru,
Which endows us, with the glorious six qualities
Like Sham, which gives the students,
The ability to go in to Eternal trance,
And which helps to get perennial
Devotion to the feet of Vishnu.

Swarchaparana Makhileshtathabhyam,
Swaha Sahayaksha Durndarabhyam,
Swanthachad Bhava Pradha Poojanabhyam,
Namo Nama Sri Guru Padukhabyam.

Salutations and salutations to the sandals of my Guru
Which bestows all desires of the serving disciples,
Who are ever involved in carrying the burden of service
And which helps the aspirants to
The state of Realization.

Kaamadhi Sarpa Vraja Garudabhyam
Viveka Vairagya Nidhi Pradhabhyam,
Bhodha Pradhabhyam Drutha Mokshathabhyam,
Namo Nama Sri Guru Padukhabyam.

Salutations and Salutations to the sandals of my Guru
Which is the Garuda, which drives away
The serpent of passion,
Which provides one, with the treasure of
Wisdom and renunciation,
Which blesses one, with enlightened knowledge,
And blesses the aspirant with Speedy salvation.

DEVI GAYATRI

Om Bhuur Bhuvah Svaha
Tat-Savitur Varennyam
Bhargo Devasya Dhiimahi
Dhiyo Yo Nah Prachodayaat

OM - That Divine illumination which pervades the
Bhu Loka - Physical Plane, Consciousness of the
Physical Plane
Bhuvar Loka - Antariksha or Intermediate Space
Consciousness of the Prana
Swar Loka - Swarga - Heaven, Consciousness of the
Divine Mind on that Savitur - Divine Illumination
Which is the Most Adorable - Varenyam and which is of
The nature of Divine Effulgence - Bhargo Devasya
I Meditate
May that Divine Intelligence - Dhiyah
Awaken - Pracodyat our Spiritual Consciousness.

GAYATRI FOR PRANAYAMA

MEDITATION

Om Bhuuh Om Bhuvah Om Svaha
Om Maha Om Janaha Om Tapaha Om Satyam
Om Tat-Savitur Varennyam Bhargo Devasya Dhiimahi
Dhiyo Yo Nah Prachodayaat

Om Aapo Jyotii Rasomritam
Brahma Bhuur Bhuvah
Svah Om

Om - I meditate on the Bhu Loka - Physical Plane
Consciousness of the Physical Plane
Om - I meditate on the Bhuvar Loka - Antariksha or
Intermediate Space, Consciousness of the Prana
Om - I meditate on the Swar Loka - Swarga, Heaven
Consciousness of the beginning of the Divine Mind
OM - I meditate on the Mahar Loka - Great, Mighty,
Still subtler Plane felt as All-Pervading Consciousness
OM - I meditate on the Janar Loka - Generating, Still
subtler Plane felt as All-Creating Consciousness
OM - I meditate on the Tapo Loka - Filled with Tejas,
Still subtler Plane felt as filled with Divine Tejas or
Illumination of Shakti

OM - I meditate on the Satya Loka - Absolute Truth,
Most subtle Plane merging with the
Consciousness of Brahman
OM – I Meditate on that Savitur - Divine Illumination
Which is most Adorable - Varenyam and which is of the
Nature of Divine Effulgence - Bhargo Devasya,
I meditate May that Divine Intelligence - Dhiyah
Awaken - Pracodyat our Spiritual Consciousness.
OM – I meditate on that Divine Consciousness which
is:
Apah - All - Pervading
Jyoti- Divine Effulgence
Rasa- Divine Essence
Amritam - Immortal and Nectar-like Blissful
Brahma - Sacchidananda Brahman has manifested in
Grosser forms as Bhu Loka - Physical Plane
Bhuvar Loka - Antariksha or Intermediate Space and
Swar Loka - Swarga or Heaven
Om In Essence.

SARASWATI DEVI

Esham Na Vidya Na Tapo Na Daanam
Gyanam Na Sheelam Na Guno Na Dharmaha
Te Mrityulokena Bhumi Bhaar Bhuta
Manushya Roopena Mrigascharanti

Those who possess neither Lore, Meditation,
Liberalism nor Knowledge, Politeness,
Virtues or Righteousness
Those humans are considered a burden in this world.
They are like animals wandering over
The earth in human form.

Ya Kundendu Tushar Haar Dhawla
Ya Shubhra Vastravita
Ya Veena Var Danda Mandit Kara
Ya Shweta Padmasana
Ya Brahmaachyuta Shankar Prabhri Tibhir
Devayi Sada Vandita
Samampatu Saraswati Bhagwati
Nihshesha Jaadyapaha

May Goddess Saraswati protect me - She who is
Immaculately white like the jasmine blossom,

The moon, and the wreath of the snow Who wears a White sari, and holds an exquisite Vina in Her hand Who is seated on a white lotus, who is ever adored by All the Gods including Brahma, Chyut - Vishnu, and Shankar - Shiva Who quickly and skillfully removes all Types of ignorance from her devotees

Shuklam Brahma Vichar Saara Paramam
Aadyam Jagad Vyapineem
Veena Pustak Dharini Mabhaydam
Jaaddyaan Dhakara Pahaam
Haste Sphatika Malikaam Vidadhatim
Padmasane Sansthitam
Vandetaam Parmeshwarim Bhagawatim
Budhhi Pradaam Sharadaam

Namaste Shaarade Devi
Kaashmiira Pura Vaasini
Tvaam Aham Praarthaye Nityam
Vidyaa Daanam Cha Dehi Me

Salutations to Devi Sharada, Who abide in the abode of Kashmira to You, O Devi, I always pray for Knowledge Please bestow on me the gift of that Knowledge Which illumines everything from within.

Sarasvati Mahaa Bhaage
Vidye Kamala Lochane
Vidyaa Ruupe Vishaal Aakshi
Vidyaam Dehi Namostute

O Devi Saraswati, the most Auspicious Goddess of Knowledge with Lotus - like Eyes
An Embodiment of Knowledge with Large Eyes,
Kindly Bless me with Knowledge. I Salute you.

Sarasvati Namastubhyam
Varade Kaama Ruupinni
Vidya Arambham Karishyaami
Siddhir Bhavatu Me Sadaa

Salutations to Devi Saraswati, Who is the giver of
Boons and fulfiller of wishes
O Devi, when I begin my studies, please bestow on me
The capacity of right understanding, always.
Prayer for wisdom

Paavakaa Nah Sarasvati
Vaajebhir Vaajani Vatii
Yajnyam Vassttu Dhiyaa Vasuh

O Saraswati, You are the purifier of our intellect and
Your strength of wisdom grows within us with sacrificial
Offerings inner and outer
May my offering in yagnya strengthen
Your wisdom within me
May your presence within me make me rich in wisdom.

Making the presence of Universal Wisdom Felt
Maho Arnnaha Sarasvati
Pra Chetayati Ketunaa
Dhiyo Vishvaa Vi Raajati

Saraswati, that great wave of Universal wisdom
Who has flowed as a river and who is the awakener of
Our intellect Who is now shining as the embodiment
of Universal wisdom in this yagnya.

Shuklaam Brahma Vichaara Saara Paramaam
Aadyaam Jagad Vyaapiniim
Veena Pustaka Dhaarinim Abhaya Daam
Jaaddya Andhakaara Apahaam
Haste Sphaatika Maalikaam Bidadhatim
Padma Asane Samsthitaam
Vande Taam Parameshvarim Bhagavatim
Buddhi Pradaam Shaaradaam

I meditate on Devi Sharada,
Who is Pure White in Colour, and Whose deepest

Essence can only be Fathomed by enquiring into the
Nature of Brahman - Absolute Consciousness
Who is Supreme and Primeval, and Her essence is
Spread across the whole Universe as consciousness
Who is holding the Veena symbolising the essence of
Music and Book symbolising the essence of Knowledge
And displaying the gesture of fearlessness arising
Out of Knowledge
The Knowledge which removes the darkness of
Ignorance from our minds
Who is holding a garland of crystal beads in Her hand,
Shining with purity and Who is abiding on the Sea of
Lotus blooming like an awakened consciousness
I Extol and worship Her, Who is the supreme Goddess
Who awakens our intelligence.

I worship Devi Sharada.

~~~
~~~

SARASWATI STOTRAM

Ya kundendu tusharaharadhavala ya shubhravastravrita Ya
vinavaradandamanditakara ya shvetapadmasana
Ya brahmachyutashankaraprabhritibhir devaissada Pujita
sa mam patu sarasvati bhagavati
Vishsheshajadyapaha dorbhiryukta chaturbhim
Sphatikamaninibhai akshamalandadhana hastenaikena
Padmam sitamapicha shukam pustakam chaparena
Bhasa kundendushankhasphatikamaninibha
Bhasamana asamana sa me vagdevateyam nivasatu Vadane
sarvada suprasanna surasurasevitapadapankaja Kare
virajatkamaniyapustaka
Virinchipatni kamalasanasthita sarasvati nrityatu vachi Me
sada Sarasvati sarasijakesaraprabha tapasvini
Sitakamalasanapriya
Ghanastani kamala vilolalochana manaswini
Bhavatu varaprasadinii

Saraswathi namastubhyam varade kamarupini
Vidyarambam karishyami siddhir bhavatu me sada

Saraswathi namastubhyam sarva devi namo namaha
Shaantarupe shashidhare sarvayoge namo namaha
Nityanande niraadhare nishkalayai namo namaha
Vidyadhare visalakshi shuddhagnana namo namaha
Suddha sphatika rupayai sukshmarupe namo namaha

Shabdabrahmi chaturhaste sarvasiddhyai namo namaha
Muktalankrita sarvangyai muladhare namo namaha
Mulamantra svarupayai mulashaktyai namo namaha
Mano manimahayoge vagishvari namo namaha
Vagbhyai varadahastayai varadayai namo namaha
Vedayai vedarupayai vedantayai namo namaha
Gunadosha vivarjinyai gunadiptyai namo namaha
Sarvagnane sadanande sarvarupe namo namaha
Sampannayai kumaryai cha sarvagne te namo namaha
Yoganarya umadevyai yogananade namo namaha
Divyagnana trinetrayai divyamurtyai namo namaha
Ardha chandra jatadhari chandrabimbe namo namaha
Chandraditya jatadhari chandrabimbe namo namaha
Anurupe maharupe vishvarupe namo namaha
Animadyashta siddhayai anandayai namo namaha
Gnana vignana rupayai gnanamurte namo namaha
Nanashastra svarupayai nanarupe namo namaha
Padmada padmavansha cha padmarupe namo namaha
Parameshthyai paramurtyai namaste papanashini
Mahadevyai mahakalyai mahalakshmyai namo namaha
Brahmavishnushivayai cha brahmanaryai namo namaha
Kamalakarapushpa cha kamarupe namo namaha
Kapali karadiptayai karmadayai namo namaha

Sayam pratah pathennityam shanmasatsiddhiruchyate
Choravyaghrbhayamnasti pathatam shrinvatamapi
Ittam sarasvati stotram agastyamuni vachakam
Sarvasiddhikaram nrinam sarvapapapranashanam

JOYTI SHLOKA

Shubham Karoti Kalyaannam
Aarogyam Dhana Sampadaa
Shatru Buddhi Vinaashaaya
Deepa Jyotir Namostute

Salutations to the Light of the Lamp which brings
Auspiciousness, health and prosperity
Which destroys inimical feelings
Salutations to the Light of the Lamp.

Deepa Jyotih Para Brahma
Deepa Jyotir Janaardanah
Deepo Haratu Me Paapam
Deepa Jyotir Namostute

Salutations to the Light of the Lamp
The Light of the Lamp represents the Supreme Brahman
The Light of the Lamp represents
Janardhana - Sri Vishnu
Let the Light of the Lamp remove my sins
Salutations to the Light of the Lamp.

~~~
~~~

LAKSHMI DEVI

Karaagre Vasate Lakshmi
Karamadhye Sarasvati
Karamuule Tu Govindah
Prabhaate Karadarshanam

At the top of the hand in the palm, dwells Devi Lakshmi and at the middle of the hand dwell Devi Saraswati at the base of the hand dwell Sri Govinda Therefore one should look at one's hands in the early Morning and contemplate on them.

~~~
~~~

MAHA LAKSHMI ASHTAKAM

Namastestu Mahaa Maaye
Shri Pithe Sura Pujite
Shankha Chakra Gadaa Haste
Mahaalakshmi Namostute

I worshipfully salute Devi Mahalakshmi
Who is the Mahamaya - the Primordial cause of
Creation and who is worshipped in Sri Pitha - Her
Abode by the Suras I worshipfully salute Her,
Who is adorned in Her beautiful form with
Shankha - conch, Chakra - Disc and Gada - mace in
Her hands I worshipfully salute Devi Mahalakshmi.

Namaste Garudaa Rudhhe
Kolaasura Bhayangkari
Sarva Paapa Hare Devi
Mahaa Lakshmi Namostute

I worshipfully salute Devi Mahalakshmi
Who is mounted on the Garuda, and who is the terror
To kolasura I worshipfully salute the Devi
Who removes all sins when we surrender to Her
I worshipfully salute Devi Mahalakshmi.

Sarvajanaye Sarva Varade
Sarva Dushta Bhayankari
Sarva Duhkha Hare Devi
Mahaa Lakshmi Namostute

I worshipfully salute Devi Mahalakshmi, Who is All-Knowing knowing even our innermost thoughts
Who gives all boons when Her compassion
Aroused I worshipfully salute Devi Mahalakshmi
Who is the terror to all the wicked - destroying our
Evil tendencies I worshipfully salute the Devi
Who Removes all sorrows when her grace is aroused
I worshipfully salute Devi Mahalakshmi.

Siddhi Buddhi Prade Devi
Bhukti Mukti Pradaayini
Mantra Muurte Sadaa Devi
Mahaa Lakshmi Namostute

I worshipfully salute the Devi Who bestows
Accomplishments when She becomes gracious and
Intelligence to direct our lives properly with those
Accomplishments I worshipfully salute the Devi
Who bestows both worldly prosperity as well as directs
Our lives towards liberation merging in Her lotus feet
I worshipfully salute the Devi who always abide as the
Subtle form of mantra behind everything
In creation & within our hearts
I worshipfully salute Devi Mahalakshmi.

Aadyanta Rahite Devi
Aadya Shakti Maheshvari
Yogaje Yoga Sambhuute
Mahaa Lakshmi Namostute

I worshipfully salute the Devi Who is without
Beginning - Aadi and End – Anta.
Being the primordial shakti behind everything
I worshipfully salute that Great Goddess
I Worshipfully salute Devi Mahalakshmi

Who is born of Yoga out of the great consciousness
And who is always United with Yoga
I worshipfully salute Devi Mahalakshmi.

Sthoola Sookshma Mahaa Raudre
Mahaa Shakti Mahodare
Mahaa Paapa Hare Devi
Mahaa Lakshmi Namostute

I worshipfully salute Devi Mahalakshmi
Whose power is present behind both gross and subtle
Forms as well as behind the
Most terrible form of Rudrani.
I worshipfully salute Devi Mahalakshmi
Who is the great womb of Mahashakti from where
Every manifestation of power arises
I worshipfully salute the Devi
Who removes great sinsfrom our Lives when Her Great
Power passes through our Lives and cleanses us
During adverse circumstances
I worshipfully salute Devi Mahalakshmi.

Padmaa Asana Sthite Devi
Para Brahma Swaruupini
Parameshi Jagan Maatar
Mahaa Lakshmi Namostute

After Her great power cleanses us we feel the peaceful
Form of the Devi Who is seated on a lotus
Lotus of Kundalini with a Gracious Face and who is
abiding as the Supreme Brahman behind all impurities
She is the Supreme Goddess and
The Mother of the Universe
I worshipfully salute Devi Mahalakshmi.

Shvetambara Dhare Devi
Naana Langkaara Bhooshite
Jagat Sthite Jagan Maatar
Mahaa Lakshmi Namostute

I worshipfully salute the Devi Who is adorned with
White garments representing our Inner Purity
I worshipfully salute the Devi Who is adorned with
Various ornaments representing our inner beauty
I worshipfully salute the Devi Who abides within the
Universe as the Mother of the Universe
Directing our lives and all activities
I worshipfully salute Devi Mahalakshmi.

Maha Lakshmy-Ashtaka Stotram
Yah Patthed Bhaktimaan Narah
Sarva Siddhim Avaapnoti
Raajyam Praapnoti Sarvadaa

He who recites this Mahalakshmi Ashtakam Stotram
With devotion, surrendering to Her power will attain all
Accomplishments including final liberation and
Prosperity both inner and outer, always,
When She Herself directs our Lives.

~~~
~~~

MAHALAKSHMI STOTRAM

Anadyanotaroopam twam janani sarwadehinam
Sri Vishnuroopine vande Mahalakshmi Parameswreem

Namajaatyathiroopena stitam twam Parameswareem
Sri Vishnuroopine vande Mahalakshmi Parameswreem

Vyaktavyakta swaroopeena katsanam vyashyavyvastitam
Sri Vishnuroopine vande Mahalakshmi Parameswreem

Bhaktanamdapradam poornam poornakama karim varam
Sri Vishnuroopine vande Mahalakshmi Parameswreem

Antaryamana viswamaapoorva hrudi samsthitam
Sri Vishnuroopine vande Mahalakshmi Parameswreem

Sarvadaithya vinasardha Lakshmiroopam vyavastitam
Sri Vishnuroopine vande Mahalakshmi Parameswreem

Bhaktim muktim cha datum samstitha karaveerake
Sri Vishnuroopine vande Mahalakshmi Parameswreem

Sarvabhayapradam deveem sarvasamsaya nasaneem
Sri Vishnuroopine vande Mahalakshmi Parameswreem

TULSI MAA

Jagad Dhaatri Namas Tubhyam
Vishnosh Cha Priya Vallabhe
Yato Brahmaadayo Devaah
Srishti Sthitey Anta Kaarinnah

Salutations to Devi Tulsi I bow down to You
O Jagaddhatri the bearer of the world
You are the most beloved of Sri Vishnu
Because of Your power, O Devi
The Devas beginning with Brahma are able to
Create, maintain and bring an end to the world.

Namas Tulsi Kalyaanni
Namo Vishnu Priye Shubhe
Namo Moksha Prade Devi
Namah Sampat Pradaayike

Salutations to Devi Tulsi Who brings goodness in life
Salutations to Devi Tulsi Who is the beloved of
Sri Vishnu and Who is auspicious
Salutations to Devi Tulsi Who grants liberation
Salutations to Devi Tulsi Who bestows prosperity.

~~~
~~~

TULSI GAYATRI

Om Tripuraya Vidmahe
Tulsi Patraya Dhimahi
Tanno Tulsi Prachodayat

Om, let me meditate on the Goddess of Ocimum,
O, Goddess who is dear to Vishnu
Give me higher intellect and let
Brindha illuminate my mind.

BHOOMI MAA
(MOTHER EARTH)

Satyam Brhad Ratam Ugram
Dikshaa Tapo Brahma
Yajnyah Prthivim Dhaarayanti
Saa No Bhuutasya Bhavayasya
Patnyi Urum Lokam
Prthivii Nah Kranotu

Salutations to Mother Earth, The Truth - Satyam
The Cosmic Divine Law - Ritam
The spiritual passion manifested in mighty
Initiations Penances and self-dedications to
The search of brahman by the sages.
These have sustained the Mother Earth for ages
Who in turn have supported these in Her bosom
She is the consort of the past and the future,
being its witness.
May She expand our Inner life in this world towards
The cosmic life through Her purity and vastness.

Om Prthvi Tvayaa Dhritaa Lokaa
Devi Tvam Vishnunaa Dhritaa
Tvam Cha Dhaaraya Maam Devi
Pavitram Kuru Chaa Asanam

OM - O Prithivi Devi, by You are borne the entire Loka - World and Devi, You in turn are borne by Sri Vishnu, Please hold me on Your lap O Devi, And make this asana - seat of the worshipper, pure.

Samudra Vasane Devi
Parvata Stana Mandale
Vishnnu Patni Namas Tubhyam
Paada Sparsham Kshamasva Me

O Mother Earth, The Devi Who is having ocean as Her Garments and mountains as Her Bosom Who is the Consort of Sri Vishnu, I bow to You Please forgive me for touching You with my Feet.

~~~
~~~

DURGA DEVI

Sarva Mangala Maanggalye
Shive Sarvaartha Saadhike
Sharannye Tryambake Gauri
Naaraayani Namostu Te

Salutations to You O Narayani
Who is the auspiciousness in all the auspicious
Auspiciousness Herself
Complete with all the auspicious attributes
Who fulfills all the objectives of the
Devotees - purusharthas
Dharma, artha, kama and moksha
Who is the Giver of Refuge,
With three eyes and a Shining face.
Salutations to You O Narayani.

Jaya Tvam Devi Chaamunde
Jaya Bhuu Taapa Haarinni
Jaya Sarva Gate Devi
Kaalaraatri Namostu Te

Victory to You, O Devi Chamunda, Victory to You
Who is the remover of worldly afflictions and sorrows
Victory to You O Devi, Who is present in all beings
Salutations to You, O Devi Kalaratri
A form of Devi Durga, literally means the Dark Night.

Jayantii Manggalaa Kaali
Bhadrakaali Kapaalini
Durgaa Kshamaa Shiva Dhaatri
Svaahaa Svadhaa Namostu Te

Salutations to Jayanti Who is ever victorious
Mangala Who is the bestower of auspiciousness
Kali Who is beyond Kala or Time
Bhadrakali Who is the controller of life and death
Being beyond kala or time
Kapalini Who wear a garland of skulls
Salutations to Durga Who is Durgati Nashini - Shiva
Who is ever - auspicious and one with
Shiva as His Consort
Kshama Who is an embodiment of forbearance
Dhatri Who is the supporter of all beings
Swaha Who is the final receiver of the sacrificial
Oblations to Gods Swadha Who is the final receiver of
The sacrificial oblations to Manes
Salutations to You.

~~~
~~~

DEVI SUKTAM

Ya Devi Sarva Bhuteshu, Shakti Rupena Sansthita |
Namastasyai Namastasyai Namastasyai Namo Namah ||

Ya Devi Sarva Bhuteshu, Bhakti Rupena Sansthita |
Namastasyai Namastasyai Namastasyai Namo Namah ||

Ya Devi Sarva Bhuteshu, Matri Rupena Sansthita |
Namastasyai Namastasyai Namastasyai Namo Namah ||

Ya Devi Sarva Bhuteshu, Shanthi Rupena Sansthita |
Namastasyai Namastasyai Namastasyai Namo Namah ||

Ya Devi Sarva Bhuteshu, Daya Rupena Sansthita |
Namastasyai Namastasyai Namastasyai Namo Namah ||

Ya Devi Sarva Bhuteshu, Shraddha Rupena Sansthita |
Namastasyai Namastasyai Namastasyai Namo Namah ||

Ya Devi Sarva Bhuteshu, Lajjaa Rupena Sansthita |
Namastasyai Namastasyai Namastasyai Namo Namah ||

Ya Devi Sarva Bhuteshu, Jaati Rupena Sansthita |
Namastasyai Namastasyai Namastasyai Namo Namah ||

Ya Devi Sarva Bhuteshu, L̃akshmi Rupena Sansthita |
Namastasyai Namastasyai Namastasyai Namo Namah ||

Ya Devi Sarva Bhuteshu, Ñidra R̃upena Sansthita |
Namastasyai Namastasyai Namastasyai Namo Namah ||

Namastasyai Namastasyai Namastasyai Namo Namah |
Namastasyai Namastasyai Namastasyai Namo Namah ||

~~~
~~~

DURGA ARGALA STOTRAM

Madhu Kaitabha Vidhvamsi
Vidhaatri Varade Namah
Ruupam Dehi Jayam Dehi
Yasho Dehi Dvisso Jahi

Salutations to Devi Durga Who destroyed the demons
Madhu and Kaitabha thus granting the boon of
Protection to Sri Brahma O Devi,
Please grant me spiritual beauty, please grant me
Spiritual victory, please grant me spiritual glory.
Please destroy my inner enemies.

Mahishaasura Nirnaashi
Bhaktaanaam Sukhade Namah
Ruupam Dehi Jayam Dehi
Yasho Dehi Dvisso Jahi

Salutations to Devi Durga Who destroyed to the very
Root the demon Mahishasura
Salutations to Her Who Gives Great Joy to the Devotees
O Devi, please grant me spiritual beauty, please grant
Me spiritual victory, please grant me spiritual glory.
Please destroy my inner enemies.

Dhumranetra Vadhe Devi
Dharma Kaama Artha Daayini
Ruupam Dehi Jayam Dehi
Yasho Dehi Dvisso Jahi

Salutations to Devi Durga Who slayed the demon
Dhumranetra Dhumralochana.
Salutations to Her Who is the giver of
Dharma - Path of righteousness, Kama - fulfilment of
Desires and artha - prosperity to Her devotees.
O Devi, please grant me spiritual beauty, please grant
Me spiritual victory, please grant me spiritual glory.
Please destroy my inner enemies.

Raktabiija Vadhe Devi
Chanda Munda Vinaashini
Ruupam Dehi Jayam Dehi
Yasho Dehi Dvisso Jahi

Salutations to Devi Durga Who slayed the demon
Raktabija and destroyed the demons
Chanda and Munda.
O Devi, please grant me spiritual beauty, please grant
Me spiritual victory, please grant me spiritual glory.
Please destroy my inner enemies.

Nishumbha Shumbha Nirnaashi
Trailokya Shubhade Namah
Ruupam Dehi Jayam Dehi
Yasho Dehi Dvisso Jahi

Salutations to Devi Durga Who destroye to the very
Root the demons Nishumbha and Shumbha.
Salutations to Her Who bestows
Auspiciousness in the three worlds
O Devi, please grant me spiritual beauty, please grant
Me spiritual victory, please grant me spiritual glory.
Please destroy my inner enemies.

Vandita Angghri Yuge Devi
Sarva Saubhaagya Daayini
Ruupam Dehi Jayam Dehi
Yasho Dehi Dvisso Jahi

Salutations to Devi Durga Whose pair of feet is
Praised by all Who is the bestower of
All welfare and good fortune
O Devi, please grant me spiritual beauty, please grant
Me spiritual victory, please grant me spiritual glory.
Please destroy my inner enemies.

Achintya Ruupa Charite
Sarva Shatru Vinaashini

Ruupam Dehi Jayam Dehi
Yasho Dehi Dvisso Jahi

Salutations to Devi Durga Whose form and acts are
Beyond comprehension, and Who is
The destroyer of all enemies
O Devi, please grant me spiritual beauty, please grant
Me spiritual victory, please grant me spiritual glory.
Please destroy my inner enemies.

Natebhyah Sarvadaa Bhaktyaa
Chaaparne Durita Pahe
Ruupam Dehi Jayam Dehi
Yasho Dehi Dvisso Jahi

Salutations to Devi Aparna - another name of
Devi Durga Whom the devotees always Bow with
devotion Who keeps away the devotees from sins
O Devi, please grant me spiritual beauty,
Please grant me spiritual victory,
Please grant me spiritual glory.
Please destroy my inner enemies.

Stuvadbhayo Bhakti Puurvam Tvaam
Chandike Vyaadhi Naashini
Ruupam Dehi Jayam Dehi
Yasho Dehi Dvisso Jahi

O Devi Chandika, those who praise you with full
Devotion You destroy their diseases and ailments.
O Devi, please grant me spiritual beauty, please grant
Me spiritual victory, please grant me spiritual glory.
Please destroy my inner enemies.

Chandike Satatam Yuddhe
Jayanti Paapa Naashini
Ruupam Dehi Jayam Dehi
Yasho Dehi Dvisso Jahi

Salutations to Devi Chandika, Who is always victorious
in the Battles, and Who is the destroyer of all Sins

O Devi, please grant me spiritual beauty, please grant
Me spiritual victory, Please grant me spiritual glory.
Please destroy my inner enemies

Dehi Saubhaagyam Aarogyam
Dehi Devi Param Sukham
Ruupam Dehi Jayam Dehi
Yasho Dehi Dvisso Jahi

O Devi, please bestow on me welfare and prosperity,
Along with health and freedom from diseases
O Devi, please give me the highest joy
O Devi, please grant me spiritual beauty, please grant
Me spiritual victory, please grant me spiritual glory.
Please destroy my inner enemies.

Vidhehi Devi Kalyaannam
Vidhehi Vipulaam Shriyam
Ruupam Dehi Jayam Dehi
Yasho Dehi Dvisso Jahi

O Devi, please bestow on me good fortune
O Devi, please give me abundant prosperity
O Devi, please grant me spiritual beauty, please grant
Me spiritual victory, please grant me spiritual glory.
Please destroy my inner enemies.

Vidhehi Dvisatam Naasham
Vidhehi Balam Uchchakaih
Ruupam Dehi Jayam Dehi
Yasho Dehi Dvisso Jahi

O Devi, please destroy my enemies
O Devi, please give me great strength
O Devi, please grant me spiritual beauty, please grant
Me spiritual victory, please grant me spiritual glory.
Please destroy my inner enemies.

Sura Asura Shiro Ratna
Nighreshta Charanembike

Ruupam Dehi Jayam Dehi
Yasho Dehi Dvisso Jahi

Salutations to Devi Ambika, to Whose feet
The devas touch their heads adorned with
Jewels out of devotion to Whose feet the heads of
The mighty asuras adorned with jewels get subdued
O Devi, Please Grant me Spiritual Beauty, please grant
Me spiritual victory, Please grant me spiritual glory.
Please destroy my inner enemies.

Vidyaavantam Yashasvantam
Lakshmivantan Cha Maam Kuru
Ruupam Dehi Jayam Dehi
Yasho Dehi Dvisso Jahi

O Devi, please make me full with knowledge
Please make me full with glory. Please make me full
With the attributes of Lakshmi - beauty and prosperity
O Devi, please grant me spiritual beauty, please grant
Me spiritual victory, please grant me spiritual glory
Please destroy my inner enemies.

Devi Prachanda Dordanda
Daitya Darpa Nissudini
Ruupam Dehi Jayam Dehi
Yasho Dehi Dvisso Jahi

Salutations to Devi Durga, Who destroys the mighty
Pride of the excessively violent and powerful demons
O Devi, please grant me spiritual beauty, please grant
Me spiritual victory, please grant me spiritual glory.
Please destroy my inner enemies.

Prachanndda Daitya Darpaghne
Chandike Pranataaya Me
Ruupam Dehi Jayam Dehi
Yasho Dehi Dvisso Jahi

My Salutations to Devi Chandika, Who is the

Destroyer of the terrible demons with mighty pride
O Devi, please grant me spiritual beauty, please grant
Me spiritual victory, please grant me spiritual glory.
Please destroy my inner enemies.

Chaturbhuje Chatur Vaktra
Samstute Parameshvari
Ruupam Dehi Jayam Dehi
Yasho Dehi Dvisso Jahi

Salutations to the supreme goddess Durga,
Who is praised by Lord Brahma with all
His four faces and all His four hands
O Devi, please grant me spiritual beauty, please grant
Me spiritual victory, please grant me spiritual glory.
Please destroy my inner enemies.

Krishnena Samstute Devi
Shashvad Bhaktyaa SadaAmbike
Ruupam Dehi Jayam Dehi
Yasho Dehi Dvisso Jahi

Salutations to the supreme Devi Ambika,
Who is always praised by Lord Krishna with
A continuous flow of devotion
O Devi, please grant me spiritual beauty, please grant
Me spiritual victory, please grant me spiritual glory.
Please destroy my inner enemies.

Himaachala Sutaa Naatha
Samstute Parameshvari
Ruupam Dehi Jayam Dehi
Yasho Dehi Dvisso Jahi

Salutations to the supreme Goddess Durga
Who is praised by the Lord of the daughter of the
Himachal Mountain - Lord Shiva
O Devi, please grant me spiritual beauty, please grant
Me spiritual victory, please grant me spiritual glory
Please destroy my inner enemies.

Indraani Pati Sadbhaava
Puujite Parameshvari
Ruupam Dehi Jayam Dehi
Yasho Dehi Dvisso Jahi

Salutations to the supreme Goddess Durga
Who is worshipped with true devotion by
The consort of Indrani - Indra Deva
O Devi, please grant me spiritual beauty, please grant
Me spiritual victory, please grant me spiritual glory
Please destroy my Inner Enemies.

Devi Bhakta Janoddaama
Datta anando dayembike
Ruupam Dehi Jayam Dehi
Yasho Dehi Dvisso Jahi

Salutations to Devi Ambika, Who gives rise to an
upsurge Of unbounded joy in the hearts of the
devotees
O Devi, please grant me spiritual beauty, please grant
Me spiritual victory, please grant me spiritual glory.
Please destroy my inner enemies

Bhaaryaa Mano Ramaam Dehi
Mano Vritta Anusaa Rinim
Ruupam Dehi Jayam Dehi
Yasho Dehi Dvisso Jahi

O Devi, please grant me a beautiful
Spouse matching my mental disposition
O Devi, please grant me spiritual beauty, please grant
Me spiritual victory, please grant me spiritual glory
Please destroy my inner enemies.

Taarini Durga Samsaara
Saagarasya Chalod Bhave
Ruupam Dehi Jayam Dehi
Yasho Dehi Dvisso Jahi

Salutations to Devi Durga, Who took birth as
The daughter of a Mountain king and
Who enables us to cross the difficult ocean of
The samsara - worldly existence
O Devi, please grant me spiritual beauty, please grant
Me spiritual victory, please grant me spiritual glory
Please destroy my inner enemies.

Idam Stotram Pathitvaa Tu
Mahaa Stotra Pathen Naraha
Sapta Shatim SamaaRaadhya
Vara Mapnoti Durlabham

Having read this stotra - The argala stotra
One should then read the great stotra the durga
Saptashati this stotra, the argala stotra is equally
Revered like the saptashati by reading this with
Devotion, one obtains the most difficult boons.

DEVI ANNAPURNA

Nitya Ananda Kari Vara Abhaya Kari
Saundarya Ratnaa Kari
Nirdhuuta Akhila Ghora Paavana Kari
Prat yaksha Maaheshvari
Praaleya Achala Vamsha Paavana Kari
Kaashi Pura Adhishvari
Bhikshaam Dehi Kripa valambana Kari
Maata Annapurn Neshvarii

Salutations to Mother Annapoorna, who always give joy
To Her devotees, along with boons and assurance of
Fearlessness under Her motherly care.
Who is a repository of great beauty and makes their
Minds beautiful by the touch of the gem of Her inner
Beauty who purifies all the poisons and sufferings of
Their minds by the touch of Her compassion and bliss
Who is the great Goddess manifested visibly in Kashi
Who sanctified the lineage of the King of the Mountain
Of Himalayas by taking birth as Devi Parvati Who is the
Ruling Mother of the city of Kashi
O Mother Annapoorneswari, please grant us the Alms
Of Your Grace, Your Grace which support all the worlds.

Naanaa Ratna Vichitra Bhushana Kari
Hema Ambara Dambari

Muktaa Haara Vilamba MaanaVilasad
Vakssoja Kumbha Antari
Kaashmira Garu Vaasita Angga Ruchire
Kaashipura Dhishvari
Bhikshaam Dehi Kripavalambana Kari
Maata Annapurnneshvari

Salutations to Mother Annapoorna, Who is adorned
With many gems shining with various colours, and with
Garments striking with the shine of gold - golden laced
Who is decorated with a garland of pearls which is
Hanging down shining within the middle of Her
Bosom whose beautiful body is fragrant with
Saffron and Agaru – Agarwood.
Who is the Ruling Mother of the city of Kasi
O Mother Annapoorneswari, please grant us the Alms
Of Your Grace, Your Grace which support all the worlds.

Yoga Ananda Kari Ripu Kshaya Kari
Dharmartha Nishthaa Kari
Chandrarkanala Bhaasamaana Lahari
Trailokya Rakshaa Kari
Sarvaishvarya Samasta Vaanchitakari
Kaashipura Dhishvari
Bhikshaam Dehi Kripavalambana Kari
Maata Annapurnneshvari

Salutations to Mother Annapoorna Who gives the bliss
Of communion with God through yoga Who destroy
The attachment to the senses, which are the enemies
Of Yogic communion who makes us devoted to
Dharma and righteous effort to earn wealth as a
Worship of God Who is like a great wave shining with
The divine energies of Moon, Sun and Fire which
Protects the three worlds who gives all prosperity
And fulfills all wishes of the devotees who is the
Ruling Mother of the city of Kashi
O Mother Annapoorneswari, please grant us the Alms
Of Your Grace Your Grace, which Support all the Worlds.

~~~
~~~

DEVI BHUVANESHWARI

Udyad Dina Dyutim Indu Kiriittaam
Tungga Kucaam Nayana Traya Yuktaam
Smera Mukhiim Varada Angkusha Paashaam
Abhiiti Karaam Prabhaje Bhuvaneshiim

Salutations to Devi Bhuvaneshwari, Who has the Splendour of the rising Sun of the day and Who holds The Moon on Her crown like an ornament Who has Three eyes containing the Sun, Moon and the Fire Who has a smiling face and shows the vara Mudra - Boon - giving gesture Who holds an Ankusha - hook And a pasha - noose and displays the Abhaya Mudra - Gesture of Fearlessness with Her hands. Salutations to Devi Bhuvaneshwari.

Sinduura Arunna Vigrahaam Tri
Nayanaam Maannikya Mauli Sphurat
Taaraa Naayaka Shekharaam Smita
Mukhiim Aapiina Vakssoruhaam
Paannibhyaam Ali Puurnna Ratna
Cassakam Sam Vibhratiim Shaashvatiim
Saumyaam Ratna Ghattastha Madhya
Carannaam Dyaayet Paraam Ambikaam

Salutations to Devi Bhuvaneshwari Whose beautiful
Form has the reddish glow of the early morning Sun
Who has three eyes and Whose head glitters with the
Or nament of gems Who holds the chief of Star -Moon
On Her head Who is cool and joyful, and rests Her
Feet on a pitcher filled with jewels we meditate on
The supreme Ambika - supreme Mother.

~~~
~~~

DEVI KALIKA
(Kali Maa)

Galad Rakta Munnddaavalii Kannttha Maalaa
Maho Ghora Raavaa Su Damssttraa Karaalaa
Vivastraa Shmashaana Alayaa Mukta Keshii
Mahaakaala Kaama Akulaa Kaalikeyam

Salutations to Devi Kalika, from Her neck is hanging a Garland of heads from which blood is dripping down She is making a very terrific sound revealing Her large Teeth. Her appearance is extremely dreadful to look at She is without any clothes and residing in the Cremation ground. Her hair is let loose and free as is Her entire appearance. Her entire being is manifesting the great yearning to merge with Mahakala to take the Devotees beyond Samsara.
She is Kalika, The Great Dark Goddess.

Bhuje Vaama Yugme Shirosim Dadhaanaa
Varam Dakssa Yugme Abhayam Vai Tathai va
Su Madhya Api Tungga-Stanaa Bhaara Namraa

Lasad Rakta Srkka Dvayaa Su Smitaasyaa

Salutations to Devi Kalika, with Her left pair of hands
She is holding a head and a sword - symbols of death
And in like manner with Her right pair of hands
She is depicting the Vara – boon giving and
Abhaya – fearlessness Mudras – gestures
Assurance of taking the devotees to the world beyond
Death. Her pair of lips is shining with redness at the
Corner of which is playing a beautiful smile of death.

Shavadvandva Karnna Avatamsaa Su Keshii
Lasat Preta Paannim Prayuktai ka Kaanchii
Shava akaara Mancha Adhi Ruuddhaa Shivaabhish
Catur Dikssu Shabdaayamaana Abhireje

Salutations to Devi Kalika, Her ear rings are displaying
The symbols of death and She is having a beautiful
Long hair her shining girdle in the waist is made up of
The severed hands of the dead she is mounted on the
Platform of corpses and jackals from all four directions
Are making howling sounds of terror and in the midst
Of all these is reigning kalika
The Great Dark Goddess.

~~~
~~~

GANGA MAA

Gange Cha Yamune Chaiva
Godaavarii Sarasvati
Narmade Sindhu Kaaveri
Jalesmin Sannidhim Kuru

O Holy Rivers, Ganga and Yamuna, and also Godavari,
Saraswati, Narmada, Sindhu and Kaveri.
Please be present in this water near me
And make it Holy.

~~~
~~~

GANGA STOTRAM

Devi Sureshvari Bhagavati Gange
Tribhuvana Taarini Tarala Tarangge
Shankara Mauli Vihaarini Vimale
Mama Mati Rastaa Tava Pada Kamale

Salutations to Devi Ganga, O Devi Bhagavati Ganga
The Goddess of the Devas, You liberate the three
Worlds with the merciful waves of Your liquid form.
O The stainless pure one Who resides in the head of
Shankara. May my devotion remain firmly
Established on Your Lotus Feet.

Bhaagirathi Sukha Daayini Maatas
Tava Jala Mahimaa Nigame Khyaatah
Naaham Jaane Tava Mahimaanam
Paahi Krpaamayi Maama Ganyaanam

Salutations to Devi Ganga, O Mother Bhagirathi,
You give joy to all and the glory of Your water is praised
In the Scriptures. I do not know Your glory fully,
But inspite of my Ignorance
Please protect me, O Compassionate Mother.

Hari Pada Paadya Taranggini Gange
Hima Vidhu Muktaa Dhavala Tarangge
Duuri Kuru Mama Dusskriti Bhaaram
Kuru Kripayaa Bhava Saagara Paaram

Salutations to Devi Ganga, O Mother Ganga,
You originate from the feet of Hari and flow down with
Pure white waves resembling the whiteness of frost
The whiteness of Moon, as well as the whiteness of
Pearl O Mother, Please remove the burden in my mind
Created by evil deeds. By Your grace finally make me
Cross the ocean of Samsara - Worldly Existence.

Tava Jala Amalam Yena Nipitam
Parama Padam Khalu Tena Grihitam
Maatar Gange Tvayi Yo Bhaktah
Kila Tam Drastum Na Yamah Shaktah

Salutations to Devi Ganga, he who has drunk Your
Pure water, indeed he will obtain the highest abode
Yama is not able to cast his glance on him
He goes to Your abode and not Yamaloka.

Patito Ddhaarini Jaanhavi Gange
Khandita Giri Vara Mandita Bhangge
Bhishma Janani Hai Muni Vara Kanye
Patita Nivaarinni Tri Bhuvana Dhanye

Salutations to Devi Ganga, O Jahnavi Ganga,
You are the uplifter of the fallen, and You flow
Meandering through the great mountains of
Himalayas, cutting through them and adorning them.
O Mother of Bhisma and the daughter of the great
Jahnu Muni, You save the fallen and bring
Prosperity to the three worlds.

Kalpa Lataamiva Phala Daam Loke
Pranamati Yastwaam Na Patati Shoke
Paaraa Vaara Vihaarini Gange
Vimukha Yuvati Krita Tarala Apaangge

Salutations to Devi Ganga, You bestow fruits to the
World like the Kalpalata, wish-fulfilling creeper.
He who reverentially bows down to You, does not fall
Into grief. O Mother Ganga, You flow into the ocean
With the sportiveness of a young maiden
Turning away with side glances.

Tava Chan Maatah Srotah Snaatah
Punarapi Jatthare Sopi Na Jaatah
Naraka Nivaarini Jaanhavi Gange
Kalussa Vinaashini Mahimottungge

Salutations to Devi Ganga, O Mother,
He who has bathed in the flow of Your pure water,
He will not again take birth from the womb of
A mother or have rebirth.
O Jahnavi Ganga, You save people from falling in the
Naraka - hell and destroy their impurities.
O Mother Ganga, Your greatness stands high.

Punarasad Angge Punnya Tarangge
Jaya Jaya Jaanhavi Karunna Apaangge
Indra Mukutta Manni Raajita Charanne
Sukha De Shubha De Bhritya Sharannye

Salutations to Devi Ganga, O Jahnavi Ganga,
Victory to you. You make the impure body pure again
by Your holy waves and compassionate glance.
O Mother Ganga, Your feet is adorned with the crown
Jewel of Indra. You give joy and bestow auspiciousness
To the servant Who takes Your refuge.

Rogam Shokam Taapam Paapam
Hara Me Bhagavati Kumati Kalaapam
Tribhuvana Saare Vasudhaa Haare
Tvam Asi Gatir Mama Khalu Samsaare

Salutations to Devi Ganga, O Bhagavati Ganga,
Please take away my diseases, sorrows, afflictions and
Sins and evil tendencies from my mind.
O Mother Ganga, You are the prosperity of the three
Worlds and the garland of the earth You verily are my
Refugein the samsara - worldly existence.

Alakaanande Parama Anande
Kuru Karunnaamayi Kaatara Vandye
Tava Tata Nikate Yasya Nivaasah
Khalu Vaikunthe Tasya Nivaasah

Salutations to Devi Ganga, O Alakananda,
O the giver of great joy please listen to my prayers and
Be gracious to me. O the merciful one Who is adored

By the helpless he who resides near Your River Bank
Is indeed residing in Vaikuntha.

Varam Iha Niire Kamattho Miinah
Kim Vaa Tiire Sharathak Sinnah
Athavaa Shvapacho Malino Diinas
Tava Na Hi Duure Nrpati Kulinah

Salutations to Devi Ganga,
O Mother, it is better to live in Your waters like a
Tortoise or Fish or in Your River Bank like
A feeble Chameleon. Or be an unclean and miserable
Low born, but living near you rather than a King or
High born and being faraway from You.

Bho Bhuvaneshvari Punnye Dhanye
Devi Dravamayi Muni Vara Kanye
Ganga Stavamaam Amalam Nityam
Pathhati Naro Yah Sa Jayati Satyam

Salutations to Devi Ganga, O Bhuvaneswari Goddess of
The world You are the bestower of holiness and
Prosperity O Devi, You are the daughter of the great
Jahnu Muni in Liquid form he who regularly recites
This pure Ganga stava – Hymn
He truly becomes successful.

Yessaam Hrdaye Gangaa Bhaktis
Tessaam Bhavati Sadaa Sukha Muktih
Madhuraa Kaantaa Pajhati Kaabhih
Parama Ananda Kalita Lalitaa Bhih

Salutations to Devi Ganga. He who fills his heart with
Devotion to Devi Ganga he always feels the joy of
Freedom within his heart. This Ganga Stotram which is
Sweet and pleasing is like a great joy formed with
Artless innocence of devotion.

Gangaa Stotram Idam Bhava Saaram
Vaanchita Phala Dam Vimalam Saaram

Shankara Sevaka Shankara Rachitam
Patthati Sukhi Stava Iti Cha Samaaptah

Salutations to Devi Ganga. This Ganga Stotram is the True substance in this samsara giving desired fruits And is the essence of purity. This hymn is composed by Shankara, Adi Shankaracharya, the servant of Shankara – Shiva. Those who read it will be filled with Joy, thus ends this Stava – Hymn.

MAA YAMUNA

Muraari Kaaya Kaalimaa Lalaama Vaari Dhaarinnii
Trnnii Krta Trivissttapaa Tri Loka Shoka Haarinnii
Mano nukuula Kuula Kunja Punja Dhuuta Durmadaa
Dhunotu Me Mano Malam Kalinda Nandinii Sadaa

Salutations to Devi Yamuna, Your River Water holds The touch of the beautiful bluish darkness of the body Of Murari - Sri Krishna, hence making the heaven Insignificant like a blade of grass due to the touch of Sri Krishna proceeds to remove the sorrows of the Three worlds. Your River Banks hold charming groves Of breeze which is touched by Krishna and which Shake and remove our arrogance and makes us Devotionally inclined. O Kalinda Nandini, Daughter of The Kalinda Mountain, please wash away the Impurities from my mind, always.

Mala Apahaari Vaari Puura Bhuuri Mannddita Amrtaa
Bhrsham Prapaataka Pravancana Ati Pannddita Anisham
Su Nanda Nandana Angga Sangga Raaga Ranjitaa Hitaa
Dhunotu Me Mano Malam Kalinda Nandinii Sadaa

Salutations to Devi Yamuna, Your River Water, which Takes away the impurities, is filled with abundant Nectar - like qualities, which is expert in washing away Deep - seated sins which is extremely beneficial, being Coloured by the touch of the body of the son of Virtuous Nanda Gopa, O Kalinda Nandini, Daughter of The Kalinda Mountain. Please wash away the Impurities from my mind, always.

Lasat Tarangga Sangga Dhuuta Bhuuta Jaata Paatakaa
Naviina Maadhurii Dhuriinna Bhakti Jaata Caatakaa
Tatta Anta Vaasa Daasa Hamsa Samsrtaa Hi Kaama Daa
Dhunotu Me Mano Malam Kalinda Nandinii Sadaa

Salutations to Devi Yamuna, the touch of Your shining And playful waves wash away the sins rising in the Living beings. On Your River Bank resides many Chataka birds who carry the fresh sweetness born of Bhakti – devotion You grant the wishes of many Hamsas – swans Who converge and dwell on the Boundary of Your River Banks O Kalinda Nandini, Daughter of the Kalinda Mountain.
Please Wash away the impurities from my mind, always.

~~~
~~~

MAA NARMADA

Sabindu Sindhu Suskhalat Tarangga Bhangga Ranjitam
Dvissatsu Paapa Jaata Jaata Kaari Vaari Samyutam
Krtaanta Duuta Kaala Bhuuta Bhiiti Haari Varma De
Tvadiiya Paada Pankajam Namaami Devi Narmade

Salutations to Devi Narmada
Your river - body illumined with sacred drops of water
Flows with mischievous playfulness, bending with waves
Your sacred water has the divine power to transform
Those who are prone to hatred, the hatred born of sins
You put an end to the fear of the messenger of death
By giving your protective armour of refuge.
O Devi Narmada, I bow down to Your Lotus Feet,
Please give me Your refuge.

Tvad Ambu Liina Diina Miina Divya Sampradaayakam
Kalau Malaugha Bhaara Haari Sarva Tiirtha Naayakam
Sumaccha Kaccha Nakra Cakra Cakravaaka Sharmade
Tvadiiya Paada Pangkajam Namaami Devi Narmade

Salutations to Devi Narmada, You confer Your Divine
Touch to the lowly fish merged in your holy waters
You take away the weight of the sins in this age of Kali.
You are the foremost among all tirthas - pilgrimage
You confer happiness to the many fishes,
Tortoises crocodiles, geese and chakra birds
Dwelling in Your water. O Devi Narmada,
I bow down to your lotus feet,
Please give me Your Refuge.

Mahaa Gabhiira Niira Puura Paapa Dhuuta Bhuutalam
Dhvanat Samasta Paata Kaari Daari Taapa Daacalam
Jagal Laye Mahaa Bhaye Mrkanndda Suunu Harmya
De Tvadiiya Paada Pangkajam Namaami Devi Narmade

Salutations to Devi Narmada, Your River - body is deep
And overflowing, with waters that remove
The sins of the earth and it flows with great force
Making a loud reverberating sound, splitting asunder
Mountains of distresses the distresses,
Which bring our downfall In the heat of this world,
You provide the place of rest and assure great
Fearlessness. You who gave the place of refuge at your
Banks to the son of Rishi Mrikandu - Rishi Markandeya
O Devi Narmada, I Bow down to Your Lotus Feet.

Please give me Your refuge.

~~~
~~~

NAUGRAHA DEVATA

BRAHMAA MURARI

Brahmaa Muraari Tripuraantakaarii
Bhaanuh Shashii Bhuumisuto Budhashcha
Gurushcha Shukrah Shani Raahu Ketavah
Kurvantu Sarve Mama Suprabhaatam

In the early morning I remember the devas Brahma
Murari - The enemy of demon
Mura - Krishna Tripuraantakari The One
Who has brought an end to Tripurasuras - Shiva
The planets Bhanu - the Sun, Shashi - the Moon
Bumisuta - Mars and Budha Mercury
Guru Jupiter, Shukra Venus,
Shani Saturn, Rahu and Ketu
May all of them make my morning auspicious.

~~~
~~~

NAVGRAHA DEVATAAS

Surya : Om hram hreem hroum sah suryaya namah
Chandra : Om shram sreem shraum sah chandraya namah
Mangala : Om kram kreem kroum sah bhaumaya namah
Budha : Om bram breem broum sah budhaya namah
Guru : Om jhram jhreem jroum sah gurave namah
Shukra : Om dram dreem droum sah shukraya namah
Shani : Om pram preem proum sah shanaischaraya namah
Rahu : Om bhram bhreem bhroum sah rahave namah
Ketu : Om shram shreem shroum sah ketave namah

~~~
~~~

NAVAGRAHA SHANTI STOTRAM

Ravi - Bheeja Mantram

Om Ghruni Suryaya namaha

~~~

Ravi Vaidika Mantram

Om Aa Krishnena rajasa vartamaanonvesay
Unnamrutam martyancha Hiranyayena savita radhena
Devo Yaati bhavanani pasyan

~~~

Ravi - Gayatri Mantram

Om Adhityaya cha vidmahe, prabhakaraya dheemahi
Tanmo Surya prachodayat

~~~

Chandra - Bheeja Mantram

Om sooom somaya namaha

~~~

Chandra - Vaidika mantram

Om Aapyayaswa sametu, te viswasooma vrushniyam
Bhavaa vajasya samgadhe

~~~

Chandra Gayatri Mantram

Om Amrutamgaya vidmahe, kalaroopaya dheemahi
tanmo soma prachodayat

~~~

Kuja - Bheeja Mantram

Om Am angarakaya namaha

~~~

Kuja - Vaidika Mantram

Om agniromdhardiva, kakutpati prudviayam
Apari retasijinwati, bhowmaaya namaha

~~~

Kuja - Gayatri Mantram
Om Angarakaya vidmahe, shaktihastaya dheemahi
Tanmo bhooma prachodayat
~~~

Budha Bheeja Mantram
Om brhum budhaya namaha
~~~

Budha - Vaidika Mantram
Om Vudbhudyasagne, pratijaagruhi twmishapoorte sa
Sprujydayam cha asminootsa, daste adyuttarasmin
Viswe deva yamanaschaseedath
~~~

Guru - Bheeja Mantram
Om brhum bruhaspatiye namaha
~~~

Guru - Vaidika mantram
Om Brhuhaspatiye atiyadaryo, arhadyumadwibhati
Kratumajjaneshu, tadasmusu dravinam deehi chitram
~~~

Guru - Gayatri Mantram
Om Amgeerasaya vidmahe, divyadhehaaya deemahi
Tanmo jaavah prachodayat
~~~

Sukra - Bheeja Mantram
Om sum sukrayanamaha
~~~

Sukra - Vaidika Mantram
Om anmat parisutorasam brahmanaa
Vyapivatkshatrayampayam, somam prajapati
Rutena satyamindriyam vipana sukramadhasa
Indrasyodriyammidam payoomrutamadhu
~~~

Sani - Beeja Mantram

Om sam sanischaraya namaha

~~~

Sani Vaidika Mantram

Om Sanmo deveerabheeshtaya apo bhavantu Peetaye
Samyorbhisravantu na

~~~

Sani - Gayatri Mantram

Om Bhavabhavaya vidmahe, mrutyuroopaya
dheemahi, Tanmo sukra prachodayat

~~~

Rahu - Bheeja Mantram

Om Ram rahave namaha

~~~

Rahu - Vaidika Mantram

Om Kayanaschitra abhuvadhooti sada vrudhah
Sakha kaya sachishta vruta

~~~

Rahu - Gayatri Mantram

Om Siroroopaya vidmahe, amrutesaya dheemahi
Tanmo rahu prachodayat

~~~

Ketu - Bheeja Mantram

Om kam kekave namaha

~~~

Ketu - Vaidika Mantram

Om Ketum krunvanna, pesomurya apesase
Samushadbhi rajayadha

~~~

Ketu - Gayatri Mantram

**Om padmaputraya vidmahe, amrutesaaya dheemahi
Tanmo ketu prachodayat**

~~~
~~~

SURYA DEVA

Aum Mitraya Namah Who is friendly to all
Aum Ravayre Namah The shining one, the radiant one
Aum Suryaya Namah Who is the dispeller of darkness
Aum Bhanave Namah One who illumines the bright one
Aum Khagaya Namah Who is all-pervading
Aum Pushne Namah Giver of nourishment and fulfillment
Aum Hiranyagarbhaya Namah Who has golden color brilliance
Aum Marichaye Namah The giver of infinite number of rays
Aum Adityaya Namah The son of Aditi the cosmic divine Mother
Aum Savitre Namah One who is responsible for life
Aum Arkaya Namah Worthy of praise and glory
Aum Bhaskaraya Namah Giver of wisdom and illumination

~~~
~~~

SURYA ASHTAKAM

Aadi Deva Namastubhyam
Prasiida Mama Bhaaskara
Divaakara Namastubhyam
Prabhaakara Namostu Te

Salutations to Sri Suryadeva, my salutations to You
O Adideva the first God.
Please be gracious to me O Bhaskara the shining one.
My salutations to You, O Divakara the maker of the day.
Salutations to You, O Prabhakara the maker of Light.

Sapta Ashva Ratham Aaruuddham
Prachannddam Kashyapa Atmajam
Shveta Padma Dharam Devam
Tam Suuryam Pranaam Mayham

Salutations to Sri Suryadeva, You are mounted on a
Chariot driven by seven horses. You are excessively
Energeticand the son of sage Kashyapa. You are the
Deva Who holds a white Lotus in Your Hand .
I Salute You, O Suryadeva.

Lohitam Ratham Aaruuddham
Sarva Loka Pitaamaham
Mahaa Paapa Haram Devam
Tam Suuryam Pranaam Mayham

Salutations to Sri Suryadeva. You are reddish in colour,
Mounted on a chariot. You are the grandfather of all
Persons being the Adideva, the first God.
You are the Deva who removes great sins from our
Minds by Your illumination. I Salute You, O Suryadeva

Trai Gunnyam Cha Mahaa Shuuram
Brahma Vishnnu Maheshvaram
Mahaa Paapa Haram Devam
Tam Suuryam Pranaam Mayham

Salutations to Sri Suryadeva. You are the heroic one
Having the three gunas of Brahma,Vishnu and
Maheswara Qualities of Creation, sustenance and
Dissolution You are the Deva Who removes great sins
from our minds by Your illumination.
I salute You, O Suryadeva.

Bramhitam Tejah Punjam Cha
Vaayum Aakaashame Va Cha
Prabhum Cha Sarva Lokaanaam
Tam Suuryam Pranaam Mayham

Salutations to Sri Suryadeva. You are a massively
Enlarged mass of fiery energy, which pervades
Everywhere like Vayu - Air and Akasha - sky
You are the Lord of all the Worlds.
I salute You, O Suryadeva.

Bandhuka Pushpa Sangkaasham
Haara Kundala Bhushitam
Eka Cakra Dharam Devam
Tam Suuryam Pranaam Mayham

Salutations to Sri Suryadeva. You appear beautiful like a
Red hibiscus flower and you are adorned with garland

And Ear Rings. You are the Deva
Who holds a discus in one hand.
I salute You, O Suryadeva.

Tam Suuryam Jagat Kartaaram
Mahaa Tejah Pradiipanam
Mahaa Paapa Haram Devam
Tam Suuryam Pranaam Mayham

Salutations to Sri Suryadeva. O Suryadeva, You are the
Agent behind the world. Who gives energy for action to
Everyone. You enliven others with great energy
Imparting the ability to work you are the Deva Who

Removes great sins from our minds by Your Illumination. I salute You, O Suryadeva.

Tam Suuryam Jagataam Naatham
Gyaana Vigyaana Mokshadam
Mahaa Paapa Haram Devam
Tam Suuryam Pranaam Mayham

Salutations to Sri Suryadeva, You, O Suryadeva are the Lord of the world, Who grants understanding and Knowledge which leads to liberation
You are the Deva Who removes great sins from our Minds by your illumination. I salute You, O Suryadeva.

~~~
~~~

ADI DEV NAMOSTUBHYAM

Adi Dev Namostubhyam
Praseed Maam Bhaskar
Divakara Namostute
Prabhakara Namostute
Saptashva Ratham
Arudhanam Prachandam
Kashya Paatmajam S̃hwetapad
Madharam Devam Twam
Suryam Pranamam Mayham
Lohitam Ratha Marudham
Sarvalok Pita Maham
Mahapaap Haram Devam
Twam Suryam Pranamaam Mayham

~~~
~~~

SHRI VISHNU

Aadyam Ranggam Iti Proktam
Vimanam Rangga Samjnyitam
Shrimusnam Vengkatadrim Cha
Saallagraamam Cha Naimisham
Toyaadrim Pusskaram Chaiva
Nara Narayana Ashramam
Asstau Me Murtayah Santi
Svayam Vyaktaa Mahitale

First, called Ranga, the great temple of Srirangam Made known by the great Lord Ranga. Then Srimushanam and Venkatadri, Salagrama and Naimisha Toyadri - Thiruneermalai, Pushkara and Indeed Nara Narayana Ashrama - Badrikashrama or Badrinath. These eight manifestations of mine present on earth are Swayam-Vyakta - self-manifested.

Shaanta Kaaram Bhujaga Shayanam
Padma Naabham Suresham
Vishva Dhaaram Gagana Sadrisham
Megha Varnam Shubha Anggam
Lakshmi Kaantam Kamala Nayanam
Yogibhir Dhyaana Gamyam
Vande Vishnum Bhava Bhaya Haram
Sarva Lokaika Naatham

Salutations to Sri Vishnu, Who has a serene Appearance, Who rests on a Serpent - Adisesha, Who has a lotus on His Navel and Who is The Lord of the Devas, Who Sustains the Universe, Who is boundless and Infinite like the sky, Whose Colour is like the cloud - Bluish and Who has a Beautiful and auspicious Body, Who is the Husband of Devi Lakshmi, Whose Eyes are like Lotus and Who is Attainable to the Yogis by meditation, Salutations to That Vishnu Who removes the fear of worldly existence And Who is the Lord of all the Lokas.

~~~

SHREE VISHNU PRATAH SMARANAM

Pratah Smarami Bhavabhiti Maharti Shantyaih
Narayanam Garunvahanam Abjanabham
Grahabhibhutavar Varanmuktihetum
Chakrayudham Tarunvarij Patra Netram

Pratarnamami Mansa Vachasa Cha Murdhana
Padarvindayugalam Paramasya Pumsah
Narayanasya Narkarnavatarnasya
Parayanah Pravanvi Prapara Yanasya

Pratam Bhajami Bhajata Abhayankaram Tam
Prakh Sarvajanmakrita Paap Bhayapatyai
Yo Grahvaktra Patitanghri Gajendra Ghora
Shoka Prana Shankaro Bhrit Shankha Chakra
Iti shreee vishnavo pratah smaranam

~~~

VISHNU AHVAHAN

Yam Brahma Varunendra Rudra Marutah
Stunvanti Divyaih Sthavair
Vedaih Sanga Pada Kramo Panishadair
Gayanti Yam Saamgah
Dhyanavasthita Tad Gatena Manasa
Pashyanti Yam Yogino
Yasyantam Na Viduh Surasura Gana
Devaya Tasmai Namah

~~~

OM SHREE ANANT HARI NARAYAN

Mangalam Bhagawaan Vishnu
Mangalam Garudadhwajah
Mangalam Pundareekaksha
Mangalaya Tanohari

~~~

VISHNU SHATNAAM STOTRAM

Vasudevam Hrishikeshwam Vamanam Jalshayinam
Janardanam Harim Krishnam Shreevaksham
Garudadhwajam
Varaham Pundarikasham Nrishimham Narkantakam
Avyaktm Shashwatam Vishnum Ananantam Ajmavyayam

Narayanam Gadadhyaksham Govindam Kirtivajanam
Govardhano Dahram Devam Bhudharam Bhuvaneshwaram
Yekaram Yagnapurusham Ygnesham Yagnavahakam
Chakrapanim Gadapanim Shankhpanim Narottamam

Vaikuntham Dushtadamanam Bhugarbham Veetvaasasam
Trivikramam Trikaalaghnam Trimurtim Nandikeshwaram
Ramam Ramam Hayagreevam
Devamrogandharvodbhawam
Shreepatim Shreedharam Shreesham Mangalam
Mangalayudham

Damodaram Damopreetam Keshavam Keshisudanam
Varenyam Varadam Vishnum Anandam Vasudevajam
Hiranyanet Samveetam Puranam Purushottamam
Sakalam Nishkalam Suddham Nirgunam Gunshashvatam

Hirnayah Dhanushankasam Suryayatah Samaprabhah

Meghashyamam Chaturbaahum Kusalam Kamalekshanam
Jyotiroopamaroopam Cha Swaroopam Roopsamsthitam
Sarvagyam Sarvaroopastam
Sarveshaam Sarvatomukham

Gyankootastamchalam Gyangam Paramam Prabhum
Yogisham Yognishrantam Yoginam Yogiroopinam
Ishwaram Sarvabhutanaam Vande Bhootmayam Prabhum
Iti Naamaksharam Divyam Vaishnavam Kalpaapaham

SHRI VISHNU STUTI

Jai jai surnayak jan sukhdayak pranat pal bhagwanta
Go dwij hitkari jai asurari sindhu suta priya kanta
Palan sur dharni adbhud karni maram na janahi koi
Jo sahaj kripala deen dayala karahu anugrah soyi
Jai jai avinasi sab ghat basi vyapak parmananda
Avigat gotitam charita punetam mayarahit mukunda Jehi
lagi biragi ati anuragi bigat moh muni brinda Nisibasar
dhyavahi gun gan ganwahi jayati satchidananda
Jehi shrishti upayi tribidh banayi sang sahaya na duja
So karahu aghari chint humari janahi bhagati na pooja Jo
bhava bhaya bhanjan muni man ranjan
Ganjan bipati barutha
Man vach kram bani chhadi sayani
saran sakal sur jhootha
Sharad shruti shesha rishaya ashesha ja
kah kou nahi jaana
Jehi deen piyare ved pukare dravau so
shree bhagwana
Bhav baridhi mandar sab vidhi sundar gun
mandir sukh punja
Muni siddha sakal sur param bhayatur
namat nath pad kanja

~~~
~~~

SHRI RAMA

***Lokaabhi Raamam Ranna Rangga Dhiiram Raajiva Netram
Raghu Vamsha Naatham Kaarunnya Rupam Karunnaa
Karantam Shri Raamacamdram Sharannam Prapadye***

I take refuge in Sri Rama, Who is pleasing to the people
Who is calm and composed in the battle field
Whose eye sare like Blue Lotuses.
Who is the Lord of the Raghu dynasty
Who is an embodiment of compassion and Shower his
Compassion to all I take refuge in
The lotus feet of Sri Ramachandra.

***Maataa Raamo Mat Pitaa Raamachandrah
Svaami Raamo Mat Sakhaa Raamachandrah
Sarvasvam Me Raamachandro Dayaalu
Nanyam Jaane Naiva Jaane Na Jaane***

Rama is my mother and Rama - Ramachandra is my
Father. Rama is my Lord and Rama - Ramachandra is
My friend. Rama is my all in all, O the Compassionate
Rama – Ramachandra is my all in all.
I do not know any other, I do not know any other.
Indeed I do not know any other.

~~~
~~~

RAAMA RAAMA RAAMETI

Rame Raame Manorame
Sahasra Naama Tat Tulyam
Raama Naama Varaanane

By meditating on "Rama Rama Rama" - the name of
Rama. My mind gets absorbed in the divine
Consciousness of Rama which is transcendental
The name of Rama is as great as the thousand
Names of God Vishnu sahasranama.

Raamo Raja Mannih Sadaa Vijayate
Raamam Ramesham Bhaje
Raamenna Abhihataa Nishaachara Camuuh
Raamaaya Tasmai Namah
Raamaan Naasti Paraayanam Parataram
Raamasya Daasosmyaham
Raame Chitta Layas Sadaa Bhavatu Me
Bho Raama Maam Uddhara

I contemplate on Sri Rama, Who is the jewel among
The kings Who always emerges victorious, and
Who is the Lord of Sita Devi
I salute Sri Rama who destroyed the mighty armies of
The demons there is no greater refuge than Sri Rama.
I am a humble servant of Sri Rama
Let my mind ever meditate on Rama
O Sri Rama. Kindly grant me Salvation

~~~
~~~

SHRI RAAM GAYATRI MANTRA

Om Dasharathaye Vidmahe
Sitavallabhaya Dhimahi
Tanno Rama Prachodayat

SHRI RAAM MEDITATION MANTRA

Om Apadamapahartaram
Dataram Sarvasampadam
Lokabhiramam Shriramam
Bhuyo Bhuyo Namamyaham

SHRI RAMAYAN JI KI SUMIRAN

Jo Sumirat Sidhi Hoye Rama
Gan Nayak Kariwar Badana

Karau Anugrah Soi Rama
Buddhi Raasi Subh Gun Sadana

Mook Hoi Baachaal Rama
Pangu Chadhai Giriwar Gahana

Jaasu Kripa So Dayaal Rama
Dravahu Sakal Kali Mal Dahana

Neel Saroruhu Syaam Rama
Tarun Arun Vaarij Nayana

Karau So Mam Ur Dhaam Rama
Sada Ksheer Sagar Sayana

Kundendu Sam Deha Rama
Uma Raman Karuna Ayana

Jaahi Deen Par Neh Rama
Karau Kripa Mardan Mayana

KASHI SATSANGH

Vandau Guru Pad Kanj Rama
Kripa Sindhu Nar Roop Hari

Maha Moh Tam Poonj Rama
Jaasu Vachan Ravi Kar Nikari

Vandau Muni Pad Kanj Rama
Ramayan Jin Nirmayu

Sakal Sukomal Manju Rama
Dosh Rahit Dushan Sahita

Vando Charahu Ved Rama
Bhaw Vaaridh Bohit Sarisa

~~~

SHRI RAAMA STOTRAM

Aapadam aphartaram, dataram sarva sampadam
Lokabhiramam Sriramam, bhuyo bhuyo namamyaham

Aartanaamaartihantaram, bheetanaam bheetinashanam
Dvishtataam kaladandam tam, Ramachandram namamyaham

Sannadhaha kavachi khadgi, chaapabaanadharo yuva
Gachhan mamagrato nityam, Ramaha paatu salakshmanaha

Namaha kodandahastaya, sandhikrita sharaya cha
Khanditakhil daityaya, Ramayapana nivaarine

Ramaya Ramabhadraya, Ramachandraya vedhase
Raghunaatahya naathaya, Sitayah pataye namaha

Agrataha prishthatashchaiva, paarshvatashcha mahabalau
Aakarnapoorna dhanvanau, rakshetaam Rama Lakshmanau

~~~

DEVI SITA

Jaanaki Tvaam Namasyaami
Sarva Paapa Pranaashinim

Hanumanji said
O Devi Janaki, I salute You.
You are the destroyer of all sins

Daaridrya Ranna Samhartrim
Bhaktaana Bhisstta Daayinim
Videha Raaja Tanayaam
Raaghavananda Kaarinnim

I salute You, You are the destroyer of poverty in the battle of life and bestower of wishes of the devotees I salute You, You are the daughter of Videha Raja - King Janaka and cause of joy of Raghava - Sri Rama.

Bhumer Duhitaram Vidyaam
Namaami Prakrtim Shivaam
Paulastya Ishvarya Samhatrim
Bhakta Abhishtam Sarasvatim

I salute You, You are the daughter of the Earth
And the embodiment of knowledge You are the
Auspicious Prakriti.
I salute You, You are the destroyer of the power and
Supremacy of oppressors like Ravana.
And at the same time fulfiller of the wishes of the
Devotees You are an embodiment of Saraswati.

Pativrata Dhurinaam Tvaam
Namaami Janaka Atmajaam
Anugraha Paraam Riddhim
Anaghaam Hari Vallabhaam

I salute You, You are the best among
Pativratas - ideal wife devoted to husband
And at the same time, the soul of Janaka
Ideal daughter devoted to her father
I salute You. You are very gracious being Yourself
The embodiment of Riddhi - Lakshmi
Pure and sinless and extremely beloved of Hari.

~~~
~~~

SHRI KRISHNA

Kara Aravindena Pada Aravindam
Mukha Aravinde Vi-Niveshay Antam
Vatasya Patrasya Putte Shayaanam
Baalam Mukundam Manasaa Smaaraami

My mind remembers that beautiful Bala Mukundam
Who with His lotus like hands holds His lotus like feet
And puts the toe in His lotus like mouth He rests on
The he fold of the banyan leaf my mind remembers
That Beautiful Bala Mukundam

Kasturitilakam lalaat Patale
Vakshasthale Kaustubham
Nasagre varmauktikam kar tale
Venu kare kankanam
Sarvange harichandanam sulalitam
Kanthe cha muktawali
Gopastri pariveshtito vijayate
Gopala chudamani

Salutations to Gopala Who is adorned with the sacred
Marks of Kasturi - Musk on His Forehead
And Kaustubha jewel on His chest
His nose is decorated with a shining pearl
The palms of His hands are gently holding a flute.
The hands themselves are beautifully decorated with
Bracelets. His whole body is smeared with sandal paste
As if playfully anointed. His neck is decorated with a
Necklace of pearls surrounded by the cowherd Women.
Gopala is shining in the middle in
Celebration like a Jewel on the Head.

Krishnaaya Vaasudevaaya
Devaki Nandanaaya Cha
Nanda Gopa Kumaraaya
Govindaaya Namo Namah

Salutations to Sri Krishna Who is the son and the joy
Of father Vasudeva and mother Devaki
Salutations to Him Who is the boy of cowherd
Nanda and Who is himself the Lord Govinda
Salutations, Salutations to Him again and again.

Vasudeva Sutham Devam
Kamsa Chaanoora Mardhanam
Devaki Paramaanandham
Krishnam Vande' Jagathgurum

~~~
~~~

TWENTY FOUR NAME MANTRA OF LORD KRISHNA

Shri Keshvay namah, Naraynay namah, Madhvay namah,
Govinday namah, Vishnve namah, Madhusudnay namah,
Trivikramay namah, Vamnay namah, Shridhray namah,
Hrshikeshay namah, Padmanabhaay namah,
Damodaray namah, Sankrshanay namah,
Vasudevay namah, Pradyumnay namah,
Aniruddhay namah, Purushottmay namah,
Adhoxjay namah, Narsimhay namah, Achyutay namah,
Janardanay namah, Upendray namah, Haraye namah,
Shri Krishnay namah.

~~~

KARARAVINDE

Kararavinde Na Padaravindam
Mukharavinde Viniveshayantam
Vatasya Patrasya Pute Shayanam
Balam Mukundam Manasa Smarami

I memorize the Lord in his infant form - Mukunda Who sleeps in a banyan leaf he is the one who puts his Lotus life feet to His mouth with the help of His hands.

~~~

SHRI KRISHNA GAYATRI

Devkinandanaye Vidmahe
Vasudevaye Dhimahi
Tanno Krishna Prachodayat

Mukam Karoti Vaacaalam
Panggum Langghayate Girim
Yat Kripaa Tamaham Vande
Param Aananda Maadhavam

I remember with devotion the Divine grace of Krishna
Who can make the dumb speak with
Eloquence and the lame cross high mountains
I remember and extol that grace which
Flows from the supreme bliss manifestation of Madhava.

Namo Brahmannya Devaaya
Go Braahmanna Hitaaya Cha
Jagat Hitaaya Krishnaaya
Govindaaya Namo Namah

Salutations to the Lord who is of the nature of
Supreme consciousness and the friend and
Benefactor of the cowsand the brahmins
Salutations to the Lord Who is the friend and
Benefactor of the whole world
Salutations to Sri Krishna, Salutations to Sri Govinda

Salutations, Salutations to Him again and again.

MADHURASHTAKAM

Adharam Madhuram Vadanam Madhuram
Nayanam Madhuram Hasitham Madhuram
Hridayam Madhuram Gamanam Madhuram
Madhuradhipate Akhilam Madhuram

Vachanam Madhuram Charitam Madhuram
Vasanam Madhuram Valitam Madhuram
Chalitam Madhuram Dravitam Madhuram
Madhuradhipate Akhilam Madhuram

Venur Madhuro Renur Madhurah
Paanir Madhurah Paadau Madhuram
Nrityam Madhuram Saktyam Madhuram
Madhuradhipate Akhilam Madhuram
Geetam Madhuram Peetam Madhuram
Bhuktam Madhuram Suptham Madhuram
Roopam Madhuram Tilakam Madhuram
Madhuradhipate Akhilam Madhuram
Karanam Madhuram Tharnam Madhuram
Harnam Madhuram Smaranam Madhuram
Vamitham Madhuram Samitham Madhuram
Madhuradhipate Akhilam Madhuram

Gunja Madhura Mala Madhura
Yamuna Madhura Veechhi Madhura
Salilam Madhuram Kamalam Madhuram
Madhuradhipate Akhilam Madhuram

Gopi Madhura Leela Madhura
Yuktam Madhuram Muktam Madhuram
Drishtam Madhuram Sishtham Madhuram
Madhuradhipate Akhilam Madhuram

Gopa Madhura Gavo Madhura
Yashthir Madhuro Shristir Madhura
Dalitam Madhuram Palitham Madhuram
Madhuradhipate Akhilam Madhu

~~~

BALAM MUKUNDAM

Kara Ra Vindena Pada Ra Vindham
Mukhara Vinde Vini Vesay Antham
Vatasya Pathrasya Pute Sayanam
Balam Mukundam Mansas Smarami.
Samhruthya Lokaan Vatapathra Madhye
Sayana Madhyantha Vihaina Roopam
Sarveshwaram Sarva Hitha Vatharam
Balam Mukundam Manasas Smarami.

Indeevara Shyamala Komal Angam
Indrathi Devarchitha Pada Padmam
Santhana Kalpa Druma Maasritha Naam
Balam Mukundam Manasas Smarami.

Lambhalakam Lambhitha Hara Yashtim
Srungara Leelangitha Dantha Pank Theem
~~~

Bimbadaram Charu Vilasa Naethram
Balam Mukundam Manasas Smarami.

Sikh Yae Nithayadhya Payo That Heeni
Bahir Gadayam Vraja Nayi Kayam
Bukthwa Yadeshtam Kapatena Suptham
Balam Mukundam Manasas Smarami.

Kalinda Jantha Sthitha Kai Yasya
Phanagrange Natana Priyantham
Thath Pucha Hastham Sara Daendu Vakthram
Balam Mukundam Manasas Smarami.

Uloo Khale Badha Mudhara Souryam
Uthunga Padmarjuna Bhanga Leelam
Uthphulla Padmaya Tha Charu Naethram
Balam Mukundam Manasas Smarami.

Aalokhya Maadur Mukha Madarena
Sthanyam Pibhantham Sasareehuaksham
Sachinmayam Devam Anantharoopam
Balam Mukundam Manasas Smarami.

~~~
~~~

KRISHNA – MAKHAN CHOR

Braje Vasantam Navneet Choram
Gopanga Nanaam Chadukul Choram
Shree Radhikaya Hridayasi Choram
Choragya Ganyam Purusham Namami
Shree Krishna Shyamam Mansa Smarami

The Butter Thief lives in Vraj and the stealer of the
Saarees of the groups of gopis.
He even stole the heart of Radha Ji.
Our acclamation to the most superior of the thieves
We remember Shree Krishna Shyam
From our deep mind.

~~~
~~~

SHREE RADHA KRISHNA STUTI

Gopalam Giriraj Raj Dharnam Gita
Girantam Guruh Rashe
Sware Rasraj Radha Priyamsi Prernadam
Prabhuvarikansup Punpriya Yaduvaram
Meera Priyam Sundaram
Krishnam Venukaram Mayur Mukutam
Mangalaye Natham Numah
Om Shree Radha Krishnaya Namo Namah

~~~
~~~

DEVI RADHA RANI

Raadhaa Raaseshvari
Raasa Vaasinii Rasi Keshvari
Krishnaa Praanaa Dhikaa
Krishnna Priyaa Krishnna Svaruupinni
Sri Narayana
The sixteen names of Radharani

Radha, Raaseshwari, Raasavasini, Rasikeshwari
Krishnapranadhika, Krishnapriya, Krishna Swarupini

Krishnna Vaamaangga Sam Bhuutaa
Parama Ananda Ruupinni
Krishnnaa Vrndaavanii Vrndaa
Vrndaavana Vinodini
The sixteen names of Radharani Contd...

Krishna Vamanga Sambhuta, Paramanandarupini
Krishnaa, Vrindavani, Vrindaa, Vrindavana Vinodini

Chandraavali Chandrakaantaa
Sharac Chandra Prabhaananaa
Naamaany Etaani Saaraanni
Tessaam-Abhyantaraanni Cha

Chandravali, Chandrakanta,
Sharat Chandra Prabhanana
These sixteen Names which are the Essence are
Included in one thousand names

~~~
~~~

KAAL BHAIRAV ASHTAKAM

Deva Raaja Sevya Maana
Paavana Angghri Pang Kajam
Vyaala Yajnya Suutram Indu
Shekharam Krpaa Karam

Naaradaadi Yogi Vrinda
Vanditam Digambaram
Kaashi Kaa Pura Adhinaatha
Kaala Bhairavam Bhaje

Salutations to Sri Kalabhairava
Whose lotus feet is served by Indra
The King of the Devas Who has a snake as His
Sacrificial thread and a moon on His head and
Who is extremely compassionate
Who is praised by sage Narada and other yogis
And Who is Digambara - clothed by sky
Signifying that He is ever-free
Salutations to Sri Kalabhairava
Who is the Supreme Lord of the City of Kasi.

Bhaanu Kotti Bhaasvaram
Bhavaabdhi Taarakam Param
Niila Kanntham Iipsita
Artha Daayakam Trilochanam

Kaala Kaalam Ambuja Akssam
Akssa Shuulam Aksharam
Kaashikaa Pura Adhinaatha
Kaalabhairavam Bhaje

Salutations to Sri Kalabhairava
Who has the brilliance of a million suns
Who rescues us from the ocean of worldly existence
And Who is supreme and Who has a blue throat
Who bestows us with dorldly prosperity

And Who has three eyes Who is the death of
The Death and is beyond death itself
Who is lotus-eyed and Who's trident supports the
Three worlds and Who is imperishable.
Salutations to Sri Kalabhairava
Who is the supreme Lord of the city of Kasi.

Shuula Ttangka Paasha Danndda
Paannim Aadi Kaarannam
Shyaama Kaayam AadiDevam
Aksharam Nir Aamayam

Bhiima Vikramam Prabhum
Vichitra Taannddava Priyam
Kaashikaa Pura Adhinaatha
Kaalabhairavam Bhaje

Salutations to Sri Kalabhairava
Who has trident, hatchet, noose and
Club in His hands and Who is the primordial cause of
The Universe whose body is dark,
Who is the primordial Lord
Who is imperishable and Who is beyond diseases of
The world Who is the Lord with terrific prowess
And Who loves the strange, vigorous tandava dance
Salutations to Sri Kalabhairava
Who is the supreme Lord of the city of Kasi.

~~~
~~~

BHAGWAN SHIVA

Kara Charanna Kritam Vaak
Kaaya Jam Karma Jam Vaa
Shravanna Nayana Jam Vaa
Maanasam Va Aparaadham
Vihitam Avihitam Vaa
Sarvam Etat Kshamasva
Jaya Jaya Karunna Abdhe
Shrii Mahaadeva Shambho

Whatever Sins have been Committed
By Actions Performed by my Hands and Feet
Produced by my Speech and Body or my Actions
Produced by my Ears and Eyes or Sins Committed by
My Mind in Thoughts While Performing Actions, which
Are Prescribed As Well as All other Actions, which are
Not explicitly Prescribed Please Forgive Them All
Victory,Victory to You, O Sri Mahadeva Shambho
I Surrender to You, You are an Ocean of Compassion.

Karpuura Gauram Karunna Avataaram
Sansaara Saaram Bhujagendra Haaram
Sadaa Vasantam Hridaya Aravinde
Bhavam Bhavaanii Sahitam Namaami

Pure White like Camphor, an Incarnation of
Compassion The Essence of Worldly Existence
Whose Garland is the King of Serpents
Always Dwelling inside the Lotus of the Heart
I Bow to Shiva and Shakti Together.

Om Try Ambakam Yajaamahe
Sugandhim Pushtti Vardhanam
Urvaarukam Iva Bandhanaan
Mrityor Mukshiiya Maamrtaat

OM - WeWorship the Three-Eyed One - Lord Shiva
Who is Fragrant - Spiritual Essence and Who Nourishes
All beings may he severe our Bondage of
Samsara - Worldly Life Like a Cucumber severed from
the Bondage of its Creeper and thus Liberate us from
the Fear of Death by making us realize that we are
Never separated from our Immortal Nature.

~~~
~~~

SHIVA GAYATRI

Om Tatpurushaya Vidmahe
Maha Devaya Dheemahi

Tannoh Rudrah Prachodayat

~~~

JYOTIRLINGAS - SHIVA PURANA

1. **Somnath Jyotirlinga** - Where Shiva relieved the curse of Chandra Deva.
2. **Mallikarjuna Jyotirlinga** - Where Shiva-Parvati came to meet Kumara.
3. **Mahakaleshwar Jyotirlinga** - Where Shiva protected devotee Veda Priya from demon Dushana.
4. **Omkareshwar Jyotirlinga** - Where Shiva granted boon to Vindhya Mountain.
5. **Kedarnath Jyotirlinga** - Where Shiva gave darshan to devotees Nara and Narayana.
6. **Bhimashankar Jyotirlinga** - Where Shiva protected devotee Sudakshina from demon Bhima.
~~~

7. **Vishwanath Jyotirlinga** - Where Shiva created Kashi and held it on his trident.
8. **Tryambakeshwar Jyotirlinga** - Where Shiva gave darshan to devotee Gautama Rishi and released the Gautami Ganga.
9. **Vaidyanath Jyotirlinga** - Where Ravana placed the Atma Linga of Shiva.
10. **Nageshwar Jyotirlinga** - Where Shiva protected devotee Supriya from demon Daruka.
11. **Rameshwar Jyotirlinga** - Where Shiva appeared before Sri Rama and gave the blessing of victory against Ravana.
12. **Grishneshwar Jyotirlinga** - Where Shiva brought back to life the dead son of devotee Ghushma.

~~~

LINGASTAKAM

Brahma Muraari Sura Aarcita Lingam
Nirmala Bhaasita Shobhita Lingam
Janmaja Duhkha Vinaashaka Lingam
Tat Prannamaami Sadaashiva Lingam

I salute that eternal Shiva Lingam, Which is adored by
Lord Brahma, Lord Vishnu and the Gods
Which is pure, shining and well adorned
~~~

Which destroys the sorrows associated with
Birth and human life.
I salute that eternal Shiva Lingam.

Deva Muni Pravara Aarchita Lingam
Kaama Dahan Karunnaa Kara Lingam
Raavanna Darpa Vinaashana Lingam
Tat Prannamaami Sadaashiva Lingam

I salute that eternal Shiva Lingam, Which is
Worshipped by the Gods and the best of sages
Which burns the desires, Which is compassionate
Which destroyed the pride of demon Ravana.
I Salute that Eternal Shiva Lingam.

Sarva Sugandhi Sulepita Lingam
Buddhi Vivardhana Kaaranna Lingam
Siddha Sura Asura Vandita Lingam
Tat Prannamaami Sadaashiva Lingam

I salute that eternal Shiva Lingam
Which is beautifully smeared with various fragrant
Pastes Which is the cause behind the elevation of
A person's spiritual, intelligence and discernment
Which is praised by the siddhas, Devas and the asuras.
I salute that eternal Shiva Lingam.

Kanaka Mahaamanni Bhuussita Lingam
Phanni Pati Vessttita Shobhita Lingam
Daksha Su Yajnya Vinaashana Lingam
Tat Prannamaami Sadaashiva Lingam

I salute that eternal Shiva Lingam
Which is decorated with Gold and other precious gems
Which is adorned with the best of the serpents
Wrapped around it Which destroyed the grand
Sacrifice yajna of daksha.
I salute that eternal Shiva Lingam.

Kungkuma Chandana Lepita Lingam
Pangkaja Haara Su Shobhita Lingam
Sancita Paapa Vinaashana Lingam
Tat Prannamaami Sadaashiva Lingam

I salute that eternal Shiva Lingam
Which is anointed with Kumkuma - Saffron and
Chandana - sandal paste which is beautifully
Decorated with garlands of lotuses
Which destroys the accumulated sins of several lives.
I salute that eternal shiva Lingam.

Deva Ganna Aarchita Sevita Lingam
Bhaavair Bhaktibhir Eva Cha Lingam
Dinakara Kotti Prabhaakara Lingam
Tat Prannamaami Sadaashiva Lingam

I salute that eternal Shiva Lingam
Which is worshipped and served by the group of Devas
- Gods with true bhava – Emotion & Contemplation
and Bhakti - Devotion
Which has the splendour of million suns.
I salute that eternal Shiva Lingam.

Asstta Dalo Parivessttita Lingam
Sarva Samudbhava Kaaranna Lingam
Asstta Daridra Vinaashita Lingam
Tat Prannamaami Sadaashiva Lingam

I salute that eternal Shiva Lingam
Which is surrounded by eight petalled flowers
Which is the cause behind all creation
Which destroys the eight poverties.
I salute that eternal Shiva Lingam.

Suraguru Suravara Puujita Lingam
Suravana Pushpa Sada Aarchita Lingam
Paraatparam Paramaatmaka Lingam
Tat Prannamaami Sadaashiva Lingam

I salute that eternal Shiva Lingam
Which is worshipped by the preceptor of Gods - Lord
Brihaspati and the best of the Gods which is always
Worshipped by the flowers from the celestial garden
Which is superior than the best
And which is the greatest.
I salute that eternal Shiva Lingam.

Lingaassttakam Idam Punnyam
Yah Patthet Shiva Sannidhau
Shivalokam Avaapnoti
Shivena Saha Modate

Whoever recites this Lingasthakam
Consisting of eight stanzas in praise of the Lingga
Will attain the abode of Shiva and enjoy His bliss.

~~~

~~~

RUDRA ASHTAKAM

Namaami Iisham Iishaana Nirvaanna Ruupam
Vibhum Vyaapakam Brahma Veda Svaruupam
Nijam Nirgunnam Nirvikalpam Niriiham
Chidaakaasham Aakaasha Vaasam Bhajeham

Salutations to Sri Rudra, I salute the Lord Ishana -
Sri Shiva Whose form represents the state of the
Highest Nirvana extinction of all desires and passions
Leading to the highest bliss who manifests in taking
A form, though in essence he is pervading everywhere
His form embodies the highest knowledge of Brahman
Present in the core of the Vedas
Who remain absorbed in his own self which is
Beyond the three gunas - Sattva, Rajas and Tamas
Which is beyond any vikalpas - change and
Manifoldness Which is free from any movement - due
To desires who abides in the sky of
The chidakasha - Spiritual sky
I Worship that Ishana.

Niraakaaram Omkara Muulam Turiiyam
Giraa Gyaana Gotiitam Iisham Giriisham
Karaalam Mahaakaala Kaalam Kripaalam
Gunnaagaara Samsaara Paaram Natoham

Salutations to Sri Rudra, Who is formless and the very
Root from where the sacred Omkara arises
Who abides in the state of turiya - the fourth state in
Which Brahman is experienced in meditation
He is the Lord Who is beyond the knowledge which
Speech can express and beyond the perception which
Sense organs can perceive He is Girisha - Sri Shiva,
Literally meaning the Lord of the Mountains
Taking the terrible form of Mahakala
He can tear apart Kala - Time himself.
At the same time He is an embodiment of
Compassion to His devotees
I bow down to him Who helps in Crossing this
Samsara - delusion of worldly existence, which is like a
Dwelling placemade of gunas.

Tushaara Adri Samkaasha Gauram Gabhiram
Mano Bhuuta Kotti Prabhaa Shrii Shariiram
Sphuran Mauli Kallolinii Chaaru Ganggaa
Lasad Bhaala Baalendu Kanntthe Bhujanggaa

Salutations to Sri Rudra
Who is shining white resembling a Mountain of snow
And his being is very very deepin the depth of whose
Mind exist millions of rays of splendour
Which expresses themselves on his auspicious body
Over whose head, the beautiful Ganga throbs and
Surges forth towards the worlds
Over Whose forehead the newly risen moon shines
Spreading its rays and around
Whose neck adorns the beautiful serpents.

Chalat Kunnddalam Bhruu Sunetram Vishaalam
Prasannaananam Niila Kanntham Dayaalam
Mriga Adhiisha Charma Ambaram Munndda Maalam
Priyam Shangkaram Sarva Naatham Bhajaami

Salutations to Sri Rudra, Whose Ear-Rings Sway near
His beautiful face, which is adorned with a striking
Eyebrow and large beautiful Eyes

Whose face is beaming with joy and grace
Whose throat is blue due to drinking
The poison during Samudra Manthana

Who is extremely compassionate
Whose clothes are the skin of the Lord of animals
Signifying Tiger and Whose neck is adorned with a
Garland of skulls I worship him
Who is beloved of His devotees
Who is Shankara and who is the Lord of All.

Prachannddam Prakrshttam Pragalbham Paresham
Akhannddam Ajam Bhaanu Kotti Prakaasham
Tryah Shuula Nirmuulanam Shuula Paannim
Bhajeham Bhavaanii Patim Bhaava Gamyam

Salutations to Sri Rudra, Who is terrible
Eminent and extremely strong
Who is the highest Lord Who is ever unborn and
Whole and with the effulgence of million suns
Who has a trident in hand
The three spikes of which uproots the bondages of
The three gunas - tamas, Rajas and sattva
I worship the consort of Devi Bhavani
Who can be attained only by devotion.

Kalaatiita Kalyaanna Kalpa Anta Kaari
Sadaa Sajjana Ananda Daataa Pura Ari
Chid Aananda Samdoha Moha Apahaari
Prasiida Prasiida Prabho Manmatha Ari

Salutations to Sri Rudra, Whose auspicious nature is
Beyond the elements of the gross material world and
Who brings an end to a Kalpa - a cycle of creation
When all gross elements are dissolved
Who always give great joy to the wise men and
Who is the enemy - signifying destroyer of the
Tripurasuras who represents adharma by taking away
The great delusion, He plunges the prepared soul in
The fullness of cidananda, the bliss of Brahman or

Pure consciousness O, The enemy - signifying
Destroyer of Manmatha please be gracious to me,
Please be gracious to me, O Lord.

Na Yaavad Umaa Naatha Paada Aravindam
Bhajanti Iha Loke Pare Vaa Naraannaam
Na Taavat Sukham Shaanti Santaapa Naasham
Prasiida Prabho Sarva Bhuuta Adhi Vaasam

Salutations to Sri Rudra
As long as the lotus feet of the Lord of Uma
Is not worshipped in this world or Late by
The Human beings so long, Till then, joy, peace and
End of sorrows will not be experienced in life.
Therefore O Lord, please be gracious You
Who reside within all beings.

Na Jaanaami Yogam Japam Naiva Puujaam
Natoham Sadaa Sarvadaa Shambhu Tubhyam
Jaraa Janma Duhkhaugha Taatapyamaanam
Prabho Paahi Aapanna Maam Iisha Shambho

Salutations to Sri Rudra
I do not know how to perform Yoga, Japa or Puja
I always at all times only bow down to You,
O Shambhu please protect me from the sorrows of
Birth and old age as well as from the sins which lead to
Sufferings please protect me O Lord from afflictions
Protect me O My Lord Shambhu.

Rudraassttaka Idam Proktam
Viprenna Hara Tossaye
Ye Patthanti Naraa Bhaktyaa
Tessaam Shambhuh Prasiidati

This Rudrashtaka - eight verses in praise of Rudra
Composed by the wise sages for pleasing
Hara - another name of Sri Shiva those persons who
Recite this with devotion with them
Sri Shambhu will be always pleased.

Iti Shrii Gosvaami Tulasiidaasa Kritam
Shrii Rudraassttakam Sampuurnnam

Thus ends Rudrashtakam composed by
Sri Goswami Tulsidas.

~~~

SHIVA MAHIMNA STOTRAM

Mahimnah Param Te Parama Vidusho Yadyasadrishi
Stutir Brahma Dina Mapitadava Sannastvayi Girah,
Atha Vachyah Sarvah Svamati Parina Mavadhi Grinan
Mamapyeshah Stotre Hara Nirapavadah Parikarah

If it is unseemly to praise You when ignorant of the Extent of Your greatness, then even the praises of Brahma and others are inadequate. If no one can be Blamed when they praise You according to their Intellectual powers, then my attempt to compose A hymn cannot be reproached.

Atitah Panthanam Tava Cha Mahima Vanmanasayor
Atad Vyavrttya Yam Chakita Mabhi Dhatte Shrutirapi
Sa Kasya Stotavyah Katividha Gunah Kasya Vishayah
Pade Tvarvacine Patati Na Manah Kasya Na Vachah
~~~

Your greatness is beyond the reach of mind and
Speech. Who can properly praise that which even the
Vedas describe with trepidation,
By means of' 'neti-neti / not this, not this'?
How many qualities does he possess? By whom can
He be perceived? Yet whose mind and speech do not
Turn to the form later taken by Him - Sagun

Madhu Sphita Vacah Paramam Amritam Nirmitavatas
Tava Brahman Kim Vag Api Suraguror Vismaya Padam
Mama Tvetam Vanim Guna Kathana Punyena Bhavatah
Punam Ityarthe'smin
Puramathana Buddhir Vyavasita

O Brahman! Do even Brihaspati's praises cause wonder
To You, the author of the nectar like sweet Vedas?
O destroyer of the three cities, the thought that by
Praising Your glories I shall purify my speech has
Prompted me to undertake this work.

Tavaisvaryam Yat Taj Jagadudaya Raksa Pralayakrit
Trayivastu Vyastam Tisrishu Guna Bhinnasu Tanushu
Abhavyanam Asmin Varada Ramaniyama Ramanim
Vihantum Vyakrosim Vidadhata Ihaike Jadadhiyah

O Giver of boons! Some stupid people produce
Arguments–pleasing to the ignorant but in fact
Hateful– to refute Your divinity, which creates,
Preserves and destroys the world, which is divided into
Three bodies - Brahma, Vishnu and Shiva according to
The three gunas, and which is
Described in the three Vedas.

Kimihah Kimkayah Sa Khalu Kimupaya Stribhuvanam
Kimadharo Dhata Srijati Kimupadana Iti Cha
Atarkyaish Varye Tvay Yanavasara Duhstho Hatadhiyah
Kutarko'yam Kamshcin Mukharayati Mohaya Jagatah

To fulfill what desire, assuming what form, with what
Instruments, support and material does that creator

Create the three worlds? This kind of futile
Argumentation about You whose divine nature is
Beyond the reach of intellect, makes the perverted
Vociferous, and brings delusion to men.

Ajanmano Lokah Kimavayava Vanto'pi Jagatam
Adhisthataram Kim Bhavavidhir Anadritya Bhavati
Anisho Va Kuryad Bhuvana Janane Kah Parikaro
Yato Mandastvam Praty Amaravara Samsherata Ime

O Lord of gods! Can the worlds be without origin,
Though they have bodies? Is their creation possible
Withrout a creator? Who else but God can initiate the
Creation of the worlds? Because they are fools they
Raise doubts about Your existence.

Trayi Sankhyam Yogah Pasupati Matam Vaishnavamiti
Prabhinne Prasthane Paramidamadah Pathyamiti Cha
Rucinam Vaicitryad Riju Kutila Nana Pathajusham
Nrinameko Gamyas Tvamsasi Payasa Marnava Iva

Different paths to realization arc enjoined by the three
Vedas, by Sankhya, Yoga, Pashupata - Shaiva doctrine
And Vaishnava Shastras. People follow different paths,
Straight or crooked, according to their temperament,
Depending on which they consider best,
Or most appropriate – and reach You alone just
As rivers enter the ocean.

Mahokshah Khatvangam Parashu Rajinam
Bhasma Haninah Kapalam Cetiyat Tava Varada Tantro
Pakaranam Surastam Tamriddhim Dadhati Tu Bhavad
Bhru Pranihitam Na Hi Svatma Ramam Vishaya Mriga
Trishna Bhramayati

O giver of boons! A great bull, a wooden hand rest, an
Axe, a tiger skin, ashes, serpents, a human skull and
Other such things–these are all You own,
Though simply by casting your eyes on gods
You gave them great treasures which they enjoy.
Indeed one whose delight is in the self cannot be

Deluded by the mirage of sense objects.

Dhruvam Kascit Sarvam Sakala Mapara Stva Dhruva Midam Paro Dhrau Vyadhrauvye Jagati Gadati Vyasta Vishaye Samaste'pye Tasmin Puramathana Tair Vismita Iva Stuvan Jihremi Tvam Na Khalu Nanu Dhrishta Mukharata

O destroyer of the demon pura, some say that the Whole universe is eternal while others say that all is Transirtory. Others still, hold that it is eternal and non-Eternal — having different characteristics. Bewildered By all this, I do not feel ashamed to praise You; indeed My loquacity is an indication of my boldness.

Tavaisvaryam Yatnad Yadupari Virinchir Hari Radhah Paricchett Um Yatav Anala Manala Skandha Vapushah Tato Bhakti Sraddha Bhara Guru Grinad Bhyam Girisha Yat Svayam Tasthe Tabhyam Tava Kim Anuvrittir Na Phalati

O Girisha, when You took the form of a pillar of fire, Brahma trying from above and Vishnu trying from Below failed to measure You. Afterwards, when they Praised You with great faith and devotion, You revealed Yourself to them of Your own accord. What does not surrender to You bear fruit?

Ayatnadapadya Tribhuvanama Vairavya Tikaram Dashasyo Yadbahun Abhrita Ranakandu Paravashan Sthirah Padmasreni Racita Charanam Bhoruhabaleh Sthiraya Stvad Bhaktes Tripurahara Visphur Jitamidam

O destroyer of tripura, it was because of that great Devotion, which prompted him to offer his heads as Lotuses to Your feet, that the ten-headed Ravana was Still with arms and eager for fresh war after he had Effortlessly rid the three worlds of all traces of enemies.

Amushya Tvatseva Samadhigata Saram Bhujavanam Balat Kailase'pi Tvadadhivasatau Vikramayatah

Alabhya Patale Pyalasa Chalitan Gustha Shirasi
Pratishtha Tvayyasid Dhruvamupachito Muhyati Khalah

But when Ravanaextended the valour of his arms
Whose strength was obtained by worshipping You- in
Kailas, Your abode, You moved the tip of Your toe,
And he did not find a resting place even in
The nether world. Truly, when affluent
The wicked become deluded.

Yadriddhim Sutramno Varada Paramo Chairapi Satim
Adhashcakre Banah Parijana Vidheya Tribhuvanah
Na Tacchitram Tasmin Varivasitari Tvach Charanayor
Na Kasya Unnatyai Bhavati Srirasastvay Yavanatih

O Giver of boons, since Bana was the worshipper of
Your feet is it to be wondered at that he had the three
Worlds at his command and put to shame the wealth of
Indra? What prosperity does not come from bowing
Down the head to You?

Akanda Brahmanda Kshaya Chakita Devasura Kripa
Vidheya Syasidyas Trinayana Visham Samhrita Vatah
Sa Kalmashah Kanthe Tava Na Kurute Na Shriya Maho
Vikaro'pi Shlaghyo Bhuvana Bhaya Bhangavyasaninah

O Three-Eyed One, who drank poison out of
Compassion for gods and demons when they were
Distraught at the sudden prospect of the destruction of
The universe, surely the dark blue stain on Your throat
Has beautified You. Even deformity is to be admired in
One who is given to freeing the world of fear.

Asiddhartha Naiva Kvachidapi Sadeva Suranare
Nivartante Nityam, Jagati Jayino Yasya Vishikhah
Sa Pashyannisa Tvam Itara Surasadharana Mabhut
Smarah Smarta Vyatma Na Hi Vasishu Pathyah Paribhavah

O Lord, the god of love, whose arrows never fail in the
World of gods and men, become nothing but an object
Of memory because he looked on You as an ordinary

God (his body being burnt by Your look of wrath). An Insult to the self-controlled is not conducive to good.

Mahi Padaghatad Vrajati Sahasa Samshaya Padam Padam Visnor Bhramyad Bhujaparigha Rugna Graha Ganam Muhur Dyaur Dausthyam Yat Yanibhrita Jata Taditata Ta Jagad Rakshayai Tvam Natasi Nanu Vamaiva Vibhuta

When You danced to save the world, the earth was Suddenly thrown into a precarious state at the striking Of Your feet; the spatial regions and the hosts of stars Felt oppressed by the movement of Your massive club-Like arms; and the heavens became miserable as their Sides were constantly struck by Your waving matted Hair. Indeed it is Your very mightiness which is the Cause of the trouble.

Viyad Vyapi Tara Gana Gunita Phenod Gama Rucih Pravaho Varam Yah Prishata Laghu Dristah Shirasi Te Jagad Dvipakaram Jaladhivalayam Tena Kritami Tyane Naivon Neyam Dhrita Mahima Divyam Tava Vapuh

The river which pervades the sky and whose foam Crests look all the more beautiful because of stars and Planets, seems no more than a drop of water when on Your head. That same river has turned the world into Islands surrounded by waters. From this can be Judged vastness of Your divine body.

Rathah Kshoni Yanta Shata Dhriti Ragendro Dhanuratho Rathange Chandrarkau Rathacarana Panih Shara Iti Didhakshoste Ko'yam Tripura Trina Madambara Vidhir Vidheyaih Kridantyo Na Khalu Paratantrah Prabhudhiyah.

When You wanted to burn the three cities of the Demons – which were but a piece of straw to You. The earth was Your chariot, Brahma Your charioteer, The great mountain Meru Your bow, the sun and the

Moon the wheels of Your chariot, Vishnu Your arrow.
Why all this involvement? The Lord is not dependent
On others. He was only playing with things
At His command.

Hariste Sahasram Kamala Balima Dhaya Padayor
Yadekone Tasmin Nija Mudaharan Netra Kamalam
Gato Bhaktyu Drekah Parinatim Asau Chakra Vapusha
Trayanam Rakshayai Tripura Hara Jagarti Jagatam

O Destroyer of the three cities, Hari rooted out his own
Lotus-eye to make up the difference when one flower
Was missing in His offering of 1,000 lotuses to
Your feet. For this great devotion You awarded
The discus - Sudarshan Chakra with which Hari
Protects the three worlds.

Kratau Supte Jagrat Tvamasi Phalayoge Kratumatam
Kva Karma Pradhvastam Phalati Purusha Radhana Mrite
Atas Tvam Sam Preksya Kratusu Phala Dana Pratibhuvam
Shrutau Shraddham Baddhva Dridha Parikarah Karmasu Janah

When a sacrifice has ended, You ever keep awake to
Bestow its fruit on the sacrificer. How can any action
Bear fruit if not accompanied by worship of You, O
Lord? Therefore, knowing You to be the Giver of fruits
Of sacrifices and putting faith in the Vedas,
People become resolute about the
Performance of sacrificial acts.

Kriyadakso Dakshah Kratupati Radhisha Stanubhritam
Rishinamartvijyam Sharanada Sadasyah Suraganah
Kratu Bhramshas Tvattah Kratuphala Vidhana Vyasanino
Dhruvam Kartuh Sraddha Vidhura Mabhicaraya Hi Makhah.

O giver of refuge, even that sacrifice where Daksha, the
Lord of creation and expert in sacrifices, was the
Sacrificer, rishis were priests, gods participants, was

Destroyred by You who are habitually the giver of fruits Of sacrifices. Surely sacrifices cause injury to the Sacrificers in the absence of faith and devotion.

Praja Natham Natha Prasabha Mabhikam Svam Duhitaram Gatam Rohid Bhutam Rira Mayishumrishyasya Vapusha Dhanus Paner Yatam Divamapi Sapatra Kritamamum Trasantam Te'dyapi Tyajati Na Mriga Vyadharabhasah

O Lord, the fury of You who became a hunter with a Bow in hand has not as yet left Brahma who, overcome By incestuous lust and finding his own daughter Transforming herself into a hind, desired to ravish her In the body of a stag and keenly pierced by your Arrows, he has fled to the sky

Svalavanya Shamsa Dhrita Dhanusha Mahnnaya Trinavat Purah Plustam Drishtva Pura Mathana Pushpa Yudhamapi Yadi Strainam Devi Yama Nirata Dehardha Ghatana Davaiti Tvam Addha Bata Varada Mugdha Yuvatayah

O destroyer of the three cities, O giver of boons, it was Parvati who saw the god of love, bow in hand, Burnt Like a piece of straw in a minute by You. Still proud of Her beauty and believing that You are Fascinated by Her, because she was allowed to occupy Half Your body Because of her austerities. Ah, surely all women are Under delusion. you have Completely Conquered your senses.

Shmashanesva Krida Smarahara Pishacah Sahacarash Chhita Bhasma Lepah Sragapi Nrikaroti Parikarah Amangalyam Shilam Tava Bhavatu Namaiva Makhilam Tathapi Smartrinam Varada Paramam Mangalamasi

O destroyer of the god of love, O giver of boons, Your Play is in cremation grounds, Your companions are Ghosts, You smear Your body with the ashes of burnt Bodies, human skulls are Your garland-all. Your Conduct is indeed inauspicious. You promote the Greatest good of those who remember You.

Manah Pratyak Chitte Savidha Mavadhayatta Marutah Prahrishyadromanah Pramada Salilot Sangitadrisah Yada Lokyah Ladam Hrada Iva Nimajya Mritamaye Dadhat Yantas Tattvam Kimapi Yaminas Tat Kila Bhavan

You are indeed that inexpressible Truth which the Yogis realize within thorough concentrating their Minds on the self and controlling the breath according To the directions laid down in the scriptures, and Realizing with truth, they experience rapturous thrills And shed profuse tears of joy, swimming as it were in a Pool of nectar they enjoy inner bliss.

Tvamarkas Tvam Somas Tvamasi Pavanas Tvam Hutavahas Tvamapas Tvam Vyoma Tvamu Dharanir Atma Tvamiti Cha Paricchinnam Evam Tvayi Parinata Bibhratu Giram Na Vidmas Tat Tattvam Vayamiha Tu Yat Tvam Na Bhavasi

The wise hold this limiting view of You. You are the sun, You are the moon, You are fire, You are air, You are water, You are space, You are the earth and You are the self. But we do not know The things which You are not.

Trayim Tisro Vrittis Tribhuvana Matho Trinapi Sura Nakaradyair Varnais Tribhir Abhi Dadhat Tirnavikri Ti Turiyam Te Dhama Dhvanibhi Rava Rundhana Manubhih Samastam Vyastam Tvam Sharanada Grinat Yomiti Padam

O Giver of refuge, with the three letters A, U, M, Indicating the three Vedas, three states, three worlds And the three gods, the word AUM describes You Separately. By its subtle sound the word Om collectively Denotes You – Your absolute transcendental state Which is free from change.

Bhavah Sarvo Rudrah Pasupati Rathograh Sahamahan Statha Bhime Shanav Iti Yadabhi Dhana Shtakam Idam Amu Shmin Pratyekam Pravicharati Deva Shrutirapi

Priyayasmai Dhamne Pravihita Namasyo'smi Bhavate

O Lord! Bhava, Sharva, Rudra, Pashupati, Ugra, Mahadeva, Bhima, and Ishana-these eight names of Yours are each treated in detail in the Vedas. To You, Most beloved Lord Shankara, of resplendent form, I offer salutations.

Namo Nedisthaya Priyadava Davishthaya Cha Namo
Namah Kshodisthaya Smarahara Mahishthaya Cha Namah
Namo Varshishthaya Trinayana Yavishthaya Cha Namo
Namah Sarvasmai Te Tadida Mitisarvaya Cha Namah

O Lover of solitude, my salutations to You who are the Nearest and the farthest. O destroyer of the god of Love, my salutations to You Who are the minutest and Also the largest. O three-eyed one, my salutations to You who are the oldest and also the youngest. My Salutations to You again and again who are All and also transcending all.

Bahala Rajase Vishvot Pattau Bhavaya Namo Namah
Prabala Tamase Tat Samhare Haraya Namo Namah
Jana Sukhakrite Sattvo Driktau Mridaya Namo Namah
Pramahasi Pade Nistraigunye Shivaya Namo Namah

Salutations to You as Brahma in whom rajas prevails for The creation of the universe. Salutations to You as Rudra in whom tamas prevails for its destruction. Salutations to You as Vishnu in whom sattva prevails for Giving happiness to the people. Salutations to You, O Shiva, who are effulgent and beyond The three attributes.

Krisha Parinati Cetah Klesha Vashyam Kva Chedam
Kva Cha Tava Gunasimol Langhini Shashva Driddhih
Iti Chakita Mamandi Kritya Mam Bhakti Radhad
Varada Charanayoste Vakya Pushpo Paharam

O giver of boons, how poor is my ill-developed mind, Subject to afflictions, and how boundless Your divinity-

Eternal and possessing infinite virtues. Though terror–
Stricken because of this, I am inspired by my devotion
To offer this hymn of garland at Your feet.

Asita Giri Samam Syat Kajjalam Sindhu Patre
Sura Taruvara Shakha Lekhani Patra Murvi
Likhati Yadi Grhitva Sharada Sarva Kalam
Tadapi Tava Gunanam Isha Param Na Yati

O Lord, if the black mountain be ink, the ocean
The inkpot, the branch of the stout wish-fulfilling tree
A pen, the earth the writing leaf, and if taking these,
The Goddess of learning writes for eternity, even then
The limit of Your virtues will not be reached.

Asura Sura Munindrair Arcita Syendu Mauler
Grathitag Una Mahimno Nirguna Syesvarasya
Sakala Gana Varisthah Pushpadanta Bhidhano
Ruchira Mal Aghu Vrittaih Stotra Metac Chakara.

The best of Gandharvas, Pushpadanta by name,
Composed in great devotion this beautiful hymn to the
Lord, who is worshipped by demons, gods, and thc best
Of sages, whose praises have been sung, who has the
Moon on His forehead, and who is attributeless.

Ahara Harana Vadyam Dhurjateh Stotra Metat
Pathati Paramabhaktya Shuddhacittah Pumanyah
Sa Bhavati Shivaloke Rudra Tulya Stathatra
Pracurata Ra Dhanayuh Putravan Kirtimanshca

The person who with purified heart and in great
Devotion always reads this beautiful and elevating
Hymn to Shiva, becomes like Shiva after death in the
Abode of Shiva, and while in this world gets abundant

Wealth, long life, progeny and fame.

Maheshannaparo Devo Mahimno Napara Stutih,
Aghorannaparo Mantro Nasti Tattvam Guroh Param

There is no God higher than Shiva, there is no hymn
Better than the hymn on the greatness of Shiva,
There is no mantra more powerful than the name of
Shiva, There is nothing higher to be known than
The real nature of the Guru.

Diksha Danam Tapas Tirtham Jnanamyaga Dikah Kriyah,
Mahimnah Stava Pathasya Kallam Narhanti Shodashim

Initiation into spiritual life, charities, austerities,
Pilgrimages, practice of yoga, performance of sacrificial
Rites – none of these give even a sixteenth part of the
Merit that one gets by reciting the hymn on
The greatness of Shiva.

Kusuma Dashana Nama Sarva Gandharva Rajah
Shishush Ashadhara Mauler Deva Devasya Dasah
Sa Khalu Nija Mahimno Bhrashta Evasya Roshat
Stavana Mida Makarsid Divya Divyam Mahimnah

The Lord of Gandharvas, Pushpadanta by name, is the servant of the God of gods who has the crescent moon on his forehead. Fallen from his glory due to the wrath of the Lord, he composed this very beautiful uplifting hymn on the greatness of Shiva to regain His favor.

Suravaramuni Pujyam Sarvaga Mokshaikahetum
Pathati Yadi Manushyah Pranjalir Nanyachetah
Vrajati Shiva Samipam Kinnaraih Stuyamanah
Stavana Mida Mamogham Puspadanta Pranitam

If one with single-minded devotion and folded palms Reads this unfailing hymn composed by Pushpadanta, Which is adored by great gods and the best of sages And which grants heaven and liberation, one goes to Shiva and is worshipped by Kinnaras (celestial beings).

Asamapta Midam Stotram Punyam Gandharva Bhashitam
Anaupamyam Manohari Shiva Mishvara Varnanam

Thus ends this unparalleled sacred hymn composed by

Pushpadanta and describing the glory of
God Shiva in a most fascinating manner.

Ityesa Vanmayi Puja Shrimac Shankara Padayoh
Arpita Tena Devesah Priyatam Me Sadashivah

This hymn worship is offered at the feet of Shiva. May
The ever-beneficent Lord of gods be
Pleased with me at this.

Tava Tattwamna Janami Kidrishosi Maheshwara
Yadrashosi Mahadeva Tadrashaya Namo Namah

I do not know the truth of your nature and who you
Are- O great God my salutations to your true nature.

Eka Kalam Dwikalam Wa Trikalam Yah Pathennarah
Sarva Papa Vinirmuktah Shivaloke Mahiyate

Whoever reads this once, twice or thrice in a day revels
In the domain of Shiva, bereft of all sins.

Sri Pushpadanta Mukha Pankaja Nirgatena
Stotrena Kilbisha Harena Hara Priyena
Kanthas Thitena Pathitena Samahitena
Suprinito Bhavati Bhutapatir Maheshah

If a person learns by heart and recites this hymn, which
Flowed from the lotus mouth of Pushpadanta, which
Destroys sins and is dear to Shiva and which equally
Promotes the good of all.Shiva, the Lord of creation,
Becomes very pleased.

Ithi Sri Pushpadanta Virachhith Shiva Mahimna Stotram
Samaptham

Thus ends the hymn called – "Shiva Mahimna Stotra"
Composed by Pushpadanta.

SHRI SHIVA RAAM STOTRAM

Shiva Hare Shiva Rama Sakhe Prabho
Trividha Thapa Nivarana Hey Vibho
Aaja Janeswara Yadava Pahi Maam
Shiva Hare Vijayam Kuru May Varam

O Shiva, O Hare, O Rama, O friend, O Lord.
O Lord ,who cures the three types of sufferings
O Lord without birth, O Lord of the people
O Yadava, protect me.
O Shiva, O Hare , grant me the victory of success.

Kamala Lochana Rama Dayanidhe
Hara Guro Gaja Rakshaka Go Pathe
Shiva Thano Bhava Shankara Pahimaam
Shiva Hare Vijayam Kuru May Varam

O Lotus eyed treasure of mercy , Lord Rama
O Hara, O teacher, O elephant protector, O Lord of cows
O God who is Shiva, O Shankara , protect me
O Shiva, O Hare , grant me the victory of success

Sujana Ranjana Mangala Mandiram
Bhajathi They Purusha Paramam Padam
Bhavathi Thasya Sukham ParamAdbutham
Shiva Hare Vijayam Kuru May Varam

O Entertainer of the good, with a form causing good
That man who prays the divine being
Reaches your most wonderful place
O Shiva, O Hare , grant me the victory of success

Jaya Yudhishtira Vallabha Bhoopathe
Jaya JayaDritha Punya Payo Nidhe
Jaya Kripa Maya Krishna Namosthu They
Shiva Hare Vijayam Kuru May Varam

Victory to the friend of Yudhishtra, O king
Victory to him who is the blessed ocean of victory
Victory to all pervading mercy, Salutations to Krishna
O Shiva, O Hare , grant me the victory of success.

Bhava Vimochana Madhava Maapathe
SukhaviManasaHamsa Shivaarathe
Janaka Jaaratha Raghava Raksha Maam
Shiva Hare Vijayam Kuru May Varam

O Madhava who removes the fear of birth
O Lord of Lakshmi
O Swan of the mind of poets, O beloved of Parvathi
O Rama, beloved of Sita, please protect me
O Shiva, O Hare, grant me the victory of success.

Avani Mandala Mangala Maapathe
Jaladha Sundara Rama Ramapathe
Nigama Keerthi Gunarnava Gopathe
Shiva Hare Vijayam Kuru May Varam

O Consort of Devi Maa who does good to the world
O Rama who is pretty with color of cloud,
O Consort of Lakshmi
O Sea of goodness described in Vedas, O Lord of the cows
O Shiva, O Hare , grant me the victory of success.

Pathitha Pavana Nama Mayee Latha
Thava Yaso Vimalam Parigeeyathe
Thadapi Madhava Maam Kimupekshase
Shiva Hare Vijayam Kuru May Varam

O Heavenly climber who likes the downtrodden
I sing about your fame which is pure
But why do you in spite of it, neglect me
O Shiva, O Hare , grant me the victory of success.

Amaratha Para Deva Rama Pathe
VijayaThasthava Nama Dhanopama

Mayi Kadham Karunarnava Jayathe
Shiva Hare Vijayam Kuru May Varam

O greatest God of devas, O consort of Lakshmi
How can I ever get wealth, O giver of mercy
Which can measure up to the victories of yours
O Shiva, O Hare , grant me the victory of success

Hanumatha Priya Chaapa Kara Prabho
Sura Sarid Dhritha Shekhara Hey Guro
Mama Vibho Kimu Vismaranam Kritham
Shiva Hare Vijayam Kuru May Varam

Lord with a bow, who is very dear to Hanuman
O Teacher who wears the holy river on your head
O Lord, why have you forgotten me
O Shiva, O Hare, grant me the victory of success.

AharaHarjana Ranghana Sundaram
Patathi Ya Shiva Rama Kritham Sthavam
Visathi Rama Ramana Charanambhuje
Shiva Hare Vijayam Kuru May Varam

That man who reads this beautiful
People friendly, Prayer written by Shiva Rama
Would become fit to enter the lotus feet of
Rama and Lakshmi
O Shiva, O Hare, grant me the victory of success.

Pratar Uthaya Yo Bhakthya Patedh Ekagara Manasa
Vijayo Jayathe Thasya Vishnumaradhyamapnuyath.

He who reads this with concentrated devotion
Would attain all around victory and would attain
Vishnu whom he worships.

KASHI SATSANGH

SHIVA TANDAVA STOTRAM

Jattaaa Ttavii Galaj-Jwala
Pravaaha Paavita Sthale
Gale Valambya Lambitaam
Bhujangga Tungga Maalikaam
Ddamadd-Ddamadd-Ddamadd-Ddaman
Ninaadavadd-Ddamar-Vayam
Chakaara Channdda-Taannddavam

TANOTU NAH SHIVAH SHIVAM

My prostrations to Lord Shiva, the description of whose Great Tandava dance sends a thrill of blessedness Through the devotees. There dances Shiva with his Great Tandava from his huge matted Hair like a forest Is pouring out and flowing downthe sacred water of The River Ganges making the ground holy on that Holy ground Shiva is dancing His great Tandava dance Supporting His neck and hanging down are the lofty Serpents which are adorning his neck like lofty Garlands his damaru is continuously weaving out the Sound Damad, Damad, Damad, Damad and filling

The air all around Shiva performed such
A Passionate Tandava O my Lord Shiva,
Please extend the auspicious Tandava
Dance withinour beings also.

***Jattaa Kattaaha Sambhrama Bhraman Nilimpa Nirjharii
Vilola-Viichi-Vallarii-Viraajamaana-Muurdhani
Dhagad-Dhagad-Dhagaj-Jvalal-Lalaatta-Patttta-Paavake
Kishora-Chandra-Shekhare Ratih Pratikssannam Mama***

My prostrations to Lord Shiva, the description of whose
Great Tandava dance sends a thrill of blessedness
Through the devotees. There dances Shiva with His
Great Tandava. His huge matted Hair like a caldron is
Revolving round and round whirling with it is the great
River Goddess Ganga the strands of His matted hair
Which are like huge creepers are moving like huge
Waves His forehead is brilliantly effulgent on the
Surface of that huge forehead is burning a blazing fire
With the sound — Dhagad, Dhagad, Dhagad -
Referring to His third eye a young crescent moon is
Shining on the peak of His head
O my Lord Shiva, your great Tandava dance is passing
A surge of delight every moment through my being.

***Dharaa-Dharendra-Nandinii-Vilaasa-Bandhu-Bandhura
Sphurad-Diganta-Santati-Pramodamaana-Maanase
Krpaa-Kattaakssa-Dhorannii-Niruddha-Durdharaa Padi
Kvacid-Digambare Mano Vinodametu Vastuni***

My prostrations to Lord Shiva, the description of whose
Great Tandava dance sends a thrill of blessedness
Through the devotees There dances Shiva His great
Tandava now He is accompanied by the beautiful
Divine Mother Who is the supporter of the earth and
The Daughter of the Mountain She is ever has
Companion in His various divine sports. The entire
Horizon is shaking with the force of that Tandava and
The subtle waves of the Tandava is entering the sphere
Of the mind and raising waves of excessive joy. That

Shiva, the flow of Whose graceful side glance can
Restrain even the unrestrainable calamities. Who is
Digambara - clothed with sky signifying He is ever-free
And without any desire sometimes in His mind,
Materializes the wish to play the divine sports and
Hence this great Tandava.

***Jattaa-Bhujangga-Pinggala-Sphurat-Phannaa-Manni Prabhaa
Kadamba-Kungkuma-Drava-Pralipta-Digvadhuu-Mukhe
Madaa andha-Sindhura-Sphurat-Tvag-Uttariiya-Medure
Mano Vinodam-Adbhutam Bibhartu Bhuuta-Bhartari***

My prostrations to Lord Shiva, the description of whose
Great Tandava dance sends a thrill of blessedness
Through the devotees. There dances Shiva His great
Tandava. The Reddish-Brown Serpents on His matted
Hairs are throbbing with their hoods. Raised with that
Throb the lustre of the Red pearls on their raised
Hoods are collectively smearing the directions in the
Sky with the liquid saffron and the sky is appearing like
The face of a bride adorned with that Red saffron.
His upper garment is flying in the breeze and shaking
Like the thick skin of an intoxicated elephant.
My mind is experiencing an extraordinary thrill in
This divine sport it is being carried away by
The sustainer of all beings, O Shiva.

***Sahasra-Lochana-Prabhrty-Ashessa-Lekha-Shekhara
Prasuuna-Dhuuli-Dhorannii Vidhuusara-
Angghri-Piittha-Bhuuh
Bhujangga-Raaja-Maalayaa Nibaddha-Jaatta-Juuttakah
Shriyai Chiraaya Jaayataam Chakora-Bandhu-Shekharah***

My prostrations to Lord Shiva, the description of whose
Great Tandava dance sends a thrill of blessedness
Through the devotees. There dances Shiva His great
Tandava. Sahasra Tocana - Thousand eyes of Indra
Deva and others forming an unending line of heads
Are being graced by the incessant dust produced by
The dancing feet. The feet which has become dust

Coloured by dancing on the great earth. His matted
Hair is bound by the garlands of the King of serpents
The shining moon on top of His head which is a
Friend of the cakara birds - because cakara birds
Drink moonlight is radiating the deep beauty and
Auspiciousness of Sri Shiva.

Lalaatta-Chatvara-Jvalad-Dhanan jaya-Sphulingga-Bhaa
Nipiita-Pancha-Saayakam Naman-Nilimpa-Naayakam
Sudhaa-Mayuukha-Lekhayaa Viraajamaana-Shekharam
Mahaa-Kapaali-Sampade-Shiro-JattaalamAstu Nah

My prostrations to Lord Shiva, the description of whose
Great Tandava dance sends a thrill of blessedness
Through the devotees. There dances Shiva His great
Tandava on the surface of his forehead is burning a
Spark of fire and spreading its lustre from his third Eye.
The fire which absorbed the five arrows of kama
Deva and made the chief god of Kama. Bow down
On the top of His head is Shining the Nectar Rayed
Stroke of the crescent moon. May we also receive a part
Of the wealth of the great Kapali – Sri
Which is contained in his matted hair.

Karaala-Bhaala-Pattttikaa-Dhagad-Dhagad-Dhagaj-Jvalad
Dhanan jayaa hutii-Krta-Pracanndda-Pancha-Saayake
Dharaa-Dhareindra-Nandinii-Kucaagra-Chitra-Patraka
Prakalpanaieka-Shilpini Tri-Locane Ratir-Mama

My prostrations to Lord Shiva, the description of whose
Great Tandava dance sends a thrill of blessedness
Through the Devotees. There dances Shiva His great
Tandava. The terrible surface of his forehead is
Burning with the sound Dhagad, Dhagad, Dhagad,
Dhagad. Burning the terrible fire which performed the
Sacrifice of the mighty possessor of the five arrows,
Kama Deva. The footsteps of His great Tandava dance
Is drawing various pictureson the bosom of the earth
Signifying creation the earth, which is a part of the
Daughter of the Mountain Devi Parvati He is the

One artist who creates accompanied by Shakti.
My mind is extremely delighted by this
Tandava of the three eyed Shiva.

Naviina-Megha-Mannddalii Niruddha-Durdhara-Sphurat Kuhuu-Nishiithinii-Tamah Prabandha-Baddha-Kandharah Nilimpa-Nirjharii-Dharas-Tanotu Krtti-Sindhurah Kalaa-Nidhaana-Bandhurah Shriyam Jagad-Dhurandharah

My prostrations to Lord Shiva, the description of whose
Great Tandava dance sends a thrill of blessedness
Through the devotees. There dances Shiva His great
Tandava. The throb of the great Tandava has
Restrained the unrestrainable orb of the new clouds
Bound. The darkness of the night of the new moon
Around His neck .O the Bearer of the River Goddess
Ganga. O the wearer of the Elephant hide
Please extend the Sri - the auspiciousness and great
Welfare associated with this great Tandava.
O the container of the curved digit of the moon
O the bearer of the Universe. Please extend
The Sri Associated with this great Tandava.

Praphulla-Niila-Pangkaja-Prapancha-Kaalima-Prabhaa Valambi-Kanntha-Kandalii-Ruchi-Prabaddha-Kandharam Smarac-Chidam Purac-Chidam Bhavac-Chidam Makhac-Chidam Gajac-Chida-Andhakac-Chidam Tam-Antakac-Chidam Bhaje

My prostrations to Lord Shiva, the description of whose
Great Tandava dance sends a thrill of blessedness
Through the devotees.
There dances Shiva His great Tandava.
The black lustre of the Universe - The halahala poison
Drunk by Him during Samudra Manthana is appearing
Like a blooming blue Lotus resting within his
Throat like a girdle which He Himself has
Restrained by His own will

I worship the destroyer of Smara - Kama Deva.
I worship the destroyer of tripurasuras.
I worship the destroyer of the delusion of
The worldly existence.
I worship the destroyer of the sacrifice of Daksha.
I worship the destroyer of Gajasura.
I Worship the Destroyer of Demon Andhaka
I also worship the restrainer of Yama
I worship my lord Shiva.

Akharva-Sarva-Manggalaa-Kalaa-Kadamba-Man Jarii
Rasa-Pravaaha-Maadhurii-Vijrmbhannaa-Madhu-Vratam
Smara-Antakam Pura-Antakam Bhava-Antakam
Makha-Antakam
Gaja-Antaka-Andhaka-Antakam Tam-
Antaka-Antakam Bhaje

My prostrations to Lord Shiva, the description of whose
Great Tandava dance sends a thrill of blessedness
Through the devotees there dances Shiva His great
Tandava. He is the non-diminishing source of
Auspiciousness for the welfare of sll, and the source of
All arts which He manifests like a cluster of blossoms
From His Tandava dance is surging forth the nectar of
Sweetness. In the form of arts expressing His sweet will
I worship Him Who brought an end to Smara - Kama
Deva. I worship Him Who brought an end to the
Tripurasuras. I worship Him Who brings an end to the
Delusion of warldworldly existence.
I Worship Him Who brought an end to the sacrifice.
I Worship Him Who brought an end to Gajasura.
I Worship Him Who brought anend to Demon
Andhaka. I alsoWorship Him Who restrained Yama.
I Worship my Lord Shiva.

Jayat-Vada-Bhra-Vibhrama-Bhramad-Bhujanggama-Shvasad
Vinirgamat-Krama-Sphurat-Karaala-Bhaala-Havya-Vaatt
Dhimid-Dhimid-Dhimidhvanan-Mrdangga-
Tungga Manggala
Dhvani-Krama-Pravartita-Prachanndda-
Taannddavah Shivah

My prostrations to Lord Shiva, the description of whose
Great Tandava dance sends a thrill of blessedness
Through the devotees. There dances Shiva His great
Tandava his Eyebrows are moving to and From
Expressing his Complete Mastership over all the World
His Movements are Rolling the Serpents on his neck
Who are spewing out their hot breath and hissing
Terribly the terrible third eye on his Forehead
Which is like an altar for Oblation is
Throbbing in Succession and Emitting Fire
The Mridangam is Incessantly Sounding the
Auspicious beats of Dhimid, Dhimid, Dhimid, Dhimid
And With that Succession of Beats which are Rolling
Out Shiva is dancing his Passionate Tandava Dance.

Drssad-Vichitra-Talpayor-Bhujangga-Mauktika-Srajor
Garissttha-Ratna-Losstthayoh Suhrd-Vipakssa-Pakssayoh
Trnna-Aravinda-Chakssussoh Prajaa-Mahii-Mahendrayoh
Sama-Pravrttikah Kadaa Sadaashivam Bhajaamy-Aham

My prostrations to Lord Shiva, the description of whose
Great Tandava dance sends a thrill of blessedness.
Through the Devotees. When will I see the sameness in
The touch between a variegated comfortable bed and
Hard ground, when will I see the sameness in value
Between the garland made of pearls of serpents
Which is a highly valued gem and a lump of clay
When will I feel the sameness in relationship between
A friend and an enemy when will I feel the sameness in
Vision between a Grass-like Eye - ordinary look and a
Lotus-like eye - beautiful look when will I feel
The sameness in the soul of an ordinary
Subject and the King of the World when will I Worship
Sadashiva with the equality of Vision and Conduct

Kadaa Nilimpa-Nirjharii-Nikunja-Kottare Vasan
Vimukta-Durmatih Sadaa Shirahstham-Anjalim Vahan
Vimukta-Lola-Lochano Lalaama-Bhaala-Lagnakah
Shiveti Mantram-Uccharan-Kadaa Sukhii Bhavaamy-Aham

My prostrations to Lord Shiva, the description of whose
Great Tandava Dance sends a thrill of blessedness
Through the devotees when will I Dwell in a cave
Within the dense woods by the side of the River
Goddess Ganga being Free Forever from
Sinful mental dispositions and worship Shiva,
Keeping my hands on the forehead. When will
I be free from the rolling of the eyes - lustful
Tendencies and worship Shiva Applying the
Sacred mark on the forehead.
When will I be happy uttering
The Mantras of Shiva

Imam Hi Nityam-Evam-Uktam-Uttamottamam Stavam
Patthan-Smaran-Bruvan-Naro Vishuddhimeti-Santatam
Hare Gurau Subhaktim-Aashu Yaati Na-Anyathaa Gatim
Vimohanam Hi Dehinaam Su-Shangkarasya Chintanam

My prostrations to Lord Shiva, the description of whose
Great Tandava dance sends a thrill of blessedness
Through the devotees. This greatest of the great
Stava– hymn, has been uttered those who regularly
Recite it and contemplate on Shiva with purity of
Mind and in an uninterrupted manner with
Great devotion in Hara the Guru will quickly
Advancetowards him. There is no other way or refuge.
The delusion of that person will be destroyed by
Deep contemplation and
Meditation on Shankara.
My prostrations to Lord Shiva, the description of whose
Great Tandava dance sends a thrill of blessedness
Through the devotees. During the time of completion
Of the Puja. Those who recite this song of the
Ten-headed Ravana recite this after completing
The Puja of Shambhu in the evening to him who is
Steadfast in this worship will come chariots yoked with
King of elephants and horses signifying prosperity,
And Devi Lakshmi will always show her
Graceful face to him Sri Shambhu will bestow this boon.

~~~
~~~

SHIVA ARCHANAM

108 NAMES OF SHIVA

1. **AUM SHIVAYA NAMAHA** Salutations to the Auspicious One
2. **AUM MAHESHVARAYA NAMAHA** Salutations to the Great God Shiva
3. **AUM SHAMBHAVE NAMAHA** Salutations to the God who exists for our happiness alone
4. **AUM PINAKINE NAMAHA** Salutations to Shiva, who guards the path of dharma
5. **AUM SHASHISHEKHARAYA NAMAHA** Salutations to the God who wears the crescent moon in his hair
6. **AUM VAMADEVAYA NAMAHA** Salutations to the God who is pleasing and auspicious in every way
7. **AUM VIRUPAKSHAYA NAMAHA** Salutations to the God of spotless form
8. **AUM KAPARDINE NAMAHA** Salutations to the Lord with thickly matted hair
9. **AUM NILALOHITAYA NAMAHA** Salutations to the God splendid as the red sun at daybreak
10. **AUM SHANKARAYA NAMAHA** Salutations to the source of all prosperity
11. **AUM SHULAPANAYE NAMAHA** Salutations to the God who carries a spear
12. **AUM KHATVANGINE NAMAHA** Salutations to the God who carries a knurled club
13. **AUM VISHNUVALLABHAYA NAMAHA** Salutations to Shiva, who is dear to Lord Vishnu
14. **AUM SHIPIVISHTAYA NAMAHA** Salutations to the Lord whose form emits great rays of light
15. **AUM AMBIKANATHAYA NAMAHA** Salutations to Ambika's Lord
16. **AUM SHRIKANTAYA NAMAHA** Salutations to he whose throat is shining blue
17. **AUM BHAKTAVATSALAYA NAMAHA** Salutations to the Lord who loves His devotees like new born calves
18. **AUM BHAVAYA NAMAHA** Salutations to the God who is existence itself

19. AUM SARVAYA NAMAHA Salutations to Shiva who is all
20. AUM TRILOKESHAYA NAMAHA Salutations to Shiva who is the Lord of all the three worlds
21. AUM SHITAKANTHAYA NAMAHA Salutations to the primal soul whose throat is deep blue
22. AUM SHIVAPRIYAYA NAMAHA Salutations to the god who is dear to Shakti
23. AUM UGRAYA NAMAHA Salutations to Shiva whose presence is awesome and overwhelming
24. AUM KAPALINE NAMAHA Salutations to the God whose begging bowl is a human skull
25. AUM KAMARAYE NAMAHA Salutations to Shiva who conquers all passions
26. AUM ANDHAKASURA SUDANAYA NAMAHA Salutations to the Lord who killed the asura Andhaka
27. AUM GANGADHARAYA NAMAHA Salutations to the God who holds the Ganges River in his hair
28. AUM LALATAKSHAYA NAMAHA Salutations to the Lord whose sport is creation
29. AUM KALAKALAYA NAMAHA Salutations to Shiva who is the death of death
30. AUM KRIPANIDHAYE NAMAHA Salutations to the God who is the treasure of ourpassion
31. AUM BHIMAYA NAMAHA Salutations to Shiva whose strength is Aum
32. AUM PARASHU HASTAYA NAMAHA Salutations to the God who wields an axe in his hands
33. AUM MRIGAPANAYAE NAMAHA Salutations to the Lord who looks after the soul in the wilderness
34. AUM JATADHARAYA NAMAHA Salutations to Shiva who bears a mass of matted hair
35. AUM KAILASAVASINE NAMAHA Salutations to the God who abides on Mount Kailas
36. AUM KAVACHINE NAMAHA Salutations to the Lord who is wrapped in armor
37. AUM KATHORAYA NAMAHA Salutations to Shiva who causes all growth
38. AUM TRIPURANTAKAYA NAMAHA Salutations to the Lord who destroyed the three demonic cities

39. AUM VRISHANKAYA NAMAHA Salutations to the God whose emblem is a bull (Nandi)
40. AUM VRISHABHARUDHAYA NAMAHA Salutations to Shiva who rides a bull
41. AUM BHASMODDHULITA VIGRAHAYA NAMAHA Salutations to the Lord covered with holy ash
42. AUM SAMAPRIYAYA NAMAHA Salutations to the God exceedingly fond of hymns from the Sama Veda
43. AUM SVARAMAYAYA NAMAHA Salutations to Shiva who creates through sound
44. AUM TRAYIMURTAYE NAMAHA Salutations to the Lord who is worshiped in three forms
45. AUM ANISHVARAYA NAMAHA Salutations to the undisputed Lord
46. AUM SARVAGYAYA NAMAHA Salutations to the God who knows all things
47. AUM PARAMATMANE NAMAHA Salutations to the Supreme Self
48. AUM SAUMASURAGNI LOCHANAYA NAMAHA Salutations to the light of the eyes of Sauma, Surya and Agni
49. AUM HAVISHE NAMAHA Salutations to Shiva who receives oblations of ghee
50. AUM YAGYAMAYAYA NAMAHA Salutations to the architect of all sacrificial rites
51. AUM SAUMAYA NAMAHA Salutations to the Moon-glow of the mystic's vision
52. AUM PANCHAVAKTRAYA NAMAHA Salutations to the God of the five activities
53. AUM SADASHIVAYA NAMAHA Salutations to the eternally auspicious benevolent Shiva
54. AUM VISHVESHVARAYA NAMAHA Salutations to the all-pervading ruler of the cosmos
55. AUM VIRABHADRAYA NAMAHA Salutations to Shiva the foremost of heroes
56. AUM GANANATHAYA NAMAHA Salutations to the God of the Ganas
57. AUM PRAJAPATAYE NAMAHA Salutations to the Creator

58. AUM HIRANYARETASE NAMAHA Salutations to the God who emanates golden souls
59. AUM DURDHARSHAYA NAMAHA Salutations to the unconquerable being
60. AUM GIRISHAYA NAMAHA Salutations to the monarch of the holy mountain Kailas
61. AUM GIRISHAYA NAMAHA Salutations to the Lord of the Himalayas
62. AUM ANAGHAYA NAMAHA Salutations to Shiva who can inspire no fear
63. AUM BUJANGABHUSHANAYA NAMAHA Salutations to the Lord adorned with golden snakes
64. AUM BHARGAYA NAMAHA Salutations to the foremost of rishis
65. AUM GIRIDHANVANE NAMAHA Salutations to the God whose weapon is a mountain
66. AUM GIRIPRIYAYA NAMAHA Salutations to the Lord who is fond of mountains
67. AUM KRITTIVASASE NAMAHA Salutations to the God who wears clothes of hide
68. AUM PURARATAYE NAMAHA Salutations to the Lord who is thoroughly at home in the wilderness
69. AUM BHAGAVATE NAMAHA Salutations to the Lord of prosperity
70. AUM PRAMATHADHIPAYA NAMAHA Salutations to the God who is served by goblins
71. AUM MRITUNJAYAYA NAMAHA Salutations to the conqueror of death
72. AUM SUKSHMATANAVE NAMAHA Salutations to the subtlest of the subtle
73. AUM JAGADVYAPINE NAMAHA Salutations to Shiva who fills the whole world
74. AUM JAGADGURAVE NAMAHA Salutations to the guru of all the worlds
75. AUM VYAUMAKESHAYA NAMAHA Salutations to the God whose hair is the spreading sky above
76. AUM MAHASENAJANAKAYA NAMAHA Salutations to the origin of Mahasena
77. AUM CHARUVIKRAMAYA NAMAHA Salutations to Shiva, the guardian of wandering pilgrims

78. AUM RUDRAYA NAMAHA Salutations to the Lord who is fit to be praised
79. AUM BHUTAPATAYE NAMAHA Salutations to the source of living creatures, including the Bhutas, or ghostly creatures
80. AUM STHANAVE NAMAHA Salutations to the firm and immovable deity
81. AUM AHIRBUDHNYAYA NAMAHA Salutations to the Lord who waits for the sleeping kundalini
82. AUM DIGAMBARAYA NAMAHA Salutations to Shiva whose robes is the cosmos
83. AUM ASHTAMURTAYE NAMAHA Salutations to the Lord who has eight forms
84. AUM ANEKATMANE NAMAHA Salutations to the God who is the one soul
85. AUM SATVIKAYA NAMAHA Salutations to the Lord of boundless energy
86. AUM SHUDDHA VIGRAHAYA NAMAHA Salutations to him who is free of all doubt and dissension
87. AUM SHASHVATAYA NAMAHA Salutations to Shiva, endless and eternal
88. AUM KHANDAPARASHAVE NAMAHA Salutations to the God who cuts through the mind's despair
89. AUM AJAYA NAMAHA Salutations to the instigator of all that occurs
90. AUM PAPAVIMOCHAKAYA NAMAHA Salutations to the Lord who releases all fetters
91. AUM MRIDAYA NAMAHA Salutations to the Lord who shows only mercy
92. AUM PASHUPATAYE NAMAHA Salutations to the ruler of all evolving souls, the animals
93. AUM DEVAYA NAMAHA Salutations to the foremost of devas, demigods
94. AUM MAHADEVAYA NAMAHA Salutations to the greatest of the gods
95. AUM AVYAYAYA NAMAHA Salutations to the one never subject to change
96. AUM HARAYE NAMAHA Salutations to Shiva who dissolves all bondage

97. AUM PASHUDANTABHIDE NAMAHA Salutations to the one who punished Pushan

98. AUM AVYAGRAYA NAMAHA Salutations to the Lord who is steady and unwavering

99. AUM DAKSHADHVARAHARAYA NAMAHA Salutations to the destroyer of Daksha's conceited sacrifice

100. AUM HARAYA NAMAHA Salutations to the Lord who withdraws the cosmos

101. AUM BHAGANETRABHIDE NAMAHA Salutations to Shiva who taught Bhaga to see more clearly

102. AUM AVYAKTAYA NAMAHA Salutations to Shiva who is subtle and unseen

103. AUM SAHASRAKSHAYA NAMAHA Salutations to the Lord of limitless forms

104. AUM SAHASRAPADE NAMAHA Salutations to the God who is standing and walking everywhere

105. AUM APAVARGAPRADAYA NAMAHA Salutations to the Lord who gives and takes all things

106. AUM ANANTAYA NAMAHA Salutations to the God who is unending

107. AUM TARAKAYA NAMAHA Salutations to the great liberator of mankind

108. AUM PARAMESHVARAYA NAMAHA Salutations to the great God

~~~
~~~

SHIVA PANCHAAKSHARA STOTRAM

Naagendra-Haaraaya Tri-Locanaaya
Bhasma-Angga-Raagaaya Maheshvaraaya
Nityaaya Shuddhaaya Dig-Ambaraaya
Tasmai Na Kaaraaya Namah Shivaaya

I meditate on Shiva, Who has the King of snakes as His Garland and Who has three eyes.
I meditate on Shiva, Whose body is smeared with Sacred ashes and Who is the great Lord.
I meditate on Shiva, Who is eternal, Who is ever pure Who has the four directions as His clothes, signifying That He is ever free salutations to that Shiva, Who is Represented by syllable "Na," the first syllable of the Panchakshara mantra "Na-Ma-Shi-Va-Ya."

Mandaakinii-Salila-Chandana-Charcitaaya
Nandi-Iishvara-Pramatha-Naatha-Maheshvaraaya
Mandaara-Pusspa-Bahu-Pusspa-Su-Puujitaaya
Tasmai Ma Kaaraaya Namah Shivaaya

I meditate on Shiva, who is worshipped with waters from the River Mandakini and smeared with sandal Paste. I meditate on Shiva, who is the Lord of Nandi And of the ghosts and goblins who is the great Lord,

I meditate on Shiva who is worshipped with Mandara
And many other flowers salutations to that Shiva, who
Is represented by syllable "Ma," the second syllable of
The Panchakshara mantra "Na-Ma-Shi-Va-Ya."

Shivaaya Gaurii-Vadana-Abja-Vrnda
Suuryaaya Daksha-Adhvara-Naashakaaya
Shrii-Niilakanntthaaya Vrisha-Dhvajaaya
Tasmai Shi Kaaraaya Namah Shivaaya

I meditate on Shiva, Who is auspicious and who is like
The sun causing the Lotus - face of Gauri Devi Parvati
To blossom. I meditate on Shiva, Who is the destroyer
Of the sacrifice - yagnya of Daksha. I meditate on
Shiva, Who has a blue throat and has
A bull as his emblem.
Salutations to that Shiva, Who is represented by
Syllable "Shi," the third syllable of the
Panchakshara Mantra "Na-Ma-Shi-Va-Ya."

Vashissttha-Kumbhodbhava-Gautama-Aarya
Muuni-Indra-Deva-Aarchita-Shekharaaya
Chandra-Aarka-Vaishvaanara-Lochanaaya
Tasmai Va Kaaraaya Namah Shivaaya

I meditate on Shiva, Who is worshipped by the best
And most respected sages like Vashistha, Pot-Born
Sage - Agastya and Gautama and also by the devas

Who is the crown of the Universe. I meditate on Shiva,
Who has the Chandra - Moon Surya - Sun Agni – Fire,
As his three eyes salutations to that Shiva, Who is
Represented by syllable "Va," the fourth syllable of the
Panchakshara mantra "Na-Ma-Shi-Va-Ya."

Yajnya-Svaruupaaya Jattaa-Dharaaya
Pinaaka-Hastaaya Sanaatanaaya
Divyaaya Devaaya Dig-Ambaraaya
Tasmai Ya Kaaraaya Namah Shivaaya

I meditate on Shiva, who is the embodiment of yagnya-Sacrifice Who has matted hair. I meditate on Shiva, Who has the trident in His hand Who is eternal. I Meditate on Shiva, Who is Divine, Who is the shining One who has the four directions as His clothes - Signifying. He is ever free salutations to That Shiva, Who is represented by syllable "Ya," The fifth syllable of The Panchakshara mantra "Na-Ma-Shi-Va-Ya."

Panchaaksharam-Idam Punnyam
Yah Patthe-Shiva-Samnidhau
Shivalokam-Aavaapnoti
Shivena Saha Modate

Whoever recites this Panchakshara - hymn in praise of The five syllables of Na-Ma-Shi-Va-Ya near Shiva Lingam will attain the abode of Shiva And enjoy His bliss.

BHAVANI MAA ASHTAKAM

Na Taato Na Maataa Na Bandhur-Na Daataa
Na Putro Na Putrii Na Bhrtyo Na Bhartaa
Na Jaayaa Na Vidyaa Na Vrttir-Mama-Iva
Gatis-Tvam Gatis-Tvam Tvam-Ekaa Bhavaani

Neither the father, nor the mother
Neither the relation and friend, nor the donor
Neither the son, nor the daughter
Neither the Servant, Nor the Husband
Neither the Wife, Nor the worldly Knowledge
Neither my Profession. You are my Refuge.
You Alone are my Refuge
Oh Mother Bhavani.

Bhavaabdhaav-Apaare Mahaa-Duhkha-Bhiiru
Papaata Prakaamii Pralobhii Pramattah
Ku-Samsaara-Paasha-Prabaddhah Sadaham
Gatis-Tvam Gatis-Tvam Tvam-Ekaa Bhavaani
In this ocean of worldly existence which is endless
I am full of sorrow and very much afraid, I have fallen
With excessive desires and greed drunken and
Intoxicated always tied in the bondage of this miserable
Samsara - worldly existence You are my Refuge.

You alone are my Refuge.
Oh Mother Bhavani.

Na Jaanaami Daanam Na Cha Dhyaana-Yogam
Na Jaanaami Tantram Na Cha Stotra-Mantram
Na Jaanaami Puujaam Na Cha Nyaasa-Yogam
Gatis-Tvam Gatis-Tvam Tvam-Ekaa Bhavaani

Neither do I know charity, nor meditation and yoga
Neither do I know the practice of Tantra,
Nor hymns and prayers
Neither do I know worship, nor dedication to Yoga
You are my Refuge, You alone are my refuge.
Oh Mother Bhavani.

Na Jaanaami Punnyam Na Jaanaami Tiirtha
Na Jaanaami Muktim Layam Vaa Kadaacit
Na Jaanaami Bhaktim Vratam Vaapi Maatar-Gatis-Tvam
Gatis-Tvam Gatis-Tvam Tvam-Ekaa Bhavaani

Neither do I know virtuous deeds, nor pilgrimage
I do not know the way to liberation and with little
Concentration and absorption I know neither
Devotion, nor religious vows nevertheless Oh Mother
You are my Refuge, You Alone are my Refuge.
Oh Mother Bhavani.

~~~
~~~

HANUMAAN SWAMI

Atulita-Bala-Dhaamam Hema-Shailaabha-Deham
Danuja-Vana-Krshaanum Jnyaaninaam-Agragannyam
Sakala-Gunna-Nidhaanam Vaanaraannaam-Adhiisham
Raghupati-Priya-Bhaktam Vaata jatam Namaami

I salute Sri Hanuman, Who is an abode of unparallel
Power and whose huge body is like a golden Mountain
Who is like a raging fire over the forest of demons
And the foremost among the jnanis - the wise ones
Who is a storehouse of all good qualities
And the master of the monkeys
Who is a dear devotee of Raghupati - Sri Rama
And the Son of Vayudeva. I salute Sri Hanuman.

Mano-Javam Maaruta-Tulya-Vegam
Jitendriyam Buddhi-Mataam Varishtham
Vaata-Atmajam Vaanara-Yuutha-Mukhyam
Shriiraama-Duutam Sharannam Prapadye

I take refuge in Sri Hanuman
Who is swift as the mind and fast as the wind
Who is the master of the senses, and honoured for His
Excellent intelligence, learning and wisdom who is son

Of the wind God and chief among the vanaras
(Who were part of the Devas incarnated in the species
Of the monkeys to serve Sri Rama during His
Incarnation) to That messenger of Sri Rama
I take refuge by prostrating before him.

Yatra Yatra Raghunaatha Kiirtanam
Tatra Tatra Krta-Mastaka-Anjalim
Vaashpa-Vaari-Paripuurnnaa-Lochanam
Maarutim Namata Raakssasa-Antakam

Wherever the glories of Raghunatha are sung
There, with hands held over his bowed head in
Salutation and eyes filled with tears, Maruti - Bhakta
Hanuman is present I salute Maruti Who puts an
End to the Rakshasas.

Amjanii-Garbha Sambhuuta
Kapiindra Sacivottama
Raama-Priya Namas-Tubhyam
Hanuman Raksha Sarvadaa

I take refuge in Hanuman
Who was born from the womb of mother Anjani
And who was the most excellent minister of the King of
Monkeys Sugriva who is extremely dear to Sri Rama
I bow to You, O Hanuman, Please protect me always.

~~~

Hanuman Gayatri Mantra

Aum Anjaneyaye Vidmahe
Vayu Puthraya Dheemahe
Tanno Hanumat Prachodayath

We pray to the son of Anjani and the son of the wind.
May Lord Hanuman propel us.

~~~

ANJANEYA STOTRAM

Anjana nandanam veeram janaki soka nasanam,
Kapeesa Maksha hantharam, Vande lanka bhayangaram.

Mano javam , maruda thulya vegam,
Jitendriyam buddhi matham varishtam,
Vatha atmajam vanara yudha mukhyam,
Sree Rama dootam sirasa namami.

Anjaneya madhi patalananam,
Kanchanadri kamaneeya vigraham,
Parijatha tharu moola vasinam,
Bhavayami bhava mana nandanam,

Yatra yatra Raghu nada keerthanam,
Thathra thathra krudha masthakanjalim,
Bhashpa vari pari poorna lochanam,
Maruthim namatha Rakshasanthakam.

PHALA SRUTHI

Budhir balam yaso dhairyam nirbhayathwam arokadha,
Ajadyam vak paduthwancha hanumath smaranath bhaveth.

~~~
~~~

HANUMAAN SWAMI STOTRAM

Sukhekadhaam-bhushnam, manoja garva-khandanam,
Anathmadhi-vigarhanam, bhajeham-anjani-sutam
Bhavam-budhititushrame, susevyamana-madbutam,
Shiva-avatarinam-param, bhajeham-anjani-sutam
Gunakaramkripakaram, sushantidam-yashachyakaram,
Nijatambuddhi-dayakam, bhajeham-anjani-sutam
Sadaivdhusta-bhanjanam, sada-sudharva-vardhanam
Mumuksha-bhaktaranjam,bhajeham-anjani-sutam
Suramapada-sevinam, suramanama-gayinam,
Suramabhakti-dayinam, bhajeham-anjani-sutam
Virakta-mandala-dhipam, sadatma-vitsusevinam,
Subhakta-vrundvandanam, bhajeham-anjani-sutam
Vimukti-vigna-nashakam, vimukti-bhakti-dayikam,
Maha-virakti-karakam, bhajeham-anjani-sutam
Sukhemya deva madvayam, brihut-meva-tatsvayam,
Itihi-bodhi-kamgurum, bhajeham-anjani-sutam
Virakti-mukti-dayakam, imam-stavan-supavanam,
Pathantiye-samadarat-na-sansaranti-te-dhruvam.

SHRI BRAHMAN

Ambhasya-Paare Bhuvanasya Madhye
Naakasya Prishthe Mahato Mahiiyaan
Shukrenna Jyotiimshi Samanupravissttah Prajaapatish
Charati Garbhe Antah

Looking at the vast nature and feeling the Lord behind It beyond the other end of the waters of this endless Ocean - Ambhasya pare is the great Lord Who has extended himself within this mighty earth - Bhubanasya madhye and has gone be yond the infinite Sky - Nakasya pristhe he is greater than the great and Consciousness infinite by the seed of the light of Consciousness he has entered within the creation as Prajapati - creator and wandering and playing within its Womb he is playing within the cosmic creation.

~~~
~~~

NIRVANA SHATAKAM

Mano-Buddhy-Ahangkaara Chittaani Naaham
Na Cha Shrotra-Jihve Na Cha Ghraanna-Netre
Na Cha Vyoma Bhuumir-Na Tejo Na Vaayuh
Chid-Aananda-Ruupah Shivoham Shivoham

Neither am I the mind, nor the intelligence or ego
Neither am I the organs of hearing – ears
Nor that of tasting - tongue, smelling - nose or seeing -
Eyes neither am I the sky, nor the earth, neither the
Fire nor the air.
I am the ever pure blissful consciousness
I am Shiva, I am Shiva
The ever pure blissful consciousness.

Na Cha Praanna-Samjnyo Na Vai Pancha-Vaayuh
Na Vaa Sapta-Dhaatuh Na Vaa Pancha-Koshah
Na Vaak-Paanni-Paadam Na Chopastha-Paayu
Chid-Aananda-Ruupah Shivoham Shivoham

Neither am I the vital breath, nor the five vital airs
Neither am I the seven ingredients of the body
Nor the five sheaths of the body.
Neither am I the organ of speech nor the organs for
Holding – hand, movement - feet.
I am the ever pure Blissful Consciousness.
I am Shiva, I am Shiva.
The Ever Pure Blissful Consciousness.

Na Me Dvessa-Raagau Na Me Lobha-Mohau
Mado Naiva Me Naiva Maatsarya-Bhaavah
Na Dharmo Na Cha-Artho Na Kaamo Na Mokssah
Chid-Aananda-Ruupah Shivoham Shivoham

Neither do I have hatred, nor attachment
Neither Greed nor infatuation.
Neither do I have pride, nor feelings of envy and Jealousy
I am not within the bounds of Dharma
Righteousness Artha -Wealth, Kama - Desire

And Moksha - Liberation the four purusarthas of life
I am the ever pure blissful consciousness
I am Shiva, I am Shiva
The ever pure blissful consciousness.

Na Punnyam Na Paapam Na Saukhyam Na Duhkham
Na Mantro Na Tiirtham Na Vedaa Na Yajnyaah
Aham Bhojanam Naiva Bhojyam Na Bhoktaa
Chid-Aananda-Ruupah Shivoham Shivoham

Neither am I bound by merits nor sins,
Neither by worldly joys nor by sorrows.
Neither am I bound by sacred hymns nor by sacred places
Neither by sacred scriptures nor by sacrifies
I am Neither enjoyment experience
Nor an object to be enjoyed experienced,
Nor the enjoyer - experiencer
I am the ever pure blissful consciousness;
I am Shiva, I am Shiva
The Ever Pure Blissful Consciousness.

Na Mrityur-Na Shangkaa Na Me Jaati-Bhedah
Pitaa Naiva Me Naiva Maataa Na Janmah
Na Bandhurna Mitram Gurur-Na-Iva Shishyam
Chid-Aananda-Ruupah Shivoham Shivoham

Neither am I bound by death and its fear
Nor by the rules of caste and its distinctions.
Neither do I have father and mother, nor do I have birth.
Neither do I have relations nor friends
Neither spiritual teacher nor disciple
I am the ever pure blissful consciousness
I am Shiva, I am Shiva
The ever pure blissful consciousness.

Aham Nirvikalpo Niraakaara-Ruupo
Vibhu-Tvaaccha Sarvatra Sarvendriyaannaam
Na Chaa-Sanggatam Naiva Muktirna Meyah
Chid-aananda-ruupah Shivoham Shivoham

~~~
~~~

PRATAH SMARAMI HRIDI SAMSPHURAD AATMA

TATTVAM MEDITATION ON THE SOUL

I am without any variation, and without any form
I am present everywhere as the underlying
Substratum of everything and behind all sense organs
Neither do I get attached to anything, nor get freed
From anything I am the ever pure blissful consciousness
I am Shiva, I am Shiva
The ever pure blissful consciousness.

Pratah Smarami Hridi Samsphurad Aatma Tattvam
Meditation On The Soul

Praatah Smaraami Hrdi Samsphurad-Aatma-Tattvam
Sac-Chit-Sukham Parama-Hamsa-Gatim Turiiyam
Yat-Svapna-Jaagara-Sussuptim-Avaiti Nityam Tad-Brahma
Nisskalam-Aham Na Cha Bhuuta-Sangghah

In the early morning I remember and meditate on the
Pure essence of the atman shining within my heart
Which gives the bliss of Sacchidananda Existence,
Consciousness and bliss which is the supreme hamsa -
Symbolically a pure white swan floating in chidakasha
And takes the mind to the state of turiya. The fourth
State superconsciousness, which knows as a witness
Beyond the three states of dream, waking and deep
Sleep That Brahman, which is without any division
Shines as the I and not this body which is a collection
Of Pancha Bhuta - Five Elements.

Praatar-Bhajaami Manasaa Vachasaam-Agamyam
Vaacho Vibhaanti Nikhilaa Yad-Anugrahenna
Yan-Neti-Neti-Vacanair-Nigamaa Avocham
Stam Deva-Devam-Ajam-Achyutam-Aahur-Agryam

In the early morning I worship that
Which is beyond the mind and the speech and by
Whose grace all speech shine that is expressed in the
Scriptures by statement "Neti Neti." Since He cannot be
Adequately expressed by words who is called the God
Of the Gods, unborn, infallible imperishable
And foremost - primordial.

Praatar-Namaami Tamasah Param-Arka-Varnnam
Puurnnam Sanaatana-Padam Purussottama Akhyam
Yasminn-Idam Jagad-Ashessam-Ashessa-Muurtau
Rajjvaam Bhujanggama Iva Pratibhaasitam Vai

In the early morning I salute that darkness signifying
Without any form, which is of the nature of supreme
Illumination which is purna - full, which is the
Primordial abode which is called Purushottama - the
Supreme Purusha in whom this endless world is settled
Endlessly from the beginning of creation.

Shloka-Trayam-Idam Punnyam
Loka-Traya-Vibhuushannam
Praatah-Kaale Patthed-Yas-Tu
Sa Gacchet-Paramam Padam

These three slokas, which are holy unites one with the
Whole and the ornaments of the three worlds
He who recites in the early morning, attains the
Supreme abode of Brahman.

Loka-Traya-Vibhuushannam
Praatah-Kaale Patthed-Yas-Tu
Sa Gacchet-Paramam Padam

These three slokas, which are holy unites one with the
Whole and the ornaments of the three worlds
He who recites in the early morning, attains
The supreme abode of Brahman.

~~~
~~~

GAYATRI MANTRAS

Sri Ganesh Gayatri Mantra

Om Tatpurushaya Vidmahe, Vakratundaya Deemahi
Tanmo Danti Prachodayat

~~~

Sri Annapoorna Devi Gayatri Mantra

Om Bagavtya Vidmahe, Maheswarai Deemahi
Tanmo Annapoorna Prachodayat

~~~

Sri Ananta Gayatri Mantra

Om Sarprarajaya Vidmahe, Nagarajaya Deemahi
Tanmonantah Prachodayat

~~~

Sri Ayyappa Gayatri Mantra

Om Bhootadhaaya Vidmahe, Mahadevaya Deemahi
Tanmo Saastra Prachodayat

~~~

Ravi Gayatri Mantra

Om Bhaskaraya Vidmahe, Diwakarayaa Deemahi
Tanmo Surya Prachodayat

~~~

Sri Adisheshu Gayatri Mantra

Om Sahasrasreeshaya Vidmahe, Vishnu talpaya deemahi
Tanmo Naga Prachodayat

~~~

Indrani Gayatri Mantra

Om Gatatwachayi Vidmahe, Vajrahastaya Deemahi
Tanmo Indrani Prachodayat

~~~

Kuja Gayatri Mantra

Om Veeradwajaya Vidmahe, Vignahastaya Deemahi
Tanmo Bhowmah Prachodayat

~~~

Kanyaka Parameswari

Om Balaroopini Vidmahe, Parameswari Deemahi
Tanma kanya Prachodayat

~~~

Kameswari Gayatri Mantra

Om Kleem Tripuradevi Vidmahe,
Kameswararaicha Deemahi
Tanmo Klinne Prachodayat

~~~

Kamadeni Gayatri Mantra

Om Subhakamai Vidmahe, Kamdhatraicha Deemahi
Tanmo Dhenu Prachodayat

~~~

Karya Veerayaya Gayatri Mantra

Om Kaartaveeryaya Vidmahe, Maha veeryaya Deemahi
Tanmorjuna Prachodayat

~~~

Sri Kalika Devi Gayatri Mantra

Om Kalikayai Cha Vidmahe, Smasana Vasinai Deemahi
Tanmo Ghoraa Prachodayat

~~~

Gayatri mantras for Mithuna Rasi and Mithuna Lagna

Om Sowmya Roopaya Vidmahe, Baanesaaya Deemahi
Tanmo Buhdhah Prachodayat

~~~

Gayatri mantras for Karkataka Rasi and Karkataka Lagna

Om Amrutamgaaya Vidmahe, Kalaroopaya Deemahi
Tanmo Somah Prachodayat

~~~

Gayatri mantras for Simha Rasi and Simha Lagna

Om Saptaturamgaaya Vidmahe, Sahasrakiranaya Deemahi
Tanmo Ravi Prachodayat

~~~

Gayatri mantras for Kanya Rasi and Kanya Lagna

Om Sowmya Roopaya Vidmahe, Baaneesaya Deemahi
Tanmo Budhah Prachodayat

~~~

Gayatri mantras for Tula Rasi and Tula Lagna

Om Bhrugujaaya Vidmahe, Divyadeehayi Deemahi
Tanmo Sukra Prachodayat

~~~

Gayatri mantras for Tula Rasi and Tula Lagna

Om Angarakaya Vidmahe, Sakthi Hastaya Deemahi
Tanmo Bhowma Prachodayat

~~~

Gayatri mantras for Tula Rasi and Tula Lagna
~~~

Om Angeerasaya Vidmahe, Amrutesaya Deemahi
Tanmo Jeevah Prachodayat

~~~

Gayatri mantras for Makara Rasi and Makara lagna

Om Bhagabavaaya Vidmahe, Mrutyuroopaya Deemahi
Tanmo Sowri Prachodayat

~~~

Gayatri mantras for Kumba Rasi and Kumba lagna

Om Bhabhavaaya Vidmahe, Mrutyuroopaya Deemahi
Tanmo Sowri Prachodayat

~~~

Gayatri mantras for Meena Rasi and Meena lagana

Om Angeerasaaya Vidmahe, Divyadeehaya Deemahi
Tanmo Jeevah Prachodayat

~~~

NAUGRAHA DEVATA GAYATRI
MANTRAS FOR THE NINE PLANETS

RAVI
Bhaskaraya Vidmahe Mahadutyathikaraya Deemahi
Tanmo Aditya Prachodayat
~~~

CHANDRA
Padma Dwajaya Vidmahe Hemaroopaya Deemahi
Tanmaspoma Prachodayat
~~~

KUJA
Seera Dwajaya Vidmahe Vittahastaya Deemahi
Tanmo Bhowma Prachodayat
~~~

BHUDHA
Rowgineyaya Vidmahe Chandraputraya Deemahi
Tanmo Bhada prachodayat
~~~

GURU
Vrushba dwajaya vidmahe Grunihastaya Deemahi
Tanmo Guru prachodayat
~~~

SUKRA
Tatpurushaya Vidmahe Swetavarnaya Deemahi
Tannasukra Prachodayat
~~~

SANI
Kaka Dwajaya Vidmahe Khadgahastaya Deemahi
Tanmo Manta Prachodayat
~~~

RAHU
Nakadwajaya Vidmahe Padmahastaya Deemahi
Tanmo Rahu Prachodayat
~~~

KETU
Aswadwajaya Vidmahe Poolahastaya Deemahi
Tannuketu Prachodayat
~~~

RAAMCHARITMANAS

SHREE RAM CHANDRA KRIPALU BHAJAMAN
SHREE RAM STUTI

Sri ram chandra kripalu bhajmana haran bhav
bhaya daarunam
Navkanj lochan kanj mukh kar kanj pad kanjarunam
Kandarp aganit amit chhavi nav neel neeraj sundaram
Pat peet manahu tadit ruchi suchi naumi janak sutavaram
Bhaju deen bahndhu dinesh daanave daitya vansh
nikandanam
Raghuvansh anandkand kaushal chand dashrath nandanam
Sir mukut kundal tilak charu udaar ang vibhushanam
Aajanubhuj sar chaap dhar sangramjit khaldushanam
Iti vadti tulsidas shankar shesh muni man ranjanam
Mam hridaya kunj nivas kuru kaamadi khal dal ganjanam

O mind! Revere the benign Shree Ramachandra, who
Can remove the intense fear of this world
Who has fresh lotus eyes, lotus face and lotus hands,
Feet like lotus and like the rising sun
His image exceeds myriad cupids, like a fresh, blue-
Hued cloud - magnificent

His amber-robes appear like lightning, pure, captivating
Revere this groom of Janaka's daughter
Sing hymns of the brother of destitute, Lord of the
Daylight, the destroyer of the clan of Danu-Diti demons
The progeny of Raghu, limitless joy, the moon to
Kosala, sing hymns of Dasharatha's son
His head bears the crown, ear pendants, tilak on
Forehead, his adorned, shapely limbs are resplendent
Arms extend to the knees, studded with bows-arrows,
Who won battles against Khara and Dooshana
Thus says Tulsidas, O joy of Shankara, Shesh - Naag,
Mind and Sages
Reside in the lotus of my heart, O slayer of the vices-
Troops of kaama and the like.

~~~

BHAYE PRAKAT KRIPALA SHREE RAM STUTI AT BIRTH

Bhaye prakat kripala deendayala kaushlya hitkari
Harshit mahtari muni manhari adbhud roop vichari
Lochan abhirama tanu ghanshyama nij aayudh bhuj chari
Bhushan banmala nayan bishala shobha sindhu kharari
Kah dui kar jori astuti tori kehi vidhi karhu ananta
~~~

Maya gun gyanatit amana ved puran bhananta
Karuna sukh sagar sab gun aagar jehi ganwahi shruti santa
Brahmand nikaya nirmit maya rom rom prati ved kahe
Mam ur so basi yah uphasi sunat dheer mati thir na dhare
Upja jab gyana prabhu muskana charit
bahut vidhi kinhi chahe
Kahi katha sunayi matu bujhayi jehi prakar sut prem lahe
Mata puni boli so mati doli tajahu taat yah roopa
Kije shishu leela ati priya sheela yah sukh param anoopa
Suni vachan sujana rodan thana hoyi balak sur bhoopa
Yah charit je ganwahi hari pad panwahi te na
pari bhava koopa
Bhaye prakat kripala deendayala kaushlya hitkari
Harshit mahtari muni manhari adbhud roop vichari

The mercyful, graceful and the beneficial to Kaushalya
Appeared Mother Kaushalya is happy, minds of sages
Have been stolen thinking of the amazing form of lord

Lochan abhirama tanu ghanshyama nij aayudh bhuj chari
Bhushan banmala nayan bishala shobha sindhu kharari

His eyes are a spectacle – beautiful, body is black like
Clouds and in his four arms he has his own armaments
Ornament is the vanamala and his eyes are large
The Kharari - The Lord is the ocean of beauty

Kah dui kar jori astuti tori kehi vidhi karu ananta
Maya gun gyanatit amana ved puran bhananta

His mother joining both hands says O Anant - Infinite
For the lord how should I praise you
You are above the maya – illusion, gun - properties of
Nature and the knowledge even Vedas and Purans
Couldnot express you

Karuna sukh sagar sab gun aagar jehi ganwahi shruti santa
Brahmand nikaya nirmit maya rom rom prati ved kahe

The ocean of grace and happiness and all meritorious
Deeds which are applauded by Vedas and the saints

Who has made his illusion to spread upto the Universe
And even his smallest deeds are narrated by the vedas

Mam ur so basi yah uphasi sunat dheer mati thir na dhare
Upja jab gyana prabhu muskana charit bahut
Vidhi kinhi chahe

This happiness that is staying in my heart, listening to
It no steady mind can be restful.
When such knowledge is provided to Kaushlaya Ji,
The Lord smiles and wanted to show his different
Characters to her

Kahi katha sunayi matu bujhayi jehi prakar sut prem lahe
Mata puni boli so mati doli tajahu taat yah roopa

Then telling all the stories to his mother, he made her
To understand him in such a way that will let her bring
A maternal love for her child the mother again said,
This is all wandering in my mind
Oh dear son, leave this form so I can see you as my Child

Kije shishu leela ati priya sheela yah sukh param anoopa ~
Suni vachan sujana rodan thana hoyi balak sur bhoopa ~

Perform like a Child that is very lovey and polite as this
Happiness is very pleasing to a Mother
Listening the kind word of Kaushalya Ji,the lord started
Crying and the King of Gods took the form of a Child

Yah charit je ganwahi hari pad panwahi te na
Pari bhava koopa

One who sings this character of Lord, reaches to the feet
Of the lord and he never falls into the well of this world.

~~~
~~~

BHAGAVAD GITA VERSES

Yadaa yadaa hi dharmasya glaanirbhavati bhaarata
Abhyuktaanamadarmasya tadaatmaanam srijaamyahamh

When there is decay of dharma - righteousness and rise
Of adharma – unrighteousness,then I,
The Lord, am born in this world.

Karmanyevaadhikaaraste maa phaleshu kadaachana
Maa karmaphalaheturbhuu maatesangot svakarmani

A person has the right towards action alone and not
Towards the fruit of action. Let not the fruit of action
Be the motive for acting. Also, let there not be any
Attachment to inaction.

Patram pushhpam phalam toyam yo me
Bhaktyaa prayachchati
Tadaham bhaktyupahritamashnaami prayat aatmanah

I accept the offering of even a leaf, a flower, fruit or
Water, when it is offered with loving devotion.

Kaama eshha krodha eshha rajogunasamudbhavah
Mahaashano mahaapaapma viddhyenamiha vairinamh

Desire and anger which are born out of passion are
Insatiable and prompt man to great sin and should be
Recognized as enemies.

Yato yato nishcharati manashchanchalamasthiramh
Tatastato niyamyaitadaat manyeva vasham nayeth

By whatever cause the mind, which is restless and
Fidgeting, wanders away, the yogi should bring it back
From that and concentrate only on the Self.

Brahmanyaadhaaya karmaani sangam tyaktvaa karoti yah
Lipyate na sa paapena Padma patramivaambhasaa
He who offers all actions to God, without attachment,
Remains untouched by sin, just as a lotus leaf by water.

Manmanaa bhava madbhakto madyaajii maam namaskuru
Maamevaishhyasi satyam te pratijaane priyo asi me

Give your mind to Me, be devoted to Me, worship Me
And bow to Me. Doing so, you will come to Me alone,
I truly promise you, for you are so
Exceptionally dear to Me.

Antakaale cha maameva smaranmuktvaa kalevaramh
Yah prayaati sa madbhaavam yaati naastyatra samshayah

He who departs from the body, thinking of Me alone,
Even at the time of death, will definitely reach Me.

Yatra yogeshvarah krishhno yatra paartho dhanurdharah
Tatra shriirvijayo bhuutirdhruvaa niitir matirmama

Wherever there is Krishna, the Lord of Yoga and the
Bow weilding Arjuna, there rein good fortune, victory,
Prosperity and justice. Such is my conviction.

~~~
~~~

MAHATMA GANDHI QUOTES

- *Simple living, higher thinking*
- *My life is my message to the world*
- *Live as if you were to die tomorrow. Learn as if you Were to live forever.*
- *A man is but a product of his thoughts. What he thinks He becomes.*
- *Be the change that you want to see in the world.*
- *The weak can never forgive. Forgiveness is an Attribute of the strong.*
- *I will not let anyone walk through my mind with their Dirty feet.*
- *Strength does not come from physical capacity. It Comes from an indomitable will.*
- *An ounce of patience is worth more than a tonne of Preaching.*
- *Change yourself – you are in control.*
- *See the good in people and help them.*
- *Without action, you aren't going anywhere.*

- *Take care of this moment.*
- *Be congruent, be authentic, be your true self.*
- *Continue to grow and evolve.*
- *A no uttered from the deepest conviction is better than A 'Yes' uttered merely to please, or worse, to avoid Trouble.*
- *Glory lies in the attempt to reach one's goal and Not in reaching it.*
- *An eye for an eye will make the whole world blind.*
- *Happiness is when what you think, what you say, and What you do are in harmony.*
- *A coward is incapable of exhibiting love; it is the Prerogative of the brave.*
- *Nobody can hurt me without my permission.*
- *In a gentle way, you can shake the world.*

~~~
~~~

AARTIS
OM JAI JAGDISH

Om Jai Jagadish Hare, Swaami Jai Jagadish Hare
Bhakta Jano Ke Sankat, Daas Janon Ke Sankat
Kshan Me Duur Kare
Om Jai Jagadish Hare

Om, Victory to You, the Lord of the Universe
Swami, Victory to You, the Lord of the Universe
The difficulties of Your devotees, The difficulties of
Your servants You remove in an instant.
Om, Victory to You, the Lord of the Universe.

Jo Dhyaave Phal Paave,Duhkh-Bin Se Man Kaa
Swaami Duhkh-Bin Se Man Kaa
Sukh Sampati Ghar Aave,Sukh Sampati Ghara Aave
Kashta Mite Tan Kaa
Om Jai Jagadish Hare

Whoever meditates on You will get Your grace
Whoever meditates with a mind free of sorrows
Swami, with a mind free of sorrows
Joy and Prosperity will come to them
Joy and Prosperity will come to them
And distress of body and mind will be relieved
Om, Victory to You, the Lord of the Universe.

Maat Pitaa Tum Mere, Sharan Gahuu Kiskii,
Swaami Sharan Gahuu Maim Kiskii
Tum Bin Aur Na Duujaa,Tum Bin Aur Na Duujaa
Aas Karuu Mai Jiskii
Om Jai Jagadish Hare

You are my Father and Mother, and my refuge
Swami, You are my refuge apart from
You there is none else
Swami, there is none else, I aspire for

Om, Victory to You, the Lord of the Universe.

Tum Purana Paramaatmaa,Tum Antarayaami
Swaami Tum Antarayaami
Paarabrahma Parameshwara, Paarabrahma Parameshwara
Tum Sab Ke Swaami
Om Jai Jagadish Hare

You are the Puran Paramatma
You are the indweller of everyone
Swami, You are the indweller of everyone
You are the Parabrahman and Parama
Ishwara - Supreme God
You are the Parabrahman and Parama
Ishwara - Supreme God
You are the Lord of everyone
Om, Victory to You, the Lord of the Universe.

Tum Karunnaa Ke Saagar,Tum Paalan-Kartaa
Swami Tum Paalan-Kartaa
Mai Muurakh Khala-Kaamii, Mai Sevak Tum Swami
Kripaa Karo Bhartaa
Om Jai Jagadish Hare

You are the ocean of compassion
You are the nurturer of everyone
Swami, You are the nurturer of everyone
I am ignorant and go after desires
I am Your servant and You are my Lord
Therefore shower Your grace on me, O Master
Om, Victory to You, the Lord of the Universe

Tum Ho Ek Agochara, Sabke Praan-Pati
Swami Sabake Praan-Pati
Kis Vidh Miluu Dayaamay, Kisa Vidh Miluu Dayaamay
Tumko Mai Kumati
Om Jai Jagadish Hare

You are the one Unseen
And the Lord of all lives
Swami, the Lord of all lives

How shall I meet You, O Merciful One
How shall I meet You,I am an ignorant
Om, Victory to You, the Lord of the Universe.

Diina-Bandhu Dukh-Hartaa,Thaakur Tuma Mere
Swami Rakshak Tum Mere
Apne Haath Uthaao, Apne Sharana Lagaao
Dwaar Padaa Tere
Om Jai Jagadish Hare

You are the friend of the helpless, and
The remover of Sorrows
You are my Lord,Swami, You are my Protector
Please raise Your hand of varada, boon-giving
And abhaya, fear-dispelling
And take me under Your protection.
I surrender myself at Your feet,
Om, Victory to You, the Lord of the Universe.

Vishaya-Vikaar Mitaao, Paap Haro Devaa
Swami Paap Haro Devaa
Shraddhaa Bhakti Baddhaao
Shraddhaa Bhakti Baddhaao
Santan Ki Sevaa
Om Jai Jagadish Hare

Remove my worldly desires
And remove my sins, O Deva
And remove my sins, O Swami
Increase my faith and devotion towards You
Increase my faith and devotion towards You
And the devotional service of this servant
Om, Victory to You, the Lord of the Universe.

GANESHA AARTI

Jai Ganesha Jai Ganesha Jai Ganesha Deva
Mata Jaiki Parvatii, Pitaa Mahadeva

Eka Danta Dayavanta, Char Bhuja Dhaari
Mathe Sinduura Sohai, Muuse Ki Savari
Jai Ganesha Jai Ganesha Jai Ganesha Deva
Mata Jakii Parvatii, Pitaa Mahaadeva
Jai Ganesha...

Andhana Ko Aankha Deta Kodhina Ko Kaayaa
Banjhana Ko Putra Deta Nirdhana Ko Maaya
Jai Ganesha Jai Ganesha Jai Ganesha Deva
Mata Jakii Parvatii, Pitaa Mahaadeva
Jai Ganesha...

Haar Chadhe, Phool Chadhe Aura Chadhe Meva
Ladduan Ka Bhoga Lage Sant Karen Seva
Jai Ganesha Jai Ganesha Jai Ganesha Deva
Mata Jakii Parvatii, Pitaa Mahadeva
Jai Ganesha...

Dinan Ki Laaj Rakho Shambhu Putra Vaari
Manorath Ko Pura Karo Jai Ho Balihaari
Jai Ganesha Jai Ganesha Jai Ganesha Deva
Mata Jakii Parvatii, Pitaa Mahaadeva
J ai Ganesha...

SARASWATI MAA AARTI

Om Jai Saraswati Mata, Maiya Jai Saraswati Mata
Sadgun Vaibhav Shalini, Tribhuvan Vikhyata
Om Jai Saraswati Mata
Jai...

Chandravadani Padmasini Dyuti Mangal Kaari
Sohe Shubh Hans Sawaari, Atul Tej Dhaari
Om Jai Saraswati Mata Jai...

Baaye Kar Mein Veena, Daaye Kar Mala
Sheesh Mukut Mani Shohe, Gale Motiyan Mala
Om Jai Saraswati Mata Jai...

Devi Sharan Jo Aaye, Unka Uddhar Kiya
Paithi Manthra Dasi, Rawan Sanhar Kiya
Om Jai Saraswati Mata Jai..

Vidhya Gyan Pradayini, Gyan Prakash Bharo
Mohagyan Timir Ka, Jag Se Nash Karo
Om Jai Saraswati Mata Jai...

Dhoop Deep Fal Meva, Maa Swikaar Karo
Gyanchkshu De Mata, Jag Nisdar Karo
Om Jai Saraswati Mata Jai...

Maa Saraswati Ji Aarti Jo Koi Nar Gave
Hitkari Shukhkari Gyan Bhakti Pave
Om Jai Saraswati Mata
Jai...

Om Jai Saraswati Mata, Maiya Jai Saraswati Mata
Sadgun Vaibhav Shalini, Tribhuvan Vikhyata
Om Jai Saraswati Mata
Jai...

LAKSHMI MAA AARTI

Om Jai Laxmi Mata, Maiya Jai Laxmi Mata,
Tumko Nis Din Sevat, Hari, Vishnu Data
Om Jai Laxmi Mata

Uma Rama Brahmaani, Tum Ho Jag Mata,
Maiya, Tum Ho Jag Mata,
Surya Chandrama Dhyaavat, Naarad Rishi Gaata.
Om Jai Laxmi Mata.

Durga Roop Niranjani, Sukh Sampati Data,
Maiya Sukh Sampati Data
Jo Koyee Tumko Dhyaataa, Ridhee Sidhee Dhan Paataa
Om Jai Laxmi Mata.

Jis Ghar Mein Tu Rehtee, Sab Sukh Guna Aataa,
Maiya Sab Sukh Guna Aataa,
Taap Paap Mit Jaataa, Man Nahi Ghabraataa.
Om Jai Laxmi Mata

Dhoop Deep Phal Meva, Ma Sweekaar Karo,
Maiya Ma Sweekaar Karo,
Gyaan Prakaash Karo Ma, Moha Agyaan Haro.
Om Jai Laxmi Mata.

Maha Laxmiji Ki Aarti, Jo Koi Nara Gaavey
Maiya Nis Din Jo Gaavey,
Ura Ananda Samata, Paap Utar Jata.
Om Jai Laxmi Mata.

HE ANDHAN KE MAHARANI

He Andhan Ki Maharani
Ho Jai Lakshmi Rani
Tujhe Ghar Ghar Puje Parani
Ho Jai Lakshmi Rani
Mandir Tihara Cham Cham Kare
Lakho Diyo Ki Jyoti Jare
Bhakto Ka Ma Bhandar Bhare
Hatho Se Dhan Ki Barsa Kare
Teri Hum Pe Bhi Ho Meharbani
Ho Jai Lakshmi Rani
He Andhan Ki Maharani
Ho Jai Lakshmi Rani
Hum Mangte Ma Sona Kaha
Hum Mangte Ma Chandi Kaha
Hum To Fakat Bas Itna Mangte
Bhukha Na Koi Soye Yaha
Sabki Rakhna Nigrani
Ho Jai Lakshmi Rani
He Andhan Ki Maharani
Ho Jai Lakshmi Rani
Man Se Jo Ma Ki Puja Kare
Ma Uske Sare Dukhde Hare
Girte Haya Ki Kismat Jo Mar
Chadti Kare Aur Bhadti Kare
Hui Devi Na Tujhse Ye Bani
Ho Jai Lakshmi Rani
He Andhan Ki Maharani
Ho Jai Lakshmi Rani
Tujhe Ghar Ghar Puje Parani
Ho Jai Lakshmi Rani

DURGA MAA AARTI

Ambe, Tu Hai Jagdambe Kali, Jay Durge Khappar Wali
Tere Hi Gun Gaye Bharti,

Ho Maiya Ham Sab Utare Teri aarti

Tere Jagat Ke Bhakt Janan Par Bheed Padi Hai Bhari Maa
Danaw Dal Par Toot Pado Maa Karke Singh Sawari
Sau Sau Singho Se Tu Balshali
Asth Bhujao Wali Dushton Ko Pal Mein Sangharti
O Maiya Hum Sab Utarey Teri Aarti

Maa Bete Ka Jai Is Jag Mein Bada Hi Nirmal Nata
Poot Kaput Sune Hai Par Na Mata Suni Kumata
Sab Par Karuna Darshane Wali Amrit Barsane Wali
Dukhiyon Ke Dukhade Nivarti
O Maiya Hum Sab Utare Teri Aarti

Nahi Mangte Dhan Aur Daulat Na Chandi Na Sona Maa
Hum To Mang Maa Tere Man Mein Ek Chhota Sa Kona
Sab Ki Bigdi Banane Wali Laaj Bachane Wali
Satiyo Ke Sat Ko Sanwarti
O Maiya Hum Sab Utare Teri Aarti

Ambe Tu Hai Jagdambe Kali Jay Durge Khappar Wali
Tere Hi Gun Gaye Bharti
Ho Maiya Ham Sab Utare Teri Aarti

AMBE MAA AARTI

Jai Ambe Gauri ,Maiya Jai Shyama Gauri
Nishdin Tumko Dhyavat, Hari Brahma Shivji,
Jai Ambe....

Mang Sindur Birajat, Tiko Mrigmadko,
Ujjvalse Dou Naina, Chandravadan Niko,
Jai Ambe....

Kanak Saman Kalevar, Raktambar Raje,
Raktapushp Galmala, Kanthhar Saje,
Jai Ambe....

Kehari Vahan Rajat, Khadg Khappar Dhari,
Sur Nar Munijan Sevat, Tinke Dukhahari,
Jai Ambe....

Kanan Kundal Khobhit, Nasagre Moti,
Kotik Chandra Divakar, Samrajat Jyoti,
Jai Ambe....

Shumbh-Nishumbh Vidare, Mahishasur Ghati,
Dhumra-Vilochan Naina, Nishdin Madmati,
Jai Ambe....

Chand-Mund Sanghare, Shunit Beej Hare
Madhu Kaitabh Dau Mare, Sur Bhayheen Kare
Jai Ambe....

Brahmani, Rudrani Tum Kamala Rani,
Agam-Nigam Bakhani, Tum Shiv Patrani,
Jai Ambe....

Chaunsath Yogini Gavat, Nritya Karat Bhairon,
Bajat Tab Mridanga, Aur Bajat Damru,
Jai Ambe...

Tum Ho Jag Ki Mata, Tum Hi Ho Bharta,
Bhaktan Ki Dukh Harta, Sukh Sampati Karta,
Jai Ambe....

Bhuja Char Ati Shobhit, Var Mudra Dhari,
Manvanchhit Phal Pavat, Sevat Nar Nari,
Jai Ambe....

~~~

SHREE JAGDAMBA AARTI

Aarti Keejay Shail Suta Jagdambaji Kee,
Aarti Keejay....
Sneh-Sudha Sukh Sundar Leejay,
Jinkay Naam Lait Drav Bheejay,
Aaisi Vah Mata Vasudha Kee.

Aarti Keejay Shail Suta Kee Jagdambaji Kee,
Aarti Keejay....
Paap Vinashini Keela-Mal-Harini,
Dayamayi Bhavsagar Tarani
Shastra Dhaarinishail Vihaarini,
Budhirashi Ganpati Mata Kee.

Aarti Keejay Shail Suta Kee Jagdambaji kee,
Aarti Keejay....
Singhvahini Maat Bhavani,
Gaurav Gaan Kare Jag Prani
Shiv Kay Hridyaasan Kee Rani,
Kare Aarti Mil-Jul Taki.

Aarti Keejay Shail Suta Kee Jagdambaji Kee,
Aarti Keejay....

~~~

SANTOSHI MAA AARTI

Jai Santoshi Mata, Maiya Jai Santoshi Mata,
Apne Sevak Jan Ki, Sukh Sampati Data,
Jai Santoshi Mata....

Sundar Chir Sunahri, Man Dharan Kinhon,
Hira Panna Damke, Tan Shringar Liyo,
Jai Santoshi Mata....

Geru Lal Chhata Chhavi, Badan Kamal Sohe
Mand Hansat Karunamayi, Tribhuvan Man Mohe,
Jai Santoshi Mata....

Svarna Sinhasan Baithi, Chanvar Dhure Pyare,
Dhup, Dip, Madhu Meva, Bhog Dhare Dyare,
Jai Santoshi Mata....

Gud Aur Chana Param Priya, Tamen Santosh Kiyo,
Santoshi Kahlai, Bhaktan Vaibhav Diyo,
Jai Santoshi Mata....

Shukravar Priya Manat, Aj Divas Sohi,
Bhakti Mandali Chhai, Katha Sunat Mohi,
Jai Santoshi Mata....

Mandir Jagmag Jyoti, Mangal Dhvani Chhai,
Vinai Kare Tere Balak, Charnan Sir Nai,
Jai Santoshi Mata....

Bhakti Bhavmai Puja Angikrit Kijai,
Jo Man Vasai Hamare Ichha Phal Dijai,
Jai Santoshi Mata....

Dhyan Dharo Jan Tero Manvanchhit Phal Payo,
Puja Katha Shravan Kar Ghar Anand Ayo,
Jai Santoshi Mata.

Sharan Gahe Ki, Lajja Rakhiyo Jagdambe,
Sankat Tu Hi Nivare, Dayamayi Ambe,
Jai Santoshi Mata....

Santoshi Man Ki Aarti Jo Koi Jan Gavai,
Riddhi-Siddhi Sukh Sampati, Ji Bhar Ke Pavai,
Jai Santoshi Mata....

SANTOSHI MAA AARTI

Yaha Waha Jaha Taha Mat Puchho
Kaha Kaha Hai Santoshee Ma
Apanee Santoshee Ma Apanee Santoshee Ma
Jal Me Bhee Thal Me Bhee Chal Me Achal Me Bhee
Atal Vital Me Bhee Ma
Apanee Santoshee Ma Apanee Santoshee Ma

Badee Anokhe Chamatkarnee
Yeh Apanee Maiya
Rai Ko Parvat Kar Saktee Parvat Ko Rayee
Duwar Khula Darbar Khula Hai
Aao Baahe Bhayee Isake Dar
Kabhee Daya Kee Kamee Nahee Aayee
Pal Me Nihal Kare Dukh Ko Nikar Kare
Pal Me Nihal Kare Dukh Ko Nikar Kare
Torat Kamal Kare
Apanee Santoshee Ma Apanee Santoshee Ma

Yaha Waha Jaha Taha Mat Puchho Kaha Kaha
Hai Santoshee Ma
Apanee Santoshee Ma Apanee Santoshee Ma

Iss Amba Me Jagdamba Me, Ajab Kee Hai Saktee
Chinta Me Dube Huye Logo, Karlo Isake Bhaktee
Apna Jivan Saup Do Isko Palo Re Muktee
Suk Sampattee Kee Data
Yeh Ma Yeh kya Nahee Kar Saktee
Bigadee Banane Walee Dukhade Mitane Walee
Bigadee Banane Ealee Dukhade Mitane Walee
Kasst Hatane Walee Apanee Santoshee Ma
Yaha Waha Jaha Taha Mat Puchho Kaha Kaha
Hai Santoshee Ma
Apanee Santoshee Ma Apanee Santoshee Ma

Gauri Sut Ganpati Kee Beti
Yeh Hai Badee Bholee
Dekh Dekh Ke Iske Mukdra Har Ek Disha Dolee

Aao Re Bhakto Yeh Mata Hai Sab Kee Hamjolee
Joh Mangoge Tumhe Milenge Bhar Lo Re Jholee
Ujwal Ujwal Nirmal Nirmal Ujwal Ujwal
Nirmal Nirmal Sundar Sundar Ma
Apanee Santoshee Ma Apanee Santoshee Ma

Yaha Waha Jaha Taha Mat Puchho Kaha Kaha
Hai Santoshee Ma
Apanee Santoshee Ma Apanee Santoshee Ma
Apanee Santoshee Ma Apanee Santoshee Ma.

PARVATI MAA AARTI

Jai Parvati Mata Jai Parvati Mata
Brahma Sanatan Devi Shubh Fal Kada Data
Arikul Pada Vinasin Jaisevak Trata
Jag Jivan Jagdamba Harihar Gun Gata.
Jai Parvati Mata

Singh Vahan Saajey Kundal Hai Saatha
Dev Vadhu Jahan Gaavat Niritya Karat Tatha.
Jai Parvati Mata

Satyug Sheel Susundar Naam Sati Kahlata
Hemachal Ghar Janmi Sakhiyan Rang Rata.
Jai Parvati Mata

Shumbh Nishumh Vidaarey Hemachal Syata
Sahas Bhuja Tanu Dharkey Chakra Liyu Hatha.
Jai Parvati Mata

Shrishti Roop Tumhi Janini Shiv Sang Rang Rata
Nandi Bhringibin Lahi Sara Mad Mata.
Jai Parvati Mata

Devan Araj Karat Hum Chit Ko Laata
Gaavat De De Taali Man Mein Rang Raata.
Jai Parvati Mata

Shri Pratap Aarti Maiya Ki Jo Koi Gaata
Sada Sukhi Rehta Sukh Sampati Paata.
Jai Parvati Mata

VAISHNO MAA AARTI

Jai Vashnavi Mata, Maiya Jai Vashnavi Mata.
Hath Jood Tere Aage, Aarti Mai Gata.
Sheesh Par Chatra Birajay, Murtiyan Pyaari.
Ganga Bhati Charnan, Jyoti Jage Nyaari.
Brahman Ved Pade Nit Dware, Shankar Dhyana Dhare.
Sevat Chanvar Dulavat, Narad Nritya Kare.
Sundar Gufa Tumhari, Mann Ko Ati Bhave.
Baar-Baar Dekhne Ko, Ae Ma Mann Chave.
Bhawan Pe Jhande Jhulay, Ghanta Dhwani Baajay.
Uncha Parvat Tera, Mata Priya Laagay.
Paan Supari Dhwaja Nariyal, Bhent Pushp Mewa.
Dass Khadde Charnon Mai, Darshan Do Deva.
Jo Jan Nischay Karke, Dwar Tere Aavay
Etni Stuti Nishidin, Jo Nar Bhi Gavay.

TULSI MAA AARTI

Jai Jai Tulsi Mata, Sab Jag Ki Sukh Daata
Sab Yugon Ke Upar, Sab Logon Ke Upar

Ruj Se Raksha Karke Bhav Trata
Jai Jai Tulsi Mata

Batu Putri He Shyama, Sur Bali hai Graamya
Vishnu Priye Jo Tumko Seve, So Nar Tar Jaata
Jai Jai Tulsi Mata

Hari Ke Sheesh Viraajat Tribhuvan Se Ho Vandit
Patit Jano Ki Taarini, Tum Ho Vikhyata
Jai Jai Tulsi Mata

Lekar Janam Vijan Mein Aayi Divya Bhavan Me
Maanavlok Tumhi Se, Sukh Sampati Paata
Jai Jai Tulsi Mata

Hari Ko Tum Ati Pyaari Shyaam Varun Kumari
Prem Ajab Hai Unka Tumse Kaisa Naata
Jai Jai Tulsi Mata

Jai Jai Tulsi Mata, Sab Jag Ki Sukh Daata
Sab Yugon Ke Upar, Sab Logon Ke Upar

Ruj Se Raksha Karke Bhav Trata
Jai Jai Tulsi Mata

GANGA MAA AARTI

Om Jai Gange Mata, Shri Jai Gange Mata
Jo nar Tumko Dhyata, Man Vanchit Phal Pata
Om Jai Gange Mata

Chandra Si Jot Tumhari, Jal Nirmal Aata
Sharan Pade Jo Teri, So Nar Tar Jata
Om Jai Gange Mata

Putra Sagar Ke Taare, Sab Jag Ko Gyata
Kripa Drishtit Tumhari, Tribhuvan Sukh Data
Om Jai Gange Mata

Ek Hi Baar Jo Teri Sharanagati Aata
Yam Ki Traas Mitakar, Paramgati Pata
Om Jai Gange Mata

Aarti Maat Tumhari, Jo Nar Nit Gata
Dass Wahi Sahaj Mein, Mukti Ko Pata
Om Jai Gange Mata

VINDHESHWARI AARTI

Sunn Meri Devi Parbatvasini, Koi Tera Par Na Paya
Paan Supari Dhwaja Nariyal, Le Teri Bhent Charaya
Sunn Meri Devi Parbatvasini, Koi Tera Par Na Paya

Suva Choli Teri Aang Virajay, Kesar Tilak Lagaya
Nange Pag Ma Akbar Aaya, Sone Ka Chatar Charaya.

Sunn Meri Devi Parbatvasini, Koi Tera Par Na Paya
Unche Parbat Banyu Devalaya, Nichhe Shahar Basaya.
Satyug, Dwapar, Treta Madhaye, Kaliyug Raaj Savaya.

Sunn Meri Devi Parbatvasini, Koi Tera Par Na Paya
Dhoop Deep Navaidya Aarti, Mohan Bhog Lagaya.
Dhyanu Bhagat Maiya Tere Gunn Gaya,
Mannvanchit Phal Paaya.

Sunn Meri Devi Parbatvasini, Koi Tera Par Na Paya

SHREE RAMCHANDRA AARTI

Shree Ramacandra Kripalu Bhaju Mana,
Harana Bhava Bhaya Darunam
Navakanja-Lochana Kanja-Mukha Kara
Kanja Pada-Kanjarunam

Kandarpa Aganita Amita Chavi
Navaneela Niraj Sundaram
Patapita Manahu tarita Ruchi Suchi
Naumi Janaka-Sutavaram

Bhaju Dinabandhu Dinesha Danava
Daitya-Vansha Nikandanam
Raghunanda Anandakanda Kaushala
Chandra Dasharatha-Nandanam

Sira Mukuta Kundala Tilaka Charu
Udaru Anga Vibhushanam
Aajanu Bhuja Sharachapa Dhara,
Sangrama-Jita Khara-Dhushanam

Iti Vadati Tulasidasa Shankara
Shesha Munimana Ranjanam
Mama Hridaya-Kanja Nivasa Kuru
Kamadi Khaladala Ganjanam

SHREE RAMAYANA JI KI AARTI

Aarti Sri Ramayan Ji Ki
Kirti Kalit Lalit Siya Pi Ki

Gaavat Brahmadik Muni Narad
Balmeek Bigyaan Bisaarad
Suk Sankaadi Sesh Aru Saarad
Barni Pavansut Kirati Neeki
Aarti Sri Ramayan Ji Ki
Kirati Kalit Lalit Siya Pi Ki

Gaavat Ved Puraan Ashtadas
Chhao Shastra Sab Granthan Ko Ras
Muni Jan Dhan Santan Ko Sabras
Saar Ansh Samat Sab Hi Ki
Aarti Sri Ramayan Ji Ki
Kirti Kalit Lalit Siya Pi Ki

Gaavat Santat Sambhu Bhavani
Aru Ghatsambhav Muni Bigyani
Vyaas Aadi Kabi Barj Bakhaani
Kaagbhusundi Garud Ke Hi Ki
Aarti Sri Ramayan Ji Ki
Kirti Kalit Lalit Siya Pi Ki

Kalimal Harni Vishya Ras Peeki
Subhag Singaar Mukti Jubati Ki
Dalan Rog Bhav Moori Ami Ki
Taat Maat Sab Vidhi Tulsi Ki
Aarti Sri Ramayan Ji Ki
Keerti Kalit Lalit Siya Pi Ki

SHIVA AARTI

Jai Shiva Omkaara

Karpoor Gauram Karunavataram Samsaarsaram
Bhujgendra Haaram
Sada Vasantam Hridayaravinde Bhawam Bhawani Sahitam
Namami
Jai Shiv Omkaara, Om Jai Shiva Omkara,
Bramha, Vishnu, Sadashiv, Ardhangi Dhaara.

Jai Shiv Omkaara, Om Jai Shiva Omkara,
Bramha, Vishnu, Sadashiv, Ardhangi Dhaara.

Ekaanan Chaturaanan Panchaanan Raje,
Hansaanan Garudaasan Vrishvaahan Saaje.
Do Bhuj Chaar Chaturbhuj Dasamukh Ati Sohe,
Trigun Rup Nirakhate Tribhuvan Jan Mohe.

Akshamaala Vanamaala Mundamaala Dhaari,
Tripuraari Kansaari Kar Maala Dhaari.
Shvetambar Pitambar Baaghambar Ange,
Sanakaadik Garunaadik Bhutaadik Sange.

Kar Ke Madhy Kamandalu Charka Trishuladhaari,
Sukhakaari Dukhahaari Jagapaalan Kaari.

Bramha Vishnu Sadaashiv Jaanat Aviveka,
Pranavaakshar Mein Shobhit Ye Tino Ekaa.

Lakshmi Va Saavitri Paarvati Sangaa,
Paarvati Ardhaangi, Shivalahari Gangaa.

Parvat Sohe Parvati, Shankar Kailasa,
Bhang Dhatur Ka Bhojan, Bhasmi Mein Vaasa.

Jataa Me Gang Bahat Hai, Gal Mundan Maala,
Shesh Naag Lipataavat, Odhat Mrigachaala.

Kashi Me Viraaje Vishvanaath, Nandi Bramhchaari,
Nit Uthh Darshan Paavat, Mahimaa Ati Bhaari.

Trigunasvamiji Ki Aarti Jo Koi Nar Gave
Kahat Shivanand Svami Sukh Sampati Pave

~~~

SHIVRATRI AARTI

Aagyi Mahashivratri Padharo Shankarji,
Ho Padharo Shankarji, Aarti Utare Paar
Utaro Shankarji, Ho Utaro Shankarji
Tum Nayan Nayanme Ho Man Man Me Dham Tera.
He Neelkanth Hai Kanth Kanth Me Naam Tera,
Ho Devon Ke Dev Jagat Ke Pyare Shankarji.
Tum Raj Mahal Me, Tum Hi Bikhari Ke Ghar Me,
Dharti Per Tera Charan Mukut Hai Ambar Pe.
Sansar Tumhara Ek Hamare Shankarji,
Tum Duniya Besa Kar Bharam Ramane Wale Ho.
Papi Ke Bhi Rakhwale Bhole Bhale Ho,
Duniya Me Bhi Do Din To Gujaro Shankarji.
Kya Bhent Cherhaye Tan Maila Ghar Suna Hai,
Le Lo Aansoo Ke Gangajal Ka Namuna Hai.
Aakerke Nayan Me Charan Pakharo Shankarji.

~~~

SHREE HANUMAAN AARTI

Aarti Kije Hanuman Lala Ki
Aarti Ki Jai Hanuman Lala Ki,
Dushat Dalan Ragunath Kala Ki.

Ja Ke Bal Se Girivar Kaanpe,
Rog Dosh Ja Ke Nikat Na Jhanke.
Anjani Putra Mahabaldaye,
Santan Ke Prabhu Sada Sahaye.

De Beeraha Raghunath Pathai,
Lanka Jaari Siya Sudhi Laiye.
Lanka So Kot Samundra Se Khaiy,
Jaat Pavan Sut Baar Na Laiye.

Lanka Jaari Asur Sab Maare,
Siya Ramji Ke Kaaj Sanvare.
Lakshman Moorchit Parhe Sakare,
Aan Sajeevan Pran Ubhaare.

Paith Pataal Tori Yamkare,
Ahiravan Ke Bhuja Ukhaare.
Baayen Bhuja Asur Dal Mare,
Daayen Bhuja Sab Santa Jana Tare.

Surnar Munijan Aarti Utare,
Jai Jai Jai Hanuman Uchaare.
Kanchan Thaar Kapoor Lo Chhai,
Aarti Karat Aajani Mai.
Jo Hanumanji Ki Aarti Gaave,
Basi Baikuntha Amar Padh Pave.

Lanka Vidvance Kiye Ragurai,
Tulsidas Swami Aarti Gaaie.

Aarti Ki Jai Hanuman Lala Ki,
Dushat Dalan Ragunath Kala Ki.

KASHI SATSANGH

Pawan Tanay Sankat Haran, Managal Moorti Roop,
Ram Lakhan Sita Sahit, Hridaya Bhasu Sur Bhoop

SHRI KRISHNA AARTI

Aarti Kunj Bihari Ki

Vasudevsutam Devam Kans Charur Mardanam
Devaki Paramanandanam Krishnam Vande Jagadgurum

Aarti Kunj Bihari Ki, Shri Girdhar Krishna Murari Ki
Gale Mein Baijanti Mala, Bajave Murali Madhur Bala
Shravan Mein Kundal Jhalakala,
Nand Ke Nand, Shri Anand, Mohan Brijchand
Radhika Raman Bihari Ki
Shri Giradhar Krishnamuraari Ki
Aarti Kunj Bihari ki ...

Gagan Sam Ang Kanti Kali, Radhika Chamak Rahi Aali
Ratan Mein Thadhe Banamali
Bhramar Si Alak, Kasturi Tilak, Chandra Si Jhalak
Lalit Chavi Shyama Pyari Ki
Shri Giradhar Krishnamuraari Ki
Aarti Kunj Bihari Ki ...

Kanakmaya Mor Mukut Bilse, Devata Darsan Ko Tarse
Gagan So Suman Raasi Barse
Baje Murchang, Madhur Mridang, Gwaalini Sang
Atul Rati Gop Kumaari Ki
Shri Giradhar Krishna Murari Ki
Aarti Kunj Bihari Ki....

Jahaan Se Pragat Bhayi Ganga, Kalush Mala
Haarini Shri Ganga,
Smaran Se Hota Moh Bhanga
Basi Shiv Shish, Jataa Ke Biich, Harei Agh Kiich
Charan Chhavi Shri Banvaari Ki,
Shri Giradhar Krishnamuraari Ki,
Aarti Kunj Bihari Ki...

Chamakati Ujjawal Tat Renu, Baj Rahi Vrindavan Benu
Chahu Disi Gopi Gwaal Dhenu
Hansat Mridu Mand, Chandani Chand,
Katat Bhav Phand
Ter Sun Diin Dukhaarii Kii
Shri Giradhar Krishnamuraari Ki
Aarti Kunj Bihari Ki

~~~

RADHA KRISHNA AARTI

Om Jai Shree Radha Jai Shree KrishnaShree Radha
Krishnayah Namah

Ghoom Ghumro Ghamar Sohay Jai Shree Radha
Pat Pitambar Muni Mann Mohay Jai Shree Krishna Jugal
Prem Ras Jham Jham Jhamke
Shree Radha Krishnaya Namah
Radha Radha Krishna Kanhiya Jai Shree Radha
Bhav Bhav Sagar Paar Lagaya Jai Shree Krishna
Mangal Murthi Mooksh Karaya
Shree Radha Krishnayah Namah

~~~

SATYANARAYAN AARTI

Jai Lakshmi Ramana Swami Jai Lakshmi Ramana,
Satyanarayan Swami Jan Patak Harana,
Jai Lakshmi Ramana.....

Ratan Ja Rat Singhasan, Adhbut Chabee Rajey,
Narad Kahat Niranjan, Ghanta Dhun Bhajey
Jai Lakshmi Ramana.....

Praghat Bhaye Kali Karan, Dwaj Ko Daras Diyo
Budha Brahman Bankey, Kanchan Mahal Kiyo
Jai Lakshmi Ramana.....

Durbal Bhil Kathier, Jan Par Kripa Karey
Chandra Choor Ik Raja, Jinaki Vipat Hari
Jai Lakshmi Ramana

Vashey Manorath Payo, Shradha Tuj Dini
So Fal Bhogyo Prabhji, Phir Sutati Kini
Jai Lakshmi Ramana

Bhav Bhagti Ke Karan, Chhin Chhin Roop Dharyo
Shardha Dharan Kini, Tin Kay Karj Saryo
Jai Lakshmi Ramana

Gwal Bal Sang Raja, Ban Mein Bhakti Karey
Man Vanchit Fal Dina, Deen Dayal Hari
Jai Lakshmi Ramana

Charhat Prasad Sawayo, Kadali Fal Mewa
Dhoop Deep Tulsi Se, Raje Sat Deva
Jai Lakshmi Ramana

Shri Satya Narayan Ji Ki, Aarti jo Koi gaavey
Kahat Shivanand Swami, ManVanchit Fal Paavey

Jai Lakshmi Ramana

~~~
~~~

SURYA DEV AARTI

Om Jai-Kashyap Nandan, Om Prabhu Jai Aditi nandan,
Tribhuvan-Timin Nikandan Bhakt-Hriday-Chandan.
Om Jai-Kashyap Nandan...

Sapt-Ashvarath Raajit Ek Chakradhar,
Dukhahar-Sukhkar, Maanas-Mal-Haar.
Om Jai-Kashyap Nandan...

Sur-Muni-Bhoosur-Vandin, Vimal Vibhavashaal,
Agh-Dal-Dalan Divaakar Divya Kiran Maal.
Om Jai-Kashyap Nandan...

Sakal-Sukarma-Prasavitaa Savita Shubhkaar,
Vishva-Vilochan Mochan Bhav Bandhan Bhaar.
Om Jai-Kashyap Nandan...

Kamal-Samooh Vikasak Nashak Tray Tapa,
Sevat Sahaj Harat Ati Manasij Santapa.
Om Jai-Kashyap Nandan...

Netra-Vyadhi-Har Suravar Bhu Peeda Haar,
Vrishti-Vimochan Santat Parahit-Vratadhar.
Om Jai-Kashyap Nandan...

Suryadev Karunakar Ab Karuna Kije,
Har Agyan-Moh Sab Sattvagyan Dijai.
Om Jai-Kashyap Nandan...

GOMATA AARTI

Aarti Shri Gaiya Maiya Ki,
Aarti Harni Viswadhaiya Ki

Arthkaam Saddharm Pradaayini,
Avichal Amal Muktipadyaini

Sur Maanav Saubhagyavidhayini,
Pyaari Pujya Nand Chaiya Ki

Akhil Vishwa Pratipaalini Maata,
Madhur Amiy Dugdhanan Prabdaata

Rog Shok Sankat Paritrata,
Bhavsaagar Hit Drid Naiya Ki

Aayu Oj Aarogyavikaashini,
Dukh Dainya Vivek Budhi Daiya Ki

Sevak Ho Chahe Dukh Daayi,
Saa Pay Sudha Piya Vati Maayi

Shatru Mitra Sabko Sukhdaayi,
Sneh Swabhaav Vishwa Jaiya Ki

VANDE MAATARAM

Aao Bachchon Tumhein Dikhayen

Aao Bachchon Tumhen Dikhaayen Jhaanki Hindustaan Ki
Is Mitti Se Tilak Karo Ye Dharati Hai Balidaan Ki
Vande Maataram, Vande Maataram...

Uttar Mein Rakhavaali Karata Parvataraaj Viraat Hai
Dakshin Men Charanon Ko Dhota Saagar Ka Samraat Hai
Jamuna Ji Ke Tat Ko Dekho, Ganga Ka Ye Ghaat Hai
Baat-Baat Pe Haat-Haat Men Yahaan Niraala Thaath Hai
Dekho Ye Tasveeren Apane, Gaurav Ki Abhimaan Ki
Is Mitti Se Tilak Karo Ye Dharati Hai Balidaan Ki
Vande Maataram, Vande Maataram...

Ye Hai Apana Raajapootaana, Naaz Ise Talavaaron Pe
Isane Saara Jeevan Kaata, Barachhi, Teer, Kataaron Pe
Ye Prataap Ka Vatan Pala Hai, Aazaadi Ke Naaron Pe
Kood Padi Thi Yahaan, Hazaaron Padminiyaan Angaaron Pe
Bol Rahi Hai Kan Kan Se Qurbaani Rajasthan Ki
Is Mitti Se Tilak Karo Ye Dharati Hai Balidaan Ki
Vande Maataram, Vande Maataram...

Dekho Mulk Maraathon Ka Ye, Yahaan Shivaaji Dola Tha
Mugalon Ki Taakat Ko Jisane, Talavaaron Pe Tola Tha
Har Paavat Pe Aag Lagi Thi, Har Patthar Ek Shola Tha
Boli Har-Har Mahaadev Ki, Bachchaa-Bachcha Bola Tha
Yahaan Shivaaji Ne Rakhi Thi, Laaj Hamaari Shaan Ki
Is Mitti Se Tilak Karo Ye Dharati Hai Balidaan Ki
Vande Maataram, Vande Maataram...

Jaliyaan Vaala Baag Ye Dekho Yahaan Chali Thi Goliyaan
Ye Mat Poochho Kisne Kheli, Yahaan Khoon Ki Holiyaan
Ek Taraf Bandooken Dan Dan, Ek Taraf Thi Toliyaan
Maranevaale Bol Rahe The, Inaqalaab Ki Boliyaan

Yahaan Laga Di Behanon Ne Bhi, Baazi Apani Jaan Ki
Is Mitti Se Tilak Karo Ye Dharati Hai Balidaan Ki
Vande Maataram, Vande Maataram...

Ye Dekho Bangaal Yahaan Ka, Har Chappa Hariyaala Hai
Yahaan Ka Bachchaa-Bachcha Apane Desh Pe Maranevaala Hai
Dhaala Hai Isko Bijali Ne, Bhoonchaalon Ne Paala Hai
Mutthi Men Toofaan Bandha Hai, Aur Praan Men Jvaala Hai
Janam-Bhoomi Hai Yahi Hamaare Veer Subhaash Mahaan Ki
Is Mitti Se Tilak Karo Ye Dharati Hai Balidaan Ki
Vande Maataram, Vande Maataram...

CHAALISAS

Ganesh Chaalisa

Doha

Jai Ganapati Sadguna Sadan,
Karivar Badan Kripal,
Vighna Haran Mangal Karan,
Jai Jai Girijaalaal

Jai Jai Jai Ganapati Ganaraaju,
Mangal Bharana Karana Shubha Kaajuu,
Jai Gajbadan Sadan Sukhdaata,
Vishva Vinaayaka Buddhi Vidhaataa

Vakra Tunda Shuchi Shunda Suhaavana,
Tilaka Tripunda Bhaal Man Bhaavan,
Raajata Mani Muktana Ura Maala,
Swarna Mukuta Shira Nayana Vishaalaa

Pustak Paani Kuthaar Trishuulam,
Modaka Bhoga Sugandhit Phuulam,
Sundara Piitaambar Tana Saajit,
Charana Paadukaa Muni Man Raajit

Dhani Shiva Suvan Shadaanana Bhraataa,
Gaurii Lalan Vishva-Vikhyaata,
Riddhi Siddhi Tav Chanvar Sudhaare,
Mooshaka Vaahan Sohat Dvaare

Kahaun Janama Shubh Kathaa Tumhari,
Ati Shuchi Paavan Mangalkaarii,
Ek Samay Giriraaj Kumaarii,
Putra Hetu Tapa Kiinhaa Bhaarii

Bhayo Yagya Jaba Poorana Anupaa,
Taba Pahunchyo Tuma Dhari Dvija Rupaa,

Atithi Jaani Kay Gaurii Sukhaarii,
Bahu Vidhi Sevaa Karii Tumhaarii

Ati Prasanna Hvai Tum Vara Diinhaa,
Maatu Putra Hit Jo Tap Kiinhaa,
Milhii Putra Tuhi, Buddhi Vishaala,
Binaa Garbha Dhaarana Yahi Kaalaa

Gananaayaka Guna Gyaan Nidhaanaa,
Puujita Pratham Roop Bhagavaanaa,
Asa Kehi Antardhyaana Roop Hvai,
Palanaa Par Baalak Svaroop Hvai

Bani Shishu Rudan Jabahi Tum Thaanaa,
Lakhi Mukh Sukh Nahin Gauri Samaanaa,
Sakal Magan Sukha Mangal Gaavahin,
Nabha Te Suran Suman Varshaavahin

Shambhu Umaa Bahudaan Lutaavahin,
Sura Munijana Suta Dekhan Aavahin,
Lakhi Ati Aanand Mangal Saajaa,
Dekhan Bhii Aaye Shani Raajaa

Nija Avaguna Gani Shani Man Maahiin,
Baalak Dekhan Chaahat Naahiin,
Girijaa Kachhu Man Bheda Badhaayo,
Utsava Mora Na Shani Tuhi Bhaayo

Kahana Lage Shani Man Sakuchaai,
Kaa Karihau Shishu Mohi Dikhayii,
Nahin Vishvaasa Umaa Ura Bhayauu,
Shani Son Baalak Dekhan Kahyau

Padatahin Shani Drigakona Prakaashaa,
Baalak Sira Udi Gayo Aakaashaa,
Girajaa Girii Vikala Hvai Dharanii,
So Dukha Dashaa Gayo Nahin Varanii

Haahaakaara Machyo Kailaashaa,
Shani Kiinhon Lakhi Suta Ko Naashaa,

Turat Garuda Chadhi Vishnu Sidhaaye,
Kaati Chakra So GajaShira Laaye

Baalak Ke Dhada Uupar Dhaarayo,
Praana Mantra Padhi Shankar Daarayo,
Naama Ganesha Shambhu Taba Kiinhe,
Pratham Poojya Buddhi Nidhi Vara Diinhe

Buddhi Pariikshaa Jab Shiva Kiinhaa,
Prithvii Kar Pradakshinaa Liinhaa,
Chale Shadaanana Bharami Bhulaai,
Rache Baithii Tum Buddhi Upaai

Charana Maatu-Pitu Ke Dhara Liinhen,
Tinake Saat Pradakshina Kiinhen
Dhani Ganesha Kahi Shiva Hiye Harashyo,
Nabha Te Suran Suman Bahu Barse

Tumharii Mahima Buddhi Badhaai,
Shesha Sahasa Mukha Sake Na Gaai,
Main Mati Heen Maliina Dukhaarii,
Karahun Kaun Vidhi Vinaya Tumhaarii
Bhajata 'Raamsundara' Prabhudaasaa,
Jaga Prayaaga Kakraa Durvaasaa,
Ab Prabhu Dayaa Deena Par Keejai,
Apnii Bhakti Shakti Kuchha Deejai

Doha

Shrii Ganesha Yeh Chaalisaa,
Paatha Karre Dhara Dhyaan
Nita Nav Mangala Graha Base,
Lahe Jagat Sanmaana
Sambandh Apna Sahasra Dash,
Rishi Panchamii Dinesha
Poorana Chaalisaa Bhayo,
Mangala Moorti Ganesha

SARASWATI CHAALISA

Doha

Janak Janani Pad Kamal Raj, Nij Mastak Par Dhaari,
Bandau Maatu Saraswati, Buddhi Bal De Daataari.
Purn Jagat Mein Vyaapt Tav, Mahima Amit Anantu,
Ramsaagar Ke Paap Ko, Maatu Tuhi Ab Hantu.

Jay Shri Sakal Buddhi Balaraasi,
Jay Sarvagya Amar Avinaasi.
Jay Jay Veenaakar Dhaari,
Karati Sadaa Suhans Savaari.

Roop Chaturbhujadhaari Maata,
Sakal Vishv Andar Vikhyaata.
Jag Mein Paap Buddhi Jab Hoti,
Jabahi Dharm Ki Phiki Jyoti.

Tabahi Maatu Le Nij Avataara,
Paap Heen Karati Mahi Taara.
Baalmiki Ji The Gyaani,
Tav Prasaad Janie Sansaara.

Raamaayan Jo Rache Banaai,
Aadi Kavi Ki Padavi Paai.
Kalidaas Jo Bhaye Vikhyaata,
Teri Kripaa Drishti Se Maata.

Tulasi Sur Aadi Vidvaana,
Bhaye Aur Jo Gyaani Nana.
Tinhahi Na Aur Raheu Avalamba,
Keval Kripa Aapaki Amba.
Karahu Kripa Soi Maatu Bhavaani,
Dukhit Din Nij Daasahi Jaani.
Putra Karai Aparaadh Bahuta,
Tehi Na Dharai Chitt Sundar Maata.
Raakhu Laaj Janani Ab Meri,

Vinay Karu Bahu Bhaanti Ghaneri.
Mein Anaath Teri Avalamba,
Kripa Karau Jay Jay Jagadamba.

Madhu Kaitabh Jo Ati Balavaana,
Baahuyuddh Vishnu Te Thaana.
Samar Hajaar Paanch Mein Ghora,
Phir Bhi Mukh Unase Nahi Mora.

Maatu Sahaay Bhai Tehi Kaala,
Buddhi Viparit Kari Khalahaala.
Tehi Mrityu Bhai Khal Keri,
Purvahu Maatu Manorath Meri.

Chand Mund Jo The Vikhyaata,
Chhan Mahu Sanhaareu Tehi Maata.
Raktabij Se Samarath Paapi,
Sur-Muni Hriday Dhara Sab Kampi.

Kaateu Sir Jim Kadali Khamba,
Baar Baar Binavau Jagadamba.
Jag Prasiddh Jo Shumbh Nishumbha,
Chhin Me Badhe Taahi Tu Amba.

Bharat-Maatu Budhi Phereu Jaai,
Ramachandra Banvaas Karaai.
Ehi Vidhi Raavan Vadh Tum Kinha,
Sur Nar Muni Sab Kahu Sukh Dinha.

Ko Samarath Tav Yash Gun Gaana,
Nigam Anaadi Anant Bakhaana.
Vishnu Rudra Aj Sakahi Na Maari,
Jinaki Ho Tum Rakshaakaari.

Rakt Dantika Aur Shataakshi,
Naam Apaar Hai Daanav Bhakshi.
Durgam Kaaj Dhara Par Kinha,
Durga Naam Sakal Jag Linha.

Durg Aadi Harani Tu Maata,

Kripa Karahu Jab Jab Sukhadaata.
Nrip Kopit Jo Maaran Chaahei,
Kaanan Mein Ghere Mrig Naahei.

Saagar Madhy Pot Ke Bhange,
Ati Toofaan Nahi Kou Sange.
Bhoot Pret Baadha Yaa Dukh Mein,
Ho Daridra Athava Sankat Mein.

Naam Jape Mangal Sab Koi,
Sanshay Isame Karai Na Koi.
Putrahin Jo Aatur Bhaai,
Sabei Chhaandi Puje Ehi Maai.

Karai Path Nit Yah Chaalisa,
Hoy Putra Sundar Gun Isa.
Dhupaadik Naivedy Chadhavei,
Sankat Rahit Avashy Ho Jaavei.

Bhakti Maatu Ki Karei Hamesha,
Nikat Na Aavei Taahi Kalesha.
Bandi Path Kare Shat Baara,
Bandi Paash Door Ho Saara.

Karahu Kripa Bhavamukti Bhavaani,
Mo Kahn Daas Sadaa Nij Jaani.

Doha

**Maata Sooraj Kaanti Tav,
Andhakaar Mam Roop,
Dooban Te Raksha Karahu,
Paru Na Mein Bhav-Koop.
Bal Buddhi Vidya Dehu Mohi,
Sunahu Sarasvati Maatu,
Adham Ramasaagarahi Tum,
Aashray Deu Punaatu.**

LAKSHMI CHAALISA

Maatu Lakshmi Kari Kripaa,
Karahu Hriday Mein Vaas
Manokaamanaa Siddh Kari,
Purvahu Jan Kii Aas ~

CHAURATHA

Sindhusutaa Main Sumiron Tohii,
Jnaan Buddhi Vidyaa Dehu Mohii
Tum Samaan Nahiin Kou Upakaarii,
Sab Vidhi Prabhu Aas Hamaarii ~

CHAUPAAI

Jai Jai Jagat Janani Jagadambaa,
Sab Kii Tumahii Ho Avalambaa
Tumahii Ho Ghat Ghat Kii Vaasii,
Bintii Yahii Hamarii Khaasii

Jagajananii Jay Sindhu Kumaarii,
Diinan Kii Tum Ho Hitakaarii
Binavon Nitya Tumhe Mahaaraanii,
Kripa Karo Jag Janani Bhavaanii

Kehi Vidhi Astuti Karon Tihaarii,
Sudhi Lijain Aparaadh Bisaarin
Krapaadrasti Chitabahu Mam Orii,
Jagat Janani Binatii Sunu Morii

Jnaan Buddhi Jay Sukh Kii Daataa,
Sankat Harahu Hamaare Maataa
Kshiir Sindhu Jab Vishnumathaayo,
Chaudah Ratn Sindhu Upajaayo

Tin Ratnan Manh Tum Sukhraasii,
Sevaa Kiinh Banin Prabhudasi
Jab Jab Janam Jahaan Prabhu Liinhaa,
Ruup Badal Tahan Sevaa Kiinhaa

Svayam Vishnu Jab Nar Tanu Dhaaraa,
Liinheu Avadhapurii Avataaraa
Tab Tum Prakati Janakapur Manhin,
Sevaa Kiinh Hraday Pulakaahii

Apanaavaa Tohi Antarayaamii,
Vishvavidit Tribhuvan Ke Svaamii
Tum Samaprabal Shakti Nahi Aanii,
Kahan Lagi Mahimaa Kahaun Bakhaanii

Man Kram Bachan Karai Sevakaaii,
Manuvaanchhint Phal Sahajay Paaii
Taji Chhal Kapat Aur Chaturaai,
Puujahi Vividh Bhaanti Man Lai

Aur Haal Main Kahahun Bujhaaii,
Jo Yah Paath Karai Man Laaii
Taakahan Kouu Kast Na Hoii,
Manavaanchhit Phal Paavay Soii

Traahimahi Jay Duhkh Nivaarini,
Vividh Tap Bhav Bandhan HaariniZ
Jo Yah Parhen Aur Parhaavay,
Dhyan Lagavay Sunay Sunavay

Taakon Kou Na Rog Sataavay,
Putr Aadi Dhan Sampati Paavay
Putrahiin Dhan Sampati Hiinaa,
Andh Vadhir Korhii Ati Diinaa

Vipr Bulaaii Ken Paath Karaavay,
Shaankaa Man Mahan Tanik Na Laavay
Path Karaavay Din Chalisa,
Taapar Krapaa Karahin Jagadiishaa

Sukh Sampatti Bahut Sii Paavay,
Kamii Nanhin Kaahuu Kii Aavay
Baarah Maash Karen Jo Puujaa,
Ta Sam Dhani Aur Nahin Duujaa

Pratidin Paath Karehi Man Manhii,
Taasam Jagat Katahun Kou Naahiin
Bahuvidhi Kaa Men Karahun Baraaii,
Lehu Pariikshaa Dhyaan Lagaaii

Kari Vishvaas Karay Brat Nemaa,
Hoi Siddh Upajay Ati Prema
Jay Jay Jay Lakshmi Mahaaraanii,
Sab Mahan Vyaapak Tum Gunkhaanii

Tumhro Tej Praval Jag Maannhin,
Tum Sam Kou Dayaalu Kahun Naahiin
Mo Anaath Kii Sudhi Ab Lijay,
Sannkat Kaati Bhakti Bar Dijay
Bhuulchuuk Karu Chhimaa Hamaarii,
Darasan Dijay Dasaa Nihaarii
Binu Darsan Byaakul Ati Bhaarii,
Tumhinn Akshat Paavat Dukh Bhaarii

Nahinn Mohi Jnaan Buddhi Hai Tan Mann,
Sab Jaanat Tum Apane Man Men
Roop Chaturbhuj Kari Nij Dhaaran,
Kasht Mor Ab Karahu Nivaaran

Kehi Prakaar Mein Karahun Baraaii,
Jnaan Buddhi Mohin Nahin Adhikaaii
Uthi Kainn Praatakaray Asanaanaa,
Jo Kachu Banay Karay So Daanaa

Ashtami Ko Brat Karay Ju Praanii,
Harashi Hraday Puujahi Mahaaraanii

Solah Din Puujaa Vidhi Karahii,
Aashvin Krishn Jo Ashtamii Parahii

Takar Sab Chhuutain Dukh Daavaa,
So Jan Sukh Sampati Niet Paavaa

Doha

**Traahi Traahi Dukh Haarini, Harahu Begi Sab Traas
Jayati Jayati Jai Lakshmi, Karahu Shatru Ko Naas
Raamadaas Dhari Dhyaan Nit, Vinay Karat Kar Jor
Maatu Lakshmiidas Pay, Karahu Krapaa Kii Kor.**

DURGA CHAALISA

Namo Namo Durge Sukh Karani,
Namo Namo Ambe Dukh Harani
Nirakar Hai Jyoti Tumhari,
Tihun Lok Pheli Ujayari

Shashi Lalat Mukh Mahavishala,
Netra Lal Bhrikutee Vikarala
Roop Matu Ko Adhika Suhave,
Daras Karat Jan Ati Sukh Pave

Tum Sansar Shakti Laya Kina,
Palan Hetu Anna Dhan Dina
Annapurna Hui Jag Pala,
Tumhi Adi Sundari Bala

Pralaya Kala Sab Nashan Hari,
Tum Gauri Shiv-Shankar Pyari
Shiv Yogi Tumhre Guna Gaven,
Brahma Vishnu Tumhen Nit Dhyaven

Roop Saraswati Ko Tum Dhara,
Day Subuddhi Rishi Munina Ubara
Dharyo Roop Narsimha Ko Amba,
Pragat Bhayin Phar Kar Khamba

Raksha Kari Prahlaad Bachayo,
Hiranakush Ko Swarga Pathayo
Lakshmi Roop Dharo Jag Mahin,
Shree Narayan Anga Samahin

Ksheer Sindhu Men Karat Vilasa,
Daya Sindhu, Deeje Man Asa
Hingalaja Men Tumhin Bhavani,
Mahima Amit Na Jat Bakhani

Matangi Dhoomavati Mata,
Bhuvneshwari Bagala Sukhdata
Shree Bhairav Lara Jog Tarani,
Chhinna Bhala Bhav Dukh Nivarani

Kehari Vahan Soh Bhavani,
Langur Veer Chalat Agavani
Kar Men Khappar Khadag Viraje,
Jako Dekh Kal Dan Bhaje

Sohe Astra Aur Trishoola,
Jase Uthata Shatru Hiya Shoola
Nagarkot Men Tumhi Virajat,
Tinahu Lok Men Danka Bajat

Shumbhu Nishumbhu Danuja Tum Mare,
Rakta-beeja Shankhan Samhare
Mahishasur Nripa Ati Abhimani,
Jehi Agha Bhar Mahi Akulani

Roop Karal Kalika Dhara,
Sen Sahita Tum Tin Samhara
Pan Garha Santon Par Jab Jab,
Bhayi Sahaya Matu Tum Tab Tab

Amarpuni Aru Basava Loka,
Tava Mahirna Sab Rahen Asoka
Jwala Men Hai Jyoti Tumhari,
Tumhen Sada Poojen Nar Nari

Prem Bhakti Se Jo Yash Gave,
Dukh-daridra Nikat Nahin Ave
Dhyave Tumhen Jo Nar Man Laee,
Janam-maran Tako Chuti Jaee

Jogi Sur-muni Kahat Pukari,
Jog Na Ho Bin Shakti Tumhari
Shankar Aacharaj Tap Keenhon,
Kam, Krodha Jeet Sab Leenhon

Nisidin Dhyan Dharo Shankar Ko,
Kahu Kal Nahini Sumiro Tum Ko
Shakti Roop Ko Maran Na Payo,
Shakti Gayi Tab Man Pachitayo

Sharnagat Hui Keerti Bakhani,
Jai Jai Jai Jagdamb Bhavani
Bhayi Prasanna Aadi Jagdamba,
Dayi Shakti Nahin Keen Vilamba

Mokon Matu Kashta Ati Ghero,
Tum Bin Kaun Hare Dukh Mero
Aasha Trishna Nipat Sataven,
Moh Madadik Sab Binsaven

Shatru Nash Keeje Maharani,
Sumiron Ekachita Tumhen Bhavani
Karo Kripa Hey Matu Dayala,
Riddhi-siddhi De Karahu Nihala

Jab Lagi Jiyoon Daya Phal Paoon,
Tumhro Yash Men Sada Sunaoon
Durga Chalisa Jo Gave,
Sab Sukh Bhog Parampad Pave

KALI MAA CHAALISA

Jaykaali Kalimalaharan,
Mahima Agam Apaar,
Mahish Mardini Kaalika,
Dehu Abhay Apaar.

Ari Mad Maan Mitaavan Haari,
Mundamaal Gal Sohat Pyaari.

Ashtabhuji Sukhdaayak Maata,
Dushtdalan Jag Me Vikhyaata.

Bhaal Vishaal Mukut Chhavi Chhajei,
Kar Me Shish Shatru Ka Saajei.
Dooje Haath Liye Madhu Pyaala,
Haath Tiisare Sohat Bhaala.

Chauthe Khappar Khadag Kar Paanche,
Chhathe Trishul Shatru Bal Jaanche.

Saptam Kar Damakat Asi Pyaari,
Shobha Adbhut Maat Tumhaari.

Ashtam Kar Bhaktan Var Data,
Jag Manharan Roop Ye Maata.

Bhaktan Me Anurakt Bhavaani,
Nishdin Rate Rishi-Muni Gyaani.

Mahaashakti Ati Prabal Punita,
Tu Hi Kaali Tu Hi Sita.
Patit Taarini He Jag Paalak,
Kalyaani Paapi Kul Ghaalak.

Shesh Suresh Na Paavat Paara,
Gauri Roop Dharyo Ek Baara.

Tum Samaan Daata Nahi Dooja,
Vidhivat Kare Bhaktajan Pooja.

Roop Bhayankar Jab Tum Dhaara,
Dushtadalan Kinhehu Sanhaara.

Naam Anekan Maat Tumhaare,
Bhaktajano Ke Sankat Taare.

Kali Ke Kasht Kaleshan Harani,
Bhav Bhay Mochan Mangal Karani.

Mahima Agam Ved Yash Gaavei,
Naarad Shaarad Paar Na Paavei.

Bhoo Par Bhaar Badhyau Jab Bhaari,
Tab Tab Tum Prakati Mahtaari.

Aadi Anaadi Abhay Varadaata,
Vishvavidit Bhav Sankat Traata.

Kusamay Naam Tumhaarau Linha,
Usako Sada Abhay Var Dinha.

Dhyaan Dhare Shruti Shesh Suresha,
Kaal Roop Lakhi Tumaro Bhesha.

Kaluaa Bhairo Sang Tumhaare,
Ari Hit Roop Bhayaanak Dhaare.

Sevak Laangur Rahat Agaari,
Chauisath Jogan Agyaakaari.

Treta Mein Raghuvar Hit Aai,
Dashkandhar Ki Sain Nasaai.

Khela Ran Ka Khel Niraala,
Bhara Maans-Majja Se Pyaala.

Raudra Roop Lakhi Daanav Bhaage,
Kiyau Gavan Bhavan Nij Tyaage.

Tab Esau Taamas Chadh Aayo,
Svajan Vijan Ko Bhed Bhulaayo.

Ye Baalak Lakhi Shankar Aaye,
Raah Rok Charanan Me Dhaaye.

Tab Mukh Jibh Nikar Jo Aai,
Yahi Roop Prachalit Hai Maai.

Baadhyo Mahishaasur Mad Bhaari,
Pidit Kiye Sakal Nar-Naari.

Karun Pukaar Suni Bhaktan Ki,
Peer Mitaavan Hit Jan-Jan Ki.

Tab Pragati Nij Sain Sameta,
Naam Pada Maa Mahish Vijeta.

Shumbh Nishumbh Hane Chhan Maahi,
Tum Sam Jag Doosar Kou Naahi.

Maan Mathanhaari Khal Dal Ke,
Sada Sahaayak Bhakt Vikal Ke.

Deen Vihin Karei Nit Seva,
Paavei Manvaanchhit Phal Meva.

Sankat Me Jo Sumiran Karahi,
Unake Kasht Maaatu Tum Harahi.

Prem Sahit Jo Kirati Gaavei,
Bhav Bandhan So Mukti Paavei.

Kaali Chaalisa Jo Padhahi,
Svarglok Binu Bandhan Chadhahi.

Daya Drishti Herau Jagadamba,
Kehi Kaaran Maa Kiyau Vilamba.

Karahu Maatu Bhaktan Rakhvaali,
Jayati Jayati Kaali Kankaali.

Sevak Deen Anaath Anaari,
Bhaktibhaav Yuti Sharan Tumhaari.

Doha

Prem Sahit Jo Kare,
Kaali Chaalisa Paath,
Tinaki Pooran Kaamana,
Hoy Sakal Jag Thaath.

RADHA CHAALISA

Doha

Shriradhe Vrishabhanuja,
Bhaktani Pranaadhar
Vrindavipin Viharinni,
Prannavom Barambar

Jaiso Taiso Ravarou,
Krishna-priya Sukhadham
Charan Sharan Nij Dijiye,
Sundar Sukhad Lalam

Choupayi

Jai Vrishabhan Kunvari Shri Shyama
Kirati Nandini Shobha Dhama

Ñitya Viharini Shyam Adhara
Amit Bodh Mangal Datara

Raas Viharini Ras Vistarini
Sahachari Subhag Yuth Man Bhavni

Nitya Kishori Radha Gori
Shyam Prannadhan Ati Jiya Bhori

Karuna Sagari Hiya Umangini
Lalitadik Sakhiyan Ki Sangani

Dinkar Kanya Kuul Viharini
Krishna Prana Priy Hiy Hulsavani
Nitya Shyam Tumharo Gun Gaven
Shri Radha Radha Kahi Harshavahin

Murali Mein Nit Naam Ucharein
Tum Karann Lila Vapu Dharein

Prema Svaroopini Ati Sukumari
Shyam Priya Vrashabhanu Dulari

Navala Kishori Ati Chabi Dhama
Dhyuti Laghu Laag Koti Rati Kaama

Gourangi Shashi Nindak Vadana
Subhag Chapal Aniyare Naina

Javak Yuth Pad Pankaj Charana
Noopur Dhvani Pritam Man Harna

Santata Sahachari Seva Karhin
Maha Mod Mangal Man Bharahin

Rasikan Jeevan Prana Adhara
Radha Naam Sakal Sukh Saara

Agam Agochar Nitya Svaroopa
Dhyan Dharat Nishidin Brajabhoopa

Upjeoo Jasu Ansh Gun Khani
Kotin Uma Rama Brahmani

Nitya Dham Golok Biharini
Jan Rakshak Dukh Dosh Nasavani

Shiv Aj Muni Sanakadik Naarad
Paar Na Paayn Sesh Aru Sharad

Radha Shubh Gun Roopa Ujari
Nirakhi Prasanna Hot Banvari

Braj Jeevan Dhan Radha Rani
Mahima Amit Na Jay Bakhani

Preetam Sang Diye Gal Baahin
Biharata Nit Vrindavan Maahin

Radha Krishna Krishna Hai Radha

Ek Roop Douu-preeti Agaadha

Shri Radha Mohan Man Harni
Jan Sukh Prada Prafullit Badani

Kotik Roop Dhare Nand Nanda
Darash Karan Hith Gokul Chanda

Raas Keli Kar Tumhen Rijhaven
Maan Karo Jab Ati Dukh Paaven

Praffullit Hoth Darash Jab Paaven
Vividh Bhanti Nit Vinay Sunaven

Vrindarannya Viharinni Shyam
Naam Leth Puran Sab Kama

Kotin Yagya Tapasya Karhu
Vividh Nem Vrat Hiy Men Dharhu

Tauu Na Shyam Bhaktahi Apnaven
Jab Lagi Naam Na Radha Gaaven

Vrinda Vipin Svamini Radha
Leela Vapu Tuva Amit Agadha

Svayam Krishna Nahin Pavahin Paara
Aur Tumhen Ko Janani Haara

Shriradha Ras Preeti Abheda
Saadar Gaan Karat Nit Veda

Radha Tyagi Krishna Jo Bhajihai
Te Sapnehun Jag Jaladhi Na Tarihai

Kirati Kumari Laadali Radha
Sumirat Sakal Mitahin Bhav Badh

Naam Amangal Mool Nasavani

Vividh Taap Har Hari Man Bhavani

Radha Naam Ley Jo Koi
Sahajahi Damodar Vash Hoyi

Radha Naam Param Sukhdayi
Sahajahin Kripa Karen Yadurai

Yadupati Nandan Peeche Phirihain
Jo Kouu Radha Naam Sumirihain

Raas Viharini Shyama Pyari
Karahu Kripa Barsane Vaari

Vrindavan Hai Sharan Tumhari
Jai Jai Jai Vrishabhanu Dulari

~~~

Doha

Shri Radha Rasikeshvar Ghanshyam
Karahun Nirantar Vaas Mai Sri Vrindavan Dham
Jai Sri Radhe, Radhe, Radhe
Jai Sri Radhe, Radhe, Radhe
Jai Sri Radhe, Radhe, Radhe

~~~

SHRI RAAM CHAALISA

Shri Raghuvir Bhagat Hitakari,
Suni Lije Prabhu Araj Hamari
Nisidin Dhyan Dhare Jo Koi,
Ta Sam Bhakt Aur Nahi Hoi
Dhyan Dhare Shivaji Man Mahi,
Brahma Indra Par Nahi Pahi
Jai Jai Jai Raghunath Kripala,
Sada Karo Santan Pratipala

Door Tumhar Veer Hanumana,
Jasu Prabhav Tihu Pur Jana
Ruv Bhujdand Prachand Kripala,
Raavan Mari Suaran Pratipala
Tum Anath Ke Nath Gosai.
Deenan Ke Ho Sada Sahai
Brhamadik Tav Par Na Paven,
Sada Eesh Tumaro Yash Gave

Chariu Ved Bharat Hai Sakhi,
Tum Bhaktan Ki Lajja Rakhi
Gun Gavat Sharad Man Mahi,
Surpatitako Par Na Pahi
Nam Tumhare Let Jo Koi,
Ta Sam Dhanya Aur Nahi Hoi
Ram Naam Hai Aparampara,
Chariu Vedan Jahi Pukara

Ganapati Naam Tumharo Linho,
Tinako Pratham Pujya Tum Kinho
Shesh Ratat Nit Naam Tumhara ,
Mahi Ko Bhar Shish Par Dhara
Phool Saman Rahat So Bhara,
Pavan Kou Tumharo Para
Bharat Naam Tumharo Ur Dharo,
Taso Kabahu Na Ran Mein Haro

Naam Shatrugna Hridaya Prakasha,
Sumirat Hot Shatru Kar Nasha
Lakhan Tumhare Agyakari,
S̃ada Karat Santan Rakhwari
Tate Ran Jeet Nahi Koi.

Yudd Jure Yamahu Kin Hoi
Mahalakshmi Dhar Avatara,
Sab Vidhi Karat Paap Ko Chhara

Seetha Naam Puneeta Gayo,
Bhuvaneshwari Prabhav Dikhayo
Ghat Sou Prakhat Bhai So Aai,
Jako Dekhat Chandra Lajai
So Tumhare Nit Paon Palotat,
Navo Nidhi Charanan Mein Lotat
Sidhi Atharah Mangalkari,
So Tum Par Jave Balhari

Aurahu Jo Anek Prabhutai,
So Seetapati Tumahi Banai
Ichchha Ke Kotin Sansara,
Rachat Na Lagat Pal Ki Bhara
Jo Tumhare Charanan Chit Lave,
Taki Mukti Avasi Ho Jave
Jai Jai Jai Prabhu Jyoti Swarupa,
Nirgun Brahma Akhand Anoopa
Satya Satya Jai Satyavrat Swami,
Satya Santan Antaryami
Satya Bhajan Tumharo Jo Gave,
So Nischay Charon Phal Pave
Satya Sapath Gauripati Kinhi,
Tumne Bhaktahi Sab S̃idhi Dinhi
Sunahu Ram Tum Tat Hamare
Tumahi Bharat Kul Poojya Prachare

Tumahi Dev Kul Dev Hamare,
Tum Gurudev Pran Ke Pyare
Jo Kuch Ho So Tumhahi Raja,
Jai Jai Jai Prabhu Rakho Laja

Ram Atma Poshan Hare
Jai Jai Jai Dasarath Ke Pyare
Gyan Hriday Do Gyanswarupa
Namo Namo Jai Jagpati Bhoopa

Dhanya Dhanya Tum Dhanya Pratapa,
Naam Tumhar Harat Sanatapa
Satya Shudh Devan Mukh Gaya,
Baji Dundibhi Shankh Bajaya
Satya Satya Tum Satya Sanatan,
Tumahi Ho Hamare Tan Man Dhan
Yako Path Kare Jo Koi
Gyan Prakat Thake Ur Hoi

Avagaman Mitai Tihi Tera,
Satya Vachana Mane Shiv Mera
Aur Aas Man Mein Jo Hoi,
Manvanchit Phal Pave Soi
Teenahu Kaal Dhyan Jo Lave,
Tulsidal Anu Phool Chadhave
Saag Patra So Bhog Lagave,
So Nar Sakal Siddhata Pave

Aant Samay Raghubarapur Jai,
Jaha Janma Haribhakta Kahai
Shri Haridas Kahai Aru Gave,
So Vaikunth Dhaam Ko Jave

~~~

Doha

Saat Divas Jo Nem Kar
Paat Kar Chi Laye
Haridas Harikripa Se
Avasi Bhakti Ko Pave

~~~

HANUMAAN CHAALISA

DOHA

Shree Guru Charan Saroj Raj
Nij Man Mukur Sudhari
Barnau Raghuvar Bimal Jasu
Jo Dayaku Phal Chari

Budhi Heen Tanu Janike
Sumirow Pavan Kumar
Bal Budhi Bidya Dehu Mohi
Harahu Kalesh Bikaar

Jai Hanuman Gyan Guna Sagar
Jai Kapis Tihun Lok Ujaagar
Ramdoot Atulit Bal Dhamaa
Anjani Putra Paavansut Naamaa

Mahabeer Bikram Bajrangi
Kumati Nivaar Sumati Ke Sangi
Kanchan Baran Biraaj Subesa
Kanan Kundal Kunchit Kesaa

Haath Bajra Aur Dhvaja Birajai
Kandhe Moonj Janeu Saajai
Shankar Suvan Kesari Nandan
Tej Pratap Maha Jag Bandan

Vidyavaan Guni Ati Chatur
Ram Kaj Karibe Ko Atur
Prabhu Charitra Sunibe Ko Rasiya
Ram Lakhan Sita Man Basiya

Sukshma Roop Dhari Siyahin Dikhawa
Bikat Roop Dhari Lank Jarawa
Bhim Roop Dhari Asur Sanhare
Ramchandra Ke Kaaj Savare

Laye Sajivan Lakhan Jiyaye
Shree Raghuvir Harshi Ur Laye
Raghupati Kinhi Bahut Badaai
Tum Mama Priya Bharat Sam Bhai

Sahasa Badan Tumhro Jas Gavein
Asa Kahi Shripati Kanth Lagaavein
Sankadik Brahmadi Muneesa
Narad Sarad Sahit Ahisaa

Jam Kuber Digpal Jahan Te
Kabi Kobid Kahin Sake Kanha Te
Tum Upakar Sugrivahi Keenha
Ram Milai Rajpad Deenha

Tumharo Mantra Bibhishan Maana
Lankeshwar Bhaye Sab Jag Jaana
Jug Sahastra Jojan Par Bhaanu
Leelyo Taahi Madhur Phal Jaanu

Prabhu Mudrika Meli Mukha Maaheen
Aladhi Langhi Gaye Acharaj Naheen
Durgam Kaaj Jagat Ke Jete
Sugam Anugrah Tumhre Te Te

Ram Duware Tum Rakhavare
Hoat Na Aagya Bin Paisare
Sab Sukh Lahen Tumhari Sarna
Tum Rakshak Kaahu Ko Darnaa

Aapan Tej Samharo Aapei
Tinhu Lok Hank Te Kanpai
Bhoot Pisaach Nikat Nahi Avei
Mahabir Jab Naam Sunavei

Nassei Rog Hare Sab Peera
Japat Nirantar Hanumat Beera
Sankat Te Hanuman Chhudavei
Man Kram Bachan Dhyan Jo Lavei

Sab Par Ram Tapsvee Raja
Tinke Kaj Sakal Tum Saja
Aur Manorath Jo Koi Lave
Soi Amit Jivan Phal Pave

Charo Jug Partap Tumhara
Hai Parsiddha Jagat Ujiyara
Sadhu Sant Ke Tum Rakhvare
Asur Nikandan Ram Dulare

Ashta Siddhi Nau Nidhi Ke Data
Asa Bar Din Janki Mata
Ram Rasayan Tumhare Pasa
Sada Raho Raghupati Ke Dasa

Tumhre Bhajan Ramko Pavei
Janam Janam Ke Dukh Bisravei
Anta Kal Raghubar Pur Jai
Janma Janma Hari Bhakta Kahai

Aur Devata Chitt Na Dharai
Hanumat Sei Sarva Sukh Karai
Sankat Kate Mitey Sab Peera
Jo Sumirei Hanumat Balbeera
Jai Jai Jai Hanuman Gosain
Kripa Karahu Gurudev Ki Nain
Jo Sat Bar Path Kar Koi
Chhutai Bandi Maha Sukh Hoi

Jo Yah Padhe Hanuman Chalisa
Hoy Siddhi Sakhi Gowrisa
Tulsidas Sada Hari Chera
Keeje Nath Hriday Mah Dera

Pavan Tanay Sankat Haran
Mangal Murati Roop
Ram Lakhan Sita Sahit
Hriday Basahu Sur Bhup

~~~
~~~

SHIVA CHAALISA

Doha

Jai Ganesh Girija Suvan
Mangal Mul Sujan
Kahat Ayodhya Das
Tum Dev Abhaya Varadan

Jai Girija Pati Dinadayala
Sada Karat Santan Pratipala
Bhala Chandrama Sohat Nike
Kanan Kundal Nagaphani Ke

Anga Gaur Shira Ganga Bahaye
Mundamala Tan Chhara Lagaye
Vastra Khala Baghambar Sohain
Chhavi Ko Dekha Naga Muni Mohain

Maina Matu Ki Havai Dulari
Vama Anga Sohat Chhavi Nyari
Kara Trishul Sohat Chhavi Bhari
Karat Sada Shatrun Chhayakari

Nandi Ganesh Sohain Tahan Kaise
Sagar Madhya Kamal Hain Jaise
Kartik Shyam Aur Gana Rauo
Ya Chhavi Ko Kahi Jata Na Kauo

Devan Jabahi Jaya Pukara
Tabahi Dukha Prabhu Apa Nivara
Kiya Upadrav Tarak Bhari
Devan Sab Mili Tumahi Juhari
Turata Shadanana Apa Pathayau
Luv nimesh Mahi Mari Girayau
Apa Jalandhara Asura Sanhara
Suyash Tumhara Vidit Sansara

Tripurasur Sana Yudha Machai

Sabhi Kripakar Lina Bachai
Kiya Tapahin Bhagiratha Bhari
Purahi Pratigya Tasu Purari

Darpa Chod Ganga Thabb Aayee
Sevak Astuti Karat Sadahin
Veda Nam Mahima Tav Gai
Akatha Anandi Bhed Nahin Pai

Pragati Udadhi Mantan te Jvala
Jarae Sura-Sur Bhaye Bihala
Mahadev Thab Kari Sahayee,
Nilakantha Tab Nam Kahai

Pujan Ramchandra Jab Kinha
Jiti Ke Lanka Vibhishan Dinhi
Sahas Kamal Men Ho Rahe Dhari
Kinha Pariksha Tabahin Purari

Ek Kamal Prabhu Rakheu Goyee
Kushal-Nain Pujan Chahain Soi
Kathin Bhakti Dekhi Prabhu Shankar
Bhaye Prasanna Diye-Ichchhit Var

Jai Jai Jai Anant Avinashi
Karat Kripa Sabake Ghat Vasi
Dushta Sakal Nit Mohin Satavai
Bhramat Rahe Man Chain Na Avai
Trahi-Trahi Main Nath Pukaro
Yahi Avasar Mohi Ana Ubaro
Lai Trishul Shatrun Ko Maro
Sankat Se Mohin Ana Ubaro

Mata Pita Bhrata Sab Hoi
Sankat Men Puchhat Nahin Koi
Swami Ek Hai Asha Tumhari
Ai Harahu Ab Sankat Bhari
Dhan Nirdhan Ko Deta Sadahin
Arat Jan Ko Peer Mitaee,
Astuti Kehi Vidhi Karai Tumhari

Shambhunath Ab Tek Tumhari
Dhana Nirdhana Ko Deta Sadaa Hii
Jo Koi Jaanche So Phala Paahiin
Astuti Kehi Vidhi Karon Tumhaarii
Kshamahu Naatha Aba Chuuka Hamaarii

Shankar Ho Sankat Ke Nashan
Vighna Vinashan Mangal Karan
Yogi Yati Muni Dhyan Lagavan
Sharad Narad Shisha Navavain

Namo Namo Jai Namah Shivaya
Sura Brahmadik Par Na Paya
Jo Yah Patha Karai Man Lai
To Kon Hota Hai Shambhu Sahai

Riniyan Jo Koi Ho Adhikari
Patha Karai So Pavan Hari
Putra-hin Ichchha Kar Koi
Nischaya Shiva Prasad Tehin Hoi
Pandit Trayodashi Ko Lavai
Dhyan-Purvak Homa Karavai
Trayodashi Vrat Kare Hamesha
Tan Nahin Take Rahe Kalesha

Dhuupa Diipa Naivedya Chadhaave
Shankara Sammukha Paatha Sunaave
Janma Janma Ke Paapa Nasaave
Anta Dhaama Shivapura Men Paave

~~~

Doha

Nitya Nema Kari Pratahi
Patha Karau Chalis
Tum Meri Man Kamana
Purna Karahu Jagadisha

~~~

KRISHNA CHAALISA

Doha

Banshi Shobhit Kar Madhur,
Neel Jalad Tanu Shyam
Arun Adhar Janu Bimba Phal,
Nayan Kamal Abhiraam
Puran Indu Arvind Mukha,
Pitaambar Shubha Saaj
Jai Manmohan Madan Chhavi,
Krishnachandra Maharaj

Chaupai

Jai Yadunandan Jai Jagvandan,
Jai Vasudev Devki Nandan
Jai Yashoda Sut Nanda Dulaare,
Jai Prabhu Bhaktan Ke Rakhavaare

Jai Natanaagar Naag Nathaiyaa,
Krishna Kanhaiya Dhenu Charaiya
Puni Nakh Par Prabhu Girivar Dhaaro,
Aao Deenan Kasht Nivaaro
Bansi Madhur Adhar Dhari Teri,
Hove Puran Manorath Meri
Aao Hari Puni Maakhan Chaakho,
Aaj Laaj Bhaktan Ki Raakho

Gol Kapol Chibuk Arunaare,
Mridul Muskaan Mohini Daare
Ranjit Raajiv Nayan Vishaalaa,
Mor Mukut Vaijanti Maalaa

Kundal Shravan Peetpat Aache,
Kati Kinkini Kaachhan Kaachhe
Neel Jalaj Sundar Tanu Sohe,

Chhavi Lakhi Sur Nar Muni Mana Mohe

Mastak Tilak Alak Ghunghraale,
Aao Shyaam Bansuri Vaale
Kari Pai Paan, Putanaahin Taaryo,
Akaa Bakaa Kaaga Sur Maaryo

Madhuvan Jalat Agni Jab Jvaala,
Bhaye Sheetal Lakhitahin Nandalala
Surpati Jab Brij Chadhyo Risaai,
Musar Dhaar Baari Barsaai

Lagat-Lagat Brij Chahan Bahaayo,
Govardhan Nakhdhari Bachaayo
Lakhi Yashodaa Man Bhram Adhikaai,
Mukh Mahan Chaudah Bhuvan Dikhaai

Dusht Kansa Ati Udham Machaayo,
Koti Kamal Kahan Phul Mangaayo
Naathi Kaaliyahin Tab Tum Linhen,
Charanchinh Dai Nirbhay Kinhe

Kari Gopin Sang Raas Vilaasa,
Sab Ki Puran Kari Abhilashaa
Ketik Mahaa Asur Sanhaaryo,
Kansahi Kesh Pakadi Dai Maaryo

Maatu Pitaa Ki Bandi Chhudaayi,
Ugrasen Kahan Raaj Dilaayi
Mahi Se Mritak Chhaho Sut Laayo,
Matu Devaki Shok Mitaayo

Bhomaasur Mura Daitya Sanhaari,
Laaye Shatdash Sahas Kumaari
Dai Bhinhin Trincheer Sanhaara,
Jaraasindhu Raakshas Kahan Maara

Asur Vrikaasur Aadik Maaryo,
Bhaktan Ke Tab Kasht Nivaaryo
Deen Sudaamaa Ke Dukh Taaryo,

Tandul Teen Muthi Mukh Daaryo

Prem Ke Saag Vidura Ghar Maange,
Duryodhan Ke Mevaa Tyaage
Laakhi Premki Mahimaa Bhaari,
Naumi Shyam Deenan Hitkaari

Maarath Ke Paarath Rath Haanke,
Liye Chakra Kar Nahin Bal Thaake
Nij Gitaa Ke Gyaan Sunaaye,
Bhaktan Hriday Sudhaa Barsaaye

Meera Thi Aisi Matvaali,
Vish Pee Gayi Bajaakar Taali
Raanaa Bhejaa Saamp Pitaari,
Shaaligraam Bane Banvaari

Nij Maayaa Tum Vidhihin Dikhaayo,
Urate Sanshay Sakal Mitaayo
Tav Shat Nindaa Kari Tatkaalaa,
Jivan Mukt Bhayo Shishupaalaa
Jabahin Draupadi Ter Lagaai,
Deenanaath Laaj Ab Jaai
Asa Anaatha Ke Naath Kanhaiyaa,
Dubat Bhanvar Bachaavat Naiyaa

Sundardaas Aas Ura Dhaari,
Dayadrishti Keeje Banwaari
Naath Sakal Mam Kumati Nivaaro,
Chhamobegi Apraadh Hamaaro

Kholo Pat Ab Darshan Deeje,
Bolo Krishna Kanhaiya Ki Jai

~~~
~~~

Doha

Yah Chalisa Krishna Ka,
Path Kare Ur Dhaari
Asht Siddhi Nav Niddhi Phal,
Lahe Padaarath Chaar

VISHNU CHAALISA

Doha

Vishnu Suniye Vinay Sevak Ki Chitlaya
Kirat Kuch Varnan Karu Dije Gyan Bataya

Namo Vishnu Bhagwan Kharari
Kashat Nashavan Akhil Vihari

Prabal Jagat Mai Shakti Tumhari
Tribhuvan Fal Rahi Ujiyari

Sundar Roop Manohar Surat
Saral Swabhav Mohini Murat

Tan Par Pitambar Ati Sohat
Bejanti Mala Maan Mohat

Shankh Chakr Kar Gada Viraje
Dekhat Detaye Asur Dal Bhaje

Satay Dharam Mad Lobh Na Gaje
Kam Krodh Mad Lobh Na Chaje

Santbhakt Sajan Manranjan
Danuj Asur Dushtan Dal Ganjan

Such Upjaye Kasht Sab Bhanjan
Dhosh Mitaye Karat Jan Sannjan

Pap Kat Bhav Sindu Utaran
Kasht Nashkar Bakat Ubharn

Karat Anek Roop Prabhu Dharan
Kaval Aap Bhagati Ke Karan

Dharani Dhenu Ban Tumhi Pukara
Tab Tum Roop Ram Ka Dhara

Bhar Utar Asur Dal Maara
Ravan Aadik Ko Sanhara

Aap Varah Roop Banaya
Hiranyaksh Ko Maar Giraya

Dhar Matyas Tan Sindu Banaya
Chodah Ratann Ko Nikalaya

Amilakh Aasur Dundu Machaya
Roop Mohini Aap Dikhaya

Devan Ko Amrat Pan Karaya
Asuran Ko Chhabi Se Bahalaya

Kurm Roop Dhar Sindu Mathaya
Mandrachal Giri Turant Uthaya

Shankar Ka Tum Fand Chudaya
Bhasmasur Ka Roop Dekhaya

Vedan Ko Jab Asur Dubaya
Kar Prabanda Unhee Tuntalaya

Mohit Banker Khalahi Nachaya
Ushi Kar Se Bhasam Karaya

Asur Jalandar Ati Baldai
Sankar Se Un Kinhi Ladayi

Har Par Shi Sakal Banaye
Kin Sati Se Chal Khal Jayi

Sumiran Kin Tumhe Shivrani
Batlai Sab Vipat Kahani

Tab Tum Bane Muneshwar Gyani
Varnda Ki Sab Surti Bhulani

KASHI SATSANGH

Ho Shaparsh Dharm Sharati Mani
Hani Asur Uur Shiv Sanatni

Tumne Dhur Prahlad Ubare
Hirnakush Aadik Khal Mare

Ganika Aur Ajamil Tare
Bhahut Bhakt Bhav Sindu Utare

Harhu Sakal Santap Hamare
Kripa Karhu Kari Sirjan Hare

Dekhhu Mai Nit Darsh Tumhare
Din Bandhu Bhaktan Hitkare

Chahat Apka Sevak Darshan
Karhu Daya Apni Madhusudan

Janu Nahi Yoga Jap Poojan
Hoye Yagy Shistuti Anumotan

Shildaya Santosh Shishan
Vidhit Nahi Vatrbhodh Vilshan

Karhu Apka Kis Vidhi Poojan
Kumati Vilok Hote Dukh Bhishan

Karhu Pranam Kon Vidhisumiran
Kon Bhati Mai Karhu Samarpan

Sur Munni Karat Sada Sivkai
Harshit Rahat Param Gati Paye

Din Dukhin Par Sada Sahai
Nij Jan Jan Lave Apnayi

Pap Dosh Santap Nashao
Bhav Bandhan Se Mukat Karayo

Sut Sampati De Such Upjao
Nij Charan Ka Das Banao

Nigam Sada Se Vanay Sunao
Patte Sune So Jan Such Pave

~~~

SURYA CHAALISA

Doha

**Shri Raviharat Aa Horat Tame, Aganit Kiran Pasari,
Vandan Karu Tan Charan Mein, Argh Devu Jal Dhari.**

**Sakal Shristi Ke Swami Ho, Sachrachar Ke Nath,
Nisdin Hot Hai Tumse Hi, Hovat Sandhya Prabhat.**

Chaupaai

Jai Bhagwan Surya Tamhari,
Jai Khagesh Dinkar Subhkari.
Tum Ho Shristi Ke Netra Swaroopa,
Trigun Dhari Trai Ved Swaroopa.

Tum Hi Karta Palak Sanharak,
Bhuvan Chaturdash Ke Sanchalak.
Sundar Vadan Chaturbhuj Dhari,
Rashmi Rathi Tum Gagan Vihari.

Chakra Shankh Aru Swet Kamaldhar,
Varmudra Sohat Chothekar.
Shish Mukat Kundal Gal Mala,
Charu Tilak Tav Bhal Vishala.
~~~

Shakht Ashwa Rat Drut Gami,
Arun Sarathi Gati Avirami.
Rakht Varan Abhusan Dharak,
Atipriya Tohe Lal Padarath.

Sarvatama Kahe Tumhi Rigveda,
Metra Kahe Tum Ko Sab Veda.
Panch Dev Mein Pooje Jate,
Man Vanchit Phal Sadhak Pate.

Dwadash Naam Jaap Aaudharak,
Rog Shok Aru Kasth Nivarak.
Maa Kunti Tav Dhyan Lagayo,
Danveer Sut Karan So Payo.

Raja Yudhisthir Tav Jas Gayo,
Akshay Patra Vo Ban Mein Payo.
Shastra Tyag Arjun Akurayo,
Ban Aditya Hriday Se Payo.

Vindyachal Tab Marg Mein Aayo,
Hahakar Timir Se Chayo.
Muni Agastya Giri Garv Mitayo,
Nijtak Ban Se Vindhya Navayo.

Muni Agastya Tav Mahima Gayi,
Sumir Bhaye Vijayi Raghurai.
Tohe Virok Madhur Phal Jana,
Mukh Mein Linhi Tohe Hanumana.

Tav Nandan Shanidev Kahave,
Pavan Te Sut Shani Tir Mitave.
Yagna Vrat Stuti Tumhari Kinhi,
Bhet Shukla Yajurved Ki Dinhi.
Suryamukhi Khari Tar Tav Roopa,
Krishna Sudarshan Bhanu Swaroopa.
Naman Tohe Omkar Swaroopa,
Naman Aatma Aru Kaal Swaroopa.

Dig-digant Tav Tej Prakashe,
Ujjwal Roop Tumahi Aakashe.
Das Digpal Karat Tav Sumiran,
Aanjan Netra Karat Hai Sumiran.

Trividh Taap Harta Tum Bhagwan,
Gyan Jyoti Karta Tum Bhagwan.
Safal Banave Tav Aaradhan,
Gayatri Jaap Sarh He Sadhan.

Sandhya Trikal Karat Jo Koi,
Pave Kripa Sada Tav Wohi.
Chitt Shanti Suryashtak Deve,
Vyadhi Upadhi Sab Har Leve.

Aasthdal Kamal Yantra Subhkari,
Pooja Upasan Tav Sukhkari.
Magh Maas Suddh Saptami Pavan,
Aarambh Ho Tav Subh Vrat Palan.

Bhanu Saptami Mangal Kari,
Bhakti Dayini Doshan Hari.
Ravi Vasar Jo Tum Ko Dhyave,
Putradik Sukh Vaibhav Pave.

Paap Roopi Parvat Ke Vinashi,
Vajr Roop Tum Ho Avinashi,
Rahu Aan Tav Gras Banave,
Grahan Surya Tab Ko Lag Jaye.

Dharm Dan Tap Karat Hai Sadhak,
Mitat Rahu Tab Pida Badhak,
Surya Dev Tab Kripa Kije,
Dirgha Aayu Bal Buddhi Dje.

Surya Upasana Kar Nit Dhyave,
Kusth Rog Se Mukti Pave.
Dakshin Disha Tori Gati Gyave,
Dakshinayan Wohi Kehlave.

Uttar Margi To Uru Rath Hove,
Utrayan Tab Wo Kehlave.
Man Aru Vachan Karm Ho Pavan,
Sanyam Karat Bhale Nit Aardhan.

Doha

Bharat Das Chintan Karat, Dhar Din Kar Tav Dhyan,
Rakhiyo Kripa Is Bhakt Pe, Tumhari Surya Bhagwan.

~~~

KAALBHAIRAV CHAALISA

Doha

Shri Ganapati, Guru, Gauri Pada,
Prema Sahita Dhari Maatha.
Chalisa Vandana Karaun,
Shri Shiva Bhairavanaatha.

Shri Bhairava Sankata Harana,
Mangala Karana Kripaala.
Shyaama Varana Vikaraala Vapu,
Lochana Laala Vishaala.

Jaya Jaya Shri Kaali Ke Laalaa,
Jayati Jayati Kaashii- Kutavaalaa.
Jayati 'Batuka- Bhairava' Bhaya Haarii,
Jayati 'Kaala- Bhairava' Balakaarii.

Jayati 'Naatha- Bhairava' Vikhyaataa,
~~~

Jayati 'Sarva-Bhairava' Sukhadaataa.
Bhairava Ruupa Kiyo Shiva Dhaarana,
Bhava Ke Bhaara Utaarana Kaarana.

Bhairava Rava Suni Hvai Bhaya Duurii,
Saba Vidhi Hoya Kaamanaa Puurii.
Shesha Mahesha Aadi Guna Gaayo,
Kaashii- Kotavaala Kahalaayo.

Jataa Juuta Shira Chandra Viraajata,
Baalaa, Mukuta, Bijaayatha Saajata.
Kati Karadhanii Ghuungharuu Baajata,
Darshana Karata Sakala Bhaya Bhaajata.

Jiivana Daana Daasa Ko Diinhyo,
Kiinhyo Kripaa Naatha Taba Chiinhyo.
Vasi Rasanaa Bani Saarada-Kaalii,
Diinhyo Vara Raakhyo Mama Laalii.

Dhanya Dhanya Bhairava Bhaya Bhanjana,
Jana Manaranjana Khala Dala Bhanjana.
Kara Trishula Damaruu Shuchi Kodaa,
Kripaa Kataaksha Suyasha Nahin Thodaa.

Jo Bhairava Nirbhaya Guna Gaavata,
Ashtasiddhi Nava Nidhi Phala Paavata.
Ruupa Vishaala Kathina Dukha Mochana,
Krodha Karaala Laala Duhun Lochana.

Aginat Bhuta Preta Sanga Dolat,
Bam Bam Bam Shiva Bam Bam Bolat.
Rudrakaaya Kaalii Ke Laalaa,
Mahaa Kaalahuu Ke Ho Kaalaa.

Batuka Naatha Ho Kaala Ganbhiiraa,
Shveta, Rakta Aru Shyaama Shariiraa.
Karata Tinhun Rupa Prakaashaa,
Bharata Subhaktana Kahan Shubha Aashaa.

Ratna Jadita Kanchana Sinhaasana,

Vyaaghra Charma Shuchi Narma Suaanana.
Tumahi Jaai Kaashihin Jana Dhyaavahin,
Ishvanaatha Kahan Darshana Paavahin..

Jaya Prabhu Sanhaaraka Sunanda Jaya,
Jaya Unnata Hara Umaa Nanda Jaya.
Bhiima Trilochana Svaana Saatha Jaya,
Vaijanaatha Shri Jagatanaatha Jaya.
Mahaa Bhiima Bhiishana Shariira Jaya,
Rudra Trayambaka Dhiira Viira Jaya.
Ashvanaatha Jaya Pretanaatha Jaya,
Svaanaarudha Sayachandra Maatha Jaya.

Nimisha Digambara Chakranaatha Jaya,
Gahata Anaathana Naatha Haatha Jaya.
Treshalesha Bhuutesha Chandra Jaya,
Krodha Vatsa Amaresha Nanda Jaya.

Shri Vaamana Nakulesha Chanda Jaya,
Krityaau Kiirati Prachanda Jaya.
Rudra Batuka Krodhesha Kaaladhara,
Chakra Tunda Dasha Paanivyaala Dhara.

Kari Mada Paana Shambhu Gunagaavata,
Chaunsatha Yogina Sanga Nachaavata.
Karata Kripaa Jana Para Bahu Dhangaa,
Kaashii Kotavaala Adabangaa.

Deyan Kaala Bhairava Jaba Sotaa,
Nasai Paapa Motaa Se Motaa.
Janakara Nirmala Hoya Shariiraa,
Mitai Sakala Sankata Bhava Piiraa.

Shri Bhairava Bhuutonke Raajaa,
Baadhaa Harata Karata Shubha Kaajaa.
Ailaadii Ke Duhkha Nivaarayo,
Sadaa Kripaakari Kaaja Samhaarayo.
Sundara Daasa Sahita Anuraagaa,
Shri Durvaasaa Nikata Prayaagaa.
"Shri Bhairava Jii Kii Jaya" Lekhyo,

Sakala Kaamanaa Puurana Dekhyo.

DOHA

Jai Jai Jai Bhairav Batuka Swami Sankat Taar,
kripa Daas Par Kijiye Shankar Ke Avataar,
Jo Yeh Chalisa Pare Prem Sahit Shat Baar,
Us Ghar Sarvanand Ho,vaibhav Baare Apaar.

~~~
~~~

GANESH BHAJANS

Gaiye Ganapati Jagvandan

Gaiye Ganapati Jagvandan
Sankar Suvan Bhawani Nandan
Gaiye Ganapati Jagvandan

Siddhi Sadan Gajvadan Vinayak
Kripa Sindhu Sundar Sab Naayak
Gaiye Ganapati Jagvandan

Modak Priya Mud Mangal Daata
Vidya Vaaridhi Buddhi Vidhata
Gaiye Ganapati Jagvandan

Maangat Tulsidas Kar Jode
Basahu Ram Siya Manas More
Gaiye Ganapati Jagvandan

Ganapati Bappa Morya

Ganapati Bappa Morya Mangal Murti Morya
Siddhivinayak Morya Girijanandan Morya

Ekdant Jai Morya Gauri Sut Jai Morya
Jai Lambodar Morya Agradev Jai Morya

Vighnavinashan Morya Jai Bhuvaneshwar Morya
Gajanana Jai Morya Vidyavaridhi Morya

Sukhkarta Jai Morya Dukhharta Jai Morya
Kripasindhu Jai Morya Buddhividhata Morya

Bhawani Nandan Morya Jai Shivnandan Morya
Jai Modak Priya Morya Astavinayak Morya

~~~

Jai ganesh Gananath Dayanidhi

Jai Ganesh Gananath Dayanidhi
Sakal Vighan Kar Door Humare
Pratham Dhare Jo Dhyan Tumharo
Tiske Tune Kaaraj Sadhe

Lambodar Gajbadan Manohar
Kar Trishul Khad Sundar Dhare

Riddhi Sidhhi Dou Chanwar Dulave
Mushak Vahan Param Suhave

Brahmanand Sahaye Karo Hit
Bhakt Jano Ke Tum Rakhware

~~~

Jai Jai Ganapati Bhaktan Hitkari

Om Gan Ganpataye Namah

Jai Jai Ganapti Bhaktan Hitkari
Bhawani Nandan Sab Dukh Bhanjan
Puran Karta Kaaraj Saare

Vighna Vinasak Subh Phal Daayak
Mangal Murati Ashtavinayak
Jai Jai ....

Sab Sukhkarta Har Dukh Harta
Buddhi Vidhata Mangal Karta
Jai Jai ...

Hey Gananayak Siddhi Vinayak
Bhakt Jano Ke Tum Ho Sahayak
Jai Jai ..

~~~

Rakh Laaj Meri Ganapati

Rakh Laaj Meri Ganapati Apni Sharan Mein Lijiye
Kar Aaj Mangal Ganapati Apni Kripa Ab Kijiye

Sidhhi Vinayak Dukh Haran Santaap Hari Sukh Karan
Karun Prarthana Main Nit Prati Vardaan Mangaldijiye

Teri Daya Teri Kripa Hey Nath Hummaange Sada
Tere Dhyan Mein Khoye Mati Parnaam Mam Ab Lijiye

Karte Pratham Tav Vandana Tera Naam
Hai Dukh Bhanjana
Karnaprabhu Meri Subh Gati Ab To Sharan Mein Lijiye

~~~

Jai Vigneshwar Jai Jai

Jai Vigneshwar Jai Jai,
Jai Lambhodar Jai Jai
Jai Gananayak Jai Sukhadayak,
Jai Jai Ganesh Jai Jai

Jai Sharda Jai Jai,
Jai Vardayanee Jai Jai,
Jai Hans Vaahini Budhi Daahini,
Jai Saraswattie Jai Jai

Jai Shakti Ma Jai Jai,
Jai Jyotir Ma Jai Jai
Jai Paap nashini mukthi dahini,
Jai Durgay jai jai

Jai Pawanputra jai jai,
Jai Ramaduta jai jai
Jai Shakti maan Bajaranj baan,
Jai Hanuman jai jai

Jai Uma kaant jai jai,
Jai Kailashpati jai jai
Jai Mahakaal lochan wishaal,
Jai Shiva Shankar jai jai

~~~
~~~

SARASWATI BHAJANS

JAI SARASWATI VARDE MAHARANI

Jai Saraswati Var De Maharani
Hum Deen Hai Maa Tu Dayadani

Taar De Tu Hi Deen Dukhon Ke
Dukh Sankat Mein Nirbhaya Karni
Tav Charnon Mein Hum Kar Jore
Karate Prarthana Bhav Bhaya Harni
Vidya Daan De Maa Gyan Nidani
Jai Saraswati ...

Shanti Sukh Maya Vatavaran Kar
Bhagwati Vidya Jyoti Jaga De
Veena Vadini Saar Varsha Se
Gyan Sarita Jag Mein Baha De
Vinati Karat Hain Hum Agyani
Jai Sarasawti ...

Sahitya Sangeet Kala Ki
Hey Maa Devi Tu Hai Vibhuti
Sharan Tihare Vignavinashini
Maane Gyan Prakash Ki Jyoti
Dayadrishti De Jagat Kalyani

Jai Saraswati ...

JAI SHARDA BHAWANI

Jaya Sharda Bhawani Bharti
Vidya Dani Maha Vakya Vani Devi Dhyaven
Sur Nar Muni Mani
Devi Ko Tribhuban Jani Jo
Jaki Man Ichcha Soyi Udaape
Mangal Budh Dani Gyan Ko Nidani
Veena Pustak Dharni Pratham Devi Dhyaven
Tansen Teri Astuti Gaayo
Sapt Sur Teen Gyan Raag Rang
Lai Aksar Aave

~~~

JAI JAGADEESHWARI

Jai Jagadeeshwari mata Saraswati
sharnagat pratipaalanhari

Chand bimb sam vadan viraje
sheesh mukut mala gale dhari

Veena vaam ang mein jhoole
saamgeet dwani madhur piyari

Shwet basan kamalaasan sundar
sang ati hisubh hans sawari

Brahmanand main das tumharo
ki darshan parbrahma dulari

~~~

JAI BHAGWATI DEVI

Jai Bhagawati Devi Namo Var De
Jai Paap Vinashini Bahu Phal De
Jai Shumbha Nishumbha Kapal Dhare
Pranamami Tu Devi Nararti Hare
Jai Bhagawati Devi Namo Var De

Jai Chandra Diwakar Netra Dhare
Jai Paavak Bhushit Vaktra Vare
Jai Bhairav Deh Nileen Pare
Jai Andhak Daitya Vishosh Kare
Jai Bhagawati Devi Namo Var De

Jai Mahisha Vimardini Shool Kare
Jai Loka Samastak Paap Hare
Jai Devi Pitamah Vishnu Nute
Jai Bhaskar Shakra Shirovante
Jai Bhagawati Devi Namo Var De

Jai Shanmukh Sayudh Ishanute
Jai Sagar Gamini Shambhu Nute
Jai Dukh Daridra Vinash Kare
Jai Putra Kalatra Vivriddhi Kare
Jai Bhagawati Devi Namo Var De

Jai Devi Samasta Shareer Dhare
Jai Nak Vidarshani Dukh Hare
Jai Vyadhi Vinashini Moksh Kare
Jai Vanchhit Dayini Siddhi Vare
Jai Bhagawati Devi Namo Var De
Jai Paap Vinashini Bahu Phal De
Jai Shumbha Nishumbha Kapal Dhare
Pranamami Tu Devi Nararti Hare
Jai Bhagawati Devi Namo Var De

~~~
~~~

LAKSHMI BHAJANS

Vishnu Priya Maha Laxmi

Vishnu Priya Maha Laxmi
Teri Jai Jai Kaar
Teri Jai Jai Kaar Jagat Mein
Teri Jai Jai Kaar

Charan Vandana Kare Sabhi
Tum Jag Ki Shobha Ho Mata
Har Aagan Mein Vas Karo Maa
Sukh Sampati Ki Data
Dharma Sudha Maa Ke
Jab Pahuchi Phir Se Aayi Bahar
Teri Jai Jai Kaar Jagat Mein
Teri Jai Jai Kaar

Dhan Ke Bina Har Dhaam Hai Suna
Ajab Tumhari Hai Teri Maya
Sabhi Kast Ho Jaye Kinare
Jisne Tumko Hai Paya
Jiski Hai Khali Jholi Vo
Tumko Raha Pukar
Teri Jai Jai Kaar Jagat Mein
Teri Jai Jai Kaar

Tum Hari Charno Ki Seva Mein
Tumsa Koi Ratan Nahi
Kaise Karu Tumhari Seva
Aaye Samajh Mein Jatan Nahi
Tum Jisse Ruthi Ho Vo Akela
Jaye Jagat Mein Haar

Teri Jai Jai Kaar Jagat Mein
Teri Jai Jai Kaar
Vishnu Priya Maha Laxmi
Teri Jai Jai Kaar

Teri Jai Jai Kaar Jagat Mein
Teri Jai Jai Kaar

~~~

Mai Hoo Aaya Hai Tere Dwar

Mai Hoon Aaya Hai Tere Dwar O Jai Laxmi Mata
Mai Hoon Aaya Hai Tere Dwar O Jai Laxmi Mata
Meri Sunle Pukar Hey Maa, Meri Sunle Pukar Hey Maa
O Maiya Naiya Paar Laga, O Jai Laxmi Mata

Maathe Pe Sindur Viraaje
Dhoop Deep Nayee Vedya Chadave
Mai To Laya Hai Phool Tere Dwar
Mai To Laya Hai Phool Tere Dwar
Hey Meri Sunle Meri Pukar Hey Maa
Hey Meri Sunle Meri Pukar Hey Maa
O Jai Laxmi Mata

Mai Hoon Aaya Hai Tere Dwar O Jai Laxmi Mata
Mai Hoon Aaya Hai Tere Dwar O Jai Laxmi Mata

Jeevan Naiya Paar Laga De,
Charan Kamal Mein Aaane Wale
Tu Hi Anteryami Maa, Tu Hi Anteryami Maa
O Maiya Sunle Meri Pukar, O Jai Laxmi Mata

Mai Hoon Aaya Hai Tere Dwar O Jai Laxmi Mata
Mai Hoon Aaya Hai Tere Dwar O Jai Laxmi Mata

Tu Hai Laxmi Sharda tu Bhi Vishnu Patni
Hai Jag Janani, Tu Deen Bandhu Hai Maa
Tu Deen Bandhu Hai Maa, O Maiya Sunle Meri Pukar
O Jai Laxmi Mata
~~~

Mai Hoon Aaya Hai Tere Dwar O Jai Laxmi Mata
Mai Hoon Aaya Hai Tere Dwar O Jai Laxmi Mata

~~~

Jai He Maha Lakshmi Maa

Jai He Maha Lakshmi Maa
Naiya Meri Paar Karo
Jholee Phailaye Khare
Maiya Bandhar Bharo
Tu Hai Dayalu Maiya Mamta Bhari
Lakhoon Dukhiyon Ki Tune Vipadha Hari
Ham Bhee Aaye Sharan Tihare
Ham Pay Bhee To Dhayan Dharo
Aayi Diwali Aao Deepak Jalaey
Teri Kripa Ho To Sabhi Phoole Phaley
Sukh Sampati Se Ghar Bhar Jaye
Itna To Upkar Karo
Jai He Maha Lakshmi Maa
Naiya Meri Paar Karo

~~~

Jai Jai Lakshmi Mata He Mata He Mata

Jai Jai Lakshmi Mata He Mata He Mata
Jai Jai Lakshmi Mata He Mata He Mata
Tu Sun Le Meri Pukar Meri Pukar Mata
Jai Jai Lakshmi Mata He Mata He Mata

Aadi Bhagvati Maa Tune Hi Jag Ko Janam Diya Hai
Tu Savitri Tu Hi Gauri Tu Hi Vishnu Priya Hai
Ho Jyoti Mai Tere Roop Kai Teri Leela Aprampar
Aprampar Mata

Jai Jai Lakshmi Mata He Mata He Mata
Teri Daya Se Pal Mein Bante Bigade Kaam Sabhi Ke
Tu Jise Chaahe Narayan Ki Kar De Kripa Usi Pe
Tera Dhyan Dharoo Gungan Karoo Meri Pooja
Meri Pooja Kar Swikaar Kar Swikaar

Jai Jai Lakshmi Mata He Mata He Mata

He Mata He Mata He Mata He Mata

~~~

Aao Aao Maa Laxmi Aao

Aao Aao Maa Laxmi Aao
Maa Darsha Dikhaoji
Hai Khade Tere Dwarji
Maa Tere Bhakt Kare Hai Pukarji

Mere Naina Darsh Tera Paye
Hai Kabse Aas Lagaye Kare Intazarji
Maa Tere Bhakt Kare Hai Pukarji

Tujhko Mann Mandir Mein Baithaya
Tera Dhyan Lagaya Maa

Maine Sada Tera Naam Pukara
Tere Naam Ko Gaya Maa
Laxmi Maiyya Laxmi Maiyya
Laxmi Maiyya Bhakt Jano Ki
Atki Bhavar Mein Naiyya
Aao Aao Maha Laxmi Maa Paar Lagao
Hai Naiyya Majdharji
Maa Tere Bhagat Kare Hai Pukarji
Andhan Ko Ankhe Dete Kodin Ko Kaya
Nirdhan Ko Maya Deti Hai
Apne Bhakt Jano Ke Maiyya Laxmi
Saare Dukh Har Leti Hai
~~~

Laxmi Maiyya Laxmi Maiyya
Laxmi Maiyya Ke Charno Mein
Jhukti Sari Duniya
Gao Gao Maiyya Ki Mahima Gao
Sheesh Navao Maa Degi Apna Pyarji
Maa Tere Bhagat Kare Hai Pukarji
Aayi Deewali Ki Ritu Badi Pyari
Maa Ki Pooja Karloji
Maiyya Ke Khule Hue Dhan Bhandare
Apni Jholi Bharloji

Laxmi Maiyya Laxmi Maiyya
Laxmi Maiyya Bhakt Jano Ko
Khali Na Lautaye
Jobhi Aaye Aakar Ke Sheesh Navaye
Gun Maiyya Ka Gaye
Paye Maiyya Ka Deedarji
Maa Tere Bhagat Kare Hai Pukarji

Aao Aao Maha Laxmi Aao
Maa Darsh Dikhao
Hai Khade Tere Dwarji
Maa Tere Bhagat kare Hai Pukarji

~~~
~~~

Jai Lakshmi Kalyani

Jai Lakshmi Kalyani Maiya
Jai Lakshmi Kalyani
Jai Kakshmi Kalyani Maiya

Sab Aaye Sharan Tihari Maiya
De Darshan Maharani

Jai Lakshmi Kalyani Maiya
Jai Lakshmi Kalyani
Jai Lakshmi Kalyani

Tu Mangalmay Pawan Maiya
Kripa Sada Barsave

Deen Dukhi Sharnagat Jan Ke
Bigade Kaaj Banave

Tu Aanant Mahadani Maiya
Jai Lakshmi Kalyani
Jai Lakshmi Kalyani

Dev Sabhi Aradhan Karte
Rishi Muni Dhyan Lagate
Is Nashwar Sansar Ke Prani Teri Kirat Gaate

Tu Devi Vardani Maiya
Jai Lakshmi Kalyani
Jai Lakshmi Kalyani

Tu Raji Jisape Ho Jave
Khole Shukh Ke Dware
Man Mein Jagave Gyan Ki Jyoti
Har Leti Andhiyare
Tu Jyotirmai Shiwani Maiya
Jai Lakshmi Kalyani
Jai Lakshmi Kalyani

~~~
~~~

DURGA BHAJANS

Durgati Haarini Durga

Durgati Haarini Durga Ambey Teri Jai Jai Kaar Ho
Bhav Bhav Taarini Bhawani Ambey Meri Namaskaar Ho

Teri Hi Abha Se Jyotir Suraj Chand Sitare Hain
Teri Hi Maa Shakti Lekar Khade Hue Yeh Saare Hain
Sukhdayi ho Shrishti Saari Halka Dukh Ka Bhaar Ho

Vishwa Amba Tav Shakti To Brahmlok Par Ant Hai
Teri Mahima Ka Hey Maiya Nahi Aadi Aur Ant Hai
Janma Janma Tak Hey Brahmani
Charan Kamal Son Pyaar Ho

Hey Maha Devi Hey Mahakali
Dushton Ka Sanhaar Karo
Mangal Maya Vardaan Do Maiya Bhav
Se Beda Paar Karo
Bhaav Bhakti Mein Sharan Mein
Aayen Vinati Ma Sweekaar Ho

Aao Meri Shera Waali Maa

Aao Meri Shera Waali Maa
O Maa O Maa O Maa
Aao Meri Jyota Waali Maa
O Maa O Maa

Mere Soye Bhag Jaga Do
O Maiya Meri Jagdambe
Meri Bigdi Aaj Bana Do
O Maiya Meri Jagdambe

Jai Maa Jai Maa, Jai Jai Maa
Jai Maa Jai Maa, Jai Jai Maa

O Sunke Mahima Teri Niraali
Aaya Dar Per Ek Sawali
Aaya Dar Per Ek Sawali
Vo Dukhiyara Janam Se Andha
Haal Bada Tha Uska Manda

Haal Bada Tha Uska Manda
Tadap Ke Bola Aakho Ke Bin
Patthar Hai Here Moti
Naina Devi Mata Hai To
De Mere Naino Ko Jyoti
De Mere Naino Ko Jyoti
Teri Daya Se Mit Gaya Uski Aakho Se Andhiyara

Ek Din Ek Abhagan Maari
Kahne Lagi Dukhda Apna
Kahne Lagi Dukhda Apna

Maa Apne Bhakton Ko Dekho
Kitna Dard Pade Sahna
Kitna Dard Pade Sahna
Tune To Kitani Maaon Ko
Bakshi Aakho Ke Tare

Daya Karon Mujhpe Itni Ki
Koi Maa Kahke Pukare
Koi Maa Kahke Pukare
Dayabhai Jab Teri Maiya Usaki God Bhari Khali

Aao Meri Jag Janani Maa

Jai Maa Jai Maa, Jai Jai Maa
Jai Maa Jai Maa, Jai Jai Maa

~~~

Ambe Charan Kamal Hain Tere

Ambe Charan Kamal Hain Tere
Hum Banware Hain Janam Janam Ke
Nis Din Lete Phere

Tu Dharti Jag Palankarti
Ambar Ka Adhaar Hai Tu Hi
Sab Sukh Jhute Sab Dukh Jhute
Is Jeevan Ka Saar Hai Tu Hi
Tu Satyam Tu Shivam Sundaram
Hum Sab Chapalit Chere

Os Mein Ansu Phool Mein Shraddha
Antar Mein Lekar Ujiyare
Tere Mandir Mein Natmastak
Nabh Ke Suraj Chand Sitare
Humne Teri Muskaano Mein
Dekhe madhur sawere

~~~

Om Shailputri Maiya

Om Shailputri Maiya Raksha Karo
Om Jaga-Janani Devi Raksha Karo
Om Nav Durga Namah
Om Jaga-Janani Namah

Om Bhramcharni Maiya Raksha Karo
Om Bhavatarani Devi Raksha Karo
Om Nav Durga Namah
Om Jaga-Janani Namah

Om Chandraghanta Chandi Raksha Karo
Om Bhayaharini Maiya Raksha Karo
Om Nav Durga Namah
Om Jaga-Janani Namah

Om Kushmanda Tum Hi Raksha Karo
Om Shaktirupa Maiya Raksha Karo
Om Nav Durga Namah
Om Jaga-Janani Namah

Om Skandmata Maiya Raksha Karo
Om Jagadamba Janani Raksha Karo
Om Nav Durga Namah
Om Jaga-Janani Namah

Om Kaatyayani Maiya Raksha Karo
Om Pap Nashini Ambe Raksha Karo
Om Nav Durga Namah
Om Jaga-Janani Namah
Om Kaalratri Kali Raksha Karo
Om Sukhadati Maiya Raksha Karo
Om Nav Durga Namah
Om Jaga Janani Namah

Om Mahagauri Maiya Raksha Karo
Om Bhaktidati Raksha Karo
Om Nav Durga Namah

Om Jaga-Janani Namah

Om Siddhiratri Maiya Raksha Karo
Om Nav Durga Devi Raksha Karo

Om Nav Durga Namah
Om Jaga-Janani Namah

~~~

Namaste Jagatharini Trahi Durge

Namaste Saranye Shive Sanukampe,
Namaste Jagad Vyapike Viswaroope,
Namaste Jagad Vandhya Padaravinde,
Namaste Jagatharini Trahi Durge.

Namaste Jagat Chinthyamana Swaroope,
Namaste Maha Yogini, Jnana Roope,
Namaste, Namaste Sadananda Roope,
Namaste Jagatharini Trahi Durge.

Anadhasya Deenasya Thrushnathurasya,
Bhayarthasya Bheethasya Vrudasya Jantho,
Thwameka Gathir Devi Nisthara Karthri,
Namaste Jagatharini Trahi Durge.

Thwameka Sadhanadhi Dha Sathya Vadi,
Anekakila Krodhanath Krodhanishta,
Ida Pingala Thwam Sushumna Cha Nadi,
Namaste Jagatharini Trahi Durge.

Aranye, Rane, Shatru Madhye
Anale Pranthare Sagare Raja Grehe,
Thwameka Gathir Devi Nisthara Hetu,
Namaste Jagatharini Trahi Durge.

Apare, Maha Dusthare Athyantha Ghore,
~~~

Vipath Sagare Majjatham Deha Bhajam,
Thwameka Gathir Devi, Nisthara Nouka,
Namaste Jagatharini Trahi Durge.
Namo Devi Durge Shive Bheema Nadhe,
Saraswathya Rundathithya Mogha Swaroope,
Vibhoothi Sachi Kala Rathri Sathi Thwam,
Namaste Jagatharini Trahi Durge.

Namaschandige, Chanda Durganda Leela,
Samuth Ganditha Aganditha Sesha Sathro,
Thwameka Gathir Devi Nisthara Beejam,
Namaste Jagatharini Trahi Durge.

~~~

Saanchi Jyoti Wali Mata
Teri Jai Jaikar

Tune Mujhe Bulaya Shera Waliye
Main Aaya Main Aaya Shere Waliye
Jyota Waliye, Pahada Waliye, Mehara Waliye

Saara Jag Hai Ek Banjara
Sab Ki Manjit Tera Dwara
Unche Parwat Lamba Rasta
Par Main Rah Na Paya, Shera Waliye

Sune Man Main Jal Gayi Bati
Tere Padh Main Mil Gaye Saathi
Munh Kholu Kya Tujhase Mangu
Bin Maange Sab Paaya, Shera Waliye

Kaun Hai Raja, Kuan Bhikhari
Ek Darbar Tere Saare Pujari
Tune Sab Ko Darshan Deke
Apne Gale Lagaya, Shera Waliye

~~~

VISHNU BHAJAN

Namostute Namostute Namostute

Hey Vishnu Bhagwaan Tumhara Dhyan Kare Kalyan
Karoon Main Tumko Barambaar
Namostute Namostute Namostute

Tum Vedon Mein Updesh Bane
Ramayana Mein Sandesh Bane
Tum Teen Lok Ke Swami Ho Natargyan Kalyani Ho
Vinati Hai Tumse Ki Sabka Tum Kara Do Uddhaar
Tumhare Dasham Dasham Avataar

Jo Jhuke Tumhare Charnan Mein
Sukh Bhar De Ape Jeevan Mein
Tum Punya Kaam Mein Rehte
Ho Tum Katha Dhyan Mein Rahte Ho
Tumse Ke Hi Har Ki Archana Hoti Hai Sakaar

Amrit Manthan Mein Roop Dhara
Devon Mein Nav Utsah Bhara
Tum Shrishti Kaal Tum Purna Dev
Tum Narayan Tum Satyamev
Sukh Pave Woh Prani Jo Nit Karta Hai Sandhaan
Bhakt Ki Bhakti Ka Aadhaar
Shreeman Narayana Narayana Narayana

Itna To Karna Swami

Itna To Karna Swami, Jab Pran Tan Se Nikale
Govind Naam Leke Tab Pran Tan Se Nikale

Shree Ganga Ji Ka Tat Ho Jamuna Ka Basivat Ho
Mera Saanwara Nikat Ho Jab Pran Tan Se Nikale

Shree Vrindavan Ka Sthal Ho Mere
Mukh Mein Tulsi Dal Ho
Vishnu Charan Ka Jal Ho Jab Pran Tan Se Nikale

Jab Kanth Pran Aave Koi Rog Na Satave
Yam Daras Na Dikhave Jab Pran Tan Se Nikale

Sudhi Hove Nahi Tan Ki Taiyari Ho Gaman Ki
Lakdi Ho Braj Ke Van Ki Jab Pran Tan Se Nikale

Ye Nek Si Araj Hai Mano To Kya Haraz Hai
Kuchh Aap Ka Pharaz Hai Jab Pran Tan Se Nikale

~~~

Insaaf Ka Mandir Hai Yeh

Insaaf Ka Mandir Hai Yeh Bhagwaan Ka Ghar Hai
Kehna Hai Jo Keh De Tujhe Kis Baat Ka Darr Hai

Hai Khot Tere Man Mein Jo Bhagwaan Se Hai Door
Hai Paanv Tere Phir Bhi Tu Aane Se Hai Mazboor
Himmat Hai To Aaja Yeh Bhalayi Ki Dagar Hai

Dukh Deke Jo Dukhiya Se Na Insaaf Karega
Bhagwaan Bhi Usko Na Kabhi Maaf Karega
Yeh Soch Le Har Baat Ki Data Ko Khabar Hai

~~~

Narayan Karunamaya Sharanam

Narayan Karunamaya Sharnam
Jai Laxmi Pati Vishnu Sharnam

Vipati Humari Tumne Taari
Shok Mita Ye Bhav Bhaya Haari
Parampita Parmeshwar Sharnam

Sampati Pai Sab Man Chahi
Bhakt Jano Ki Laaj Bachayi
Deenbandhu Jagdeeshwar Sharnam

~~~

Jap Le Hari Ka Naam

Jap Le Hari Ka Naam Saanjh Sakare
Antaryami Data Hare Dukh Saare

Jagat Pita Ka Dhyan Na Aaya
Madmate Pprani Tune Janam Gavaya
Kabhi Nahi Khole Tune Antardware

Swanson Ki Tu Jap Le Mala
Guru Kirpa Se Hovenihala
Bhava Saagar Se Paar Utaare

Sharan Pade Bin Nishphal Jeena
Jeevan Mein Shubh Karam Na Kina
Yun Hi Na Prani Heera Janam Ganva Re

~~~

KRISHNA BHAJANS

Sham Piya Mori Rang De Chunariya

Sham Piya Mori Rang De Chunariya
Bina Ragai Mai Ghar Nahi Jaungi
Beet Jaye Chahe Sari Umariya
Hari Na Ragaungi Mai To Peeli Na Rangaungi
Apne Hi Rang Me Hi Rang De Swarariya
Are Aisi Rang De Ki Rang Na Chhote

Dhobiya Dohe Sare Sari Umariya
Jo Nahi Rango To Mol Hi Magayedo
Braj Me Khuli Hai Prem Bajariya
Ya Chunari Odd Mai Yamuna Ko Jaungi
Shyam Ki Mope Padegi Nazariya
Jeevan Ki Naiya Leja Uspaar Saware

~~~

Rahe Mere Mukh Mein

Rahe Mere Mukh Mein Sada Tera Naam

Oh Radha Ke Shyam Oh Meera Ke Shyam
Koi Duniya Ki Taakat Juda Na Kare
Mile Jo Mujhe Radha Radha Kare
Mujhe To Hai Pyara Prabhu Tera Naam
Oh Radha Ke Shyam
Charnon Mein Apni Bula Hi Liya
Mujhe Apna Tune Bana Hi Liya
Kahe Tumko Sab Hi Yasoda Ke Laal
Chahe Koi Bhi Mujhko Deewani Kahe
Deewani Kahe Mastani Kahe

Mujhe To Hai Pyara Prabhu Tera Naam

~~~

Tere Sang Me Rahenge O Mohana

Tere Sang Me Rahenge O Mohana
O Mohana O Sohana
Tum Chandan Bano Main Pani Banu
Mastak Par Milenge O Mohana
Tere Sang Me Rahenge O Mohana
Tum Chandan Pushpa Main Dhaga Banu
Mala Me Milenge O Mohana
Tere Sang Me Rahenge O Mohana
Tum Murli Bano Main Taan Banu
Adharon Par Milenge O Mohana
Tere Sang Me Rahenge O Mohana
Tum Vakta Bano Main Shrota Banu
Satsang Me Milenge O Mohana
Tere Sang Me Rahenge O Mohana

~~~

Achyutam Keshavam Krishna Damodaram

Achyutam Keshavam Krishna Damodaram
Rama Naraynam Janaki Vallabham
Kaun Kehta Hai Bhagvan Aate Nahi
Tum Meera Ke Jaise Bulate Nahi

Achyutam Keshavam Krishna Damodaram
Rama Naraynam Janaki Vallabham
Kaun Kehta Hai Bhagvan Khaate Nahi
Ber Shabri Ke Jaise Khilate Nahi
Achyutam Keshavam Krishna Damodaram
Rama Naraynam Janaki Vallabham
Kaun Kehta Hai Bhagvan Sote Nahi
Maa Yashoda Ke Jaise Sulate Nahin
Achyutam Keshavam Krishna Damodaram
Rama Naraynam Janaki Vallabham
Kaun Kehta Hai Bhagvan Nachthe Nahi
Gopiyo Ki Tarah Tum Nachate Nahi
~~~

Achyutam Keshavam Krishna Damodaram,
Rama Naraynam Janaki Vallabham,
Naam Japate Chalo Kaam Karte Chalo
Har Samay Krishna Ka Dhyaan Karte Chalo

Achyutam Keshavam Krishna Damodaram,
Rama Naraynam Janaki Vallabham,
Yaad Aayegi Unko Kabhi Na Kabhi
Krishan Darshan To Denge Kabhi Na Kabhi
Achyutam Keshavam Krishna Damodaram
Rama Naraynam Janaki Vallabham

~~~

Man Mohana

Man Mohana, Man Mohana
Kanha Suno Na, Tum Bin Paaon Kaise Chain
Tarsoo Tumhi Ko Din Rain
Chodke Apne Kashi Mathura
Aake Baso More Nain
Tum Bin Paaon Kaise Chain
Tarsoo Tumhi Ko Din Rain
Ik Pal Ujiyaara Aaye, Ik Pal Andhiyara Chhaye
Man Kyu Na Ghabraye, Kaise Na Ghabraye
Man Jo Koi Doraha Apni Raho Mein Paaye
Koun Disha Jaaye Tum Bin Koun Samjhaye
Raas Rachaiyya Vrindavan Ke Gokul Ke Vaasi
Radha Tumhri Daasi
Darshan Ko Hai Pyaasi
Shyam Salone Nandlala Krishna Banvari
Tumhri Chhab Hai Nyaari
Main To Hoon Tan Man Haari
Man Mohana Man Mohana
Kanha Suno Na Tum Bin Paaon Kaise Chain
Tarsoo Tumhi Ko Din Rain
~~~

Jeevan Ik Nadiyaa Hain, Lehro Lehro Behti Jaaye
Is Mein Man Ki Naiyya Doobey Kabhi Utar Jaaye
Tum Na Khevaiyya Ho To Koi Tat Kaise Paaye
Majhdhaar Behlaaye, Toh Tumri Sharan Aaye
Main Hoon Tumhari, Hain Tumhara Mera Yeh Jeevan
Tumko Hi Dekhoon Main, Dekhoon Koi Darpan
Bansi Ban Jaaongi, In Hoton Ki Ho Jaaongi
In Sapno Ke Chalkar Hain Mera Man Aangan

~~~

Mohan Hamaare Madhuban

Mohan Hamaare Madhuban Me Tum Aayaa Naa Karo
Jadoo Bharee Yaa Baasuree Bajaayaa Naa Karo

Soorat Tumhaaree Dekh Ke Salonee Saanwaaree
Sun Baasuree Ke Raagko Ham Hogayee Baawree
Maakhan Churaane Waale Dil Churaayaa Naa Karo
Mohan Hamaare Madhuban Me Tum Aayaa Naa Karo

Jadoo Bharee Yaa Baasuree Bajaayaa Naa Karo
Maathe Mukut, Galmaal Kati Me Kachhnee Sohe
Kanon Me Kundal Jhoomke Man Mere Ko Mohe
Is Chandraama Ke Roop Ko Lubhaayaa Naa Karo
Mohan Hamaare Madhuban Me Tum Aayaa Naa Karo

Jadoo Bharee Yaa Baasuree Bajaayaa Naa Karo
Apnee Yashodaa Maat Kee Saugandh Hai Tumko
Yamunaa Nadee Ke Teer Pe Tum Naa Milo Hamko
Is Baasuree Kee Taan Pe Bilmaayaa Naa Karo
Mohan Hamaare Madhuban Me Tum Aayaa Naa Karo

Jadoo Bharee Yaa Baasuree Bajaayaa Naa Karo
Isee Tumhaaree Baasuree Ne Mohinee Daaree
Bhav Sakhee Kee Beenti Tum Suniyo Banwaree
~~~

Darshan Dikhaa De Saawaraa Ab Der Na Karo
Mohan Hamaare Madhuban Me Tum Aayaa Naa Karo
Jadoo Bharee Yaa Baasuree Bajaayaa Naa Karo

~~~

Jai Krishna Hare

Jai Krishña Hare, Shri Krishña Hare
Dukhiyon Ke Dukh Door Kare
Jai Jai Jai Krishna Hare

Jab Chãron Taraf Andhiãrã Ho
Ãshã Ka Door Kinãrã Ho
Jab Koi Na Kheyan Hãrã Ho
Tab Tu Hi Beda Pãr Kare
Jai Jai Jai Krishña Hare

Tu Chãhe To Sab Kuchh Kar De
Vish Ko Bhi Amrit Karde
Puran Karde Uski Ãshã
Jo Bhi Terã Dhyãn Dhare
Jai Jai Jai Krishña Hare

~~~

Jaya Mādhava Madana Murārī

Jaya Mādhava Madana Murārī
Jaya Keśava Kali-Mala-Hārī
Jaya Mādhava Madana Murārī
Sundara Kuṇḍala Naina Viśāla,
Gale Sohe Vaijantī-Mālā
Yā Chavi Kī Balihārī Rādhe Śyāma Śyāma-Śyāma
Jaya Mādhava Madana Murārī

Kabahūn Luṭa Dadhi Khāyo,
Kabahūṅ Madhuvana Rāsa Racāyo
Nācata Vipina-Vihārī Rādhe Syāma Śyāmā-Śyāma
Jaya Mādhava Madana Murārī

Gvāla-Bāla Saṅga Dhenu Carāi,
Vana-Vana Brahmata Phire Yadu-Rāi
Kāṅdhe Kāmara Kārī Rādhe Śyāma Śyāmā-Śyāma
Jaya Mādhava Madana Murārī

Curā Curā Nava-Nīta Jo Khāyo,
Vraja-Vanitana Pai Nāma Dharāyo
Mākhanachora Murārī Rādhe Śyāma Śyāmā-Śyāma
Jaya Mādhava Madana Murārī

Eka-Dina Māna Indra Ko Māryo,
Nakha Upara Govardhana Dhāryo
Nama Paḍayo Giridhārī Rādhe Śyāma Śyāmā-Śyāma
Jaya Mādhava Madana Murārī

Duryodhana Ko Bhoga Na Khāyo,
Rūkho Sāga Vidura Ghara Khāyo
Aise Prema Pujārī Rādhe Śyāma Śyāmā-Śyāma
Jaya Mādhava Madana Murārī

Karuṇā Kara Draupadī Pukārī,
Paṭa Lipaṭa Gaye Vanavārī
Nirakha Rahe Nara Nārī Rādhe Śyāma Śyāmā-Śyāma
Jaya Mādhava Madana Murārī

Bhakta-Bhakta Saba Tumane Tāre
Bin Bhakti Hama Ṭhāḍe Dvāre
Lījo Khabara Hamārī Rādhe Śyāma Śyāmā-Śyāma
Jaya Mādhava Madana Murārī

Arjuna Ke Ratha Hāṅkana Hāre
Gītā Ke Upadeśa Tumhāre
Cakra-Sudarśana-Dhārī Rādhe Śyāma Śyāmā-Śyāma
Jaya Mādhava Madana Murārī

~~~

Nandlala Krishna Murari

Nandlala Krishna Murari
Tere Charnon Pe Balhaari
Tu Hi Raas Rachaiyya
Tu Hi Hai Gopala

Tu Hi Murliwala
Tu Hi Giridhaari
Nandlala Krishna Murari
Tere Charnon Pe Balhaari
Shyam Varn Pitaambar Dhaari Gal Vaijyantimala
Kunj Galan Mein Bansi Bajaye Gowardhan Gopala
Mormukut Ki Shobha Nyaari Kitni Sundar Chhabi Tumhari
Nandlala Krishna Murari
Tere Charnon Pe Balhaari
Tu Hi Raas Rachaiyya, Tu Hi Hai Gopala
~~~

Tu Hi Murliwala, Tu Hi Giridhaari
Nandlala Krishna Murari, Tere Charnon Pe Balhaari
Bas Gayi Tere Saanwli Surat Bhakt Janon Ke Mann Mein
Hamne Chaaron Dhaam Hai Paaye Tere Hi Charnon Mein
Pooje Tujhako Duniya Saari Jai Gopala Jai Banwaari
Nandlala Krishna Murari Tere Charnon Pe Balhaari
Tu Hi Raas Rachaiyya, Tu Hi Hai Gopala
Tu Hi Murliwala, Tu Hi Giridhaari
Nandlala Krishna Murari, Tere Charnon Pe Balhaari

~~~

Radhika Gori Se

Radhika Gori Se, Biraj Ki Chhori Se
Maiya Karade Mero Byah
Umar Teri Chhoti Hai, Nazar Teri Khoti Hai
Kaise Karadu Tero Byah
Jo Nahi Byah Karaye, Teri Gaiya Nahi Charau
Aaj Ki Baad Meri Maiya, Teri Dehali Par Na Aau
Aayega, Re Mazza, Re Mazza, Ab Jeet Haar Ka
Radhika Gori Se, Biraj Ki Chhori Se
Maiya Karade Mero Byah
Umar Teri Chhoti Hai, Nazar Teri Khoti Hai
Kaise Karadu Tero Byah

Chandan Ki Chowki Par, Maiya Tujhko Bithaun
Aapni Radha Se Main, Charan Tere Dabwaaun
Bhojan Mai Banwaunga, Banwaunga, Chapaan Prakar Ke
Radhika Gori Se, Biraj Ki Chhori Se
Maiya Karade Mero Byah
Umar Teri Chhoti Hai, Nazar Teri Khoti Hai
Kaise Karadu Tero Byah
Chhoti Si Dulhaniya, Jab Angana Me Dolegi
Tere Samne Maiya, Wo Ghunghat Na Kholegi
Daau Se, Ja Kaho, Ja Kaho, Bethenge Dawar Pe
~~~

Radhika Gori Se, Biraj Ki Chhori Se
Maiya Karade Mero Byah
Umar Teri Chhoti Hai, Nazar Teri Khoti Hai
Kaise Karadu Tero Byah
Sun Baate Kanha Ki, Maiya Bethi Muskayen
Leke Balaiyan Maiya, Hridaya Se Apne Lagaaye
Nazar Kahi, Lag Jaye Na, Lag Jaye Na, Mere Lal Ko
Radhika Gori Se, Biraj Ki Chhori Se
Maiya Karade Mero Byah
Umar Teri Chhoti Hai, Nazar Teri Khoti Hai
Kaise Karadu Tero Byah
Radhika Gori Se, Biraj Ki Chhori Se
Kanha Karadu Tero Byah

Radhe Rani Ki Jai Maharani Jai
Ho Bolo Barsane Waali Ki Jai Jai Jai
Radhe Rani Ki Jai Maharani Jai
Ho Vraj Bhanu Dulari Ki Jai Jai Jai
Radhe Rani Ki Jai Maharani Ki

~~~

Chitta Chora Yashoda Ke Baal

Chitta Chora Yashoda Ke Baal
Navanita Chora Gopaal

Gopaal... Gopaal... Gopaal... Gopaal...Govardhana Dhara Gopaal
Gopaal... Gopaal... Gopaal... Gopaal... Govardhana Dhara Gopaal
Chitta Chora Yashoda Ke Baal
Navanita Chora Gopaal

Keshava Madhava Jaya Deva Madhusudhana
Netra Kamala Dhala Ativa Manohara
Antaryami Prabho Parameshwara
Maya Manusha Vesha Lila Dhara
~~~

Gopala Gopala Nacho Gopala
Nacho Nacho Sai Nandalala
Rhuma Jhuma Rhuma Jhuma Nacho Gopala
Nacho Nacho Sai Nandalala
Mana Mohana Nandalal
Mana Mohana Madhusudhana Brindavana Nandala
Mana Mohana Nandalal
Brindavana Nandalal
Mana Mohana Madhusudhana Brindav Nandalal

~~~

Choti Choti Gaiya Chotay Chotay Gwaal

Choti Choti Gaiya Chotay Chotay Gwaal
Chotoso Mero Madan Gopal
Aage Aage Gaiya Pichay Pichay Gwaal
Beech-May Mero Madan Gopal
Choti Choti Gaiya Chotay Chotay Gwaal
Chotoso Mero Madan Gopal
Kaari Kaari Gaiya Goray Goray Gwaal
Shyam Baran Mero Madan Gopal
Choti Choti Gaiya Chotay Chotay Gwaal
Chotoso Mero Madan Gopal
Ghaas Khaavay Gaiya Dhudh Peevay Gwaal
Maakhan Khaavay Mero Madan Gopal
Choti Choti Gaiya Chotay Chotay Gwaal
Chotoso Mero Madan Gopal
Choti Choti Lakuti Chotay Chotay Haath
Bansi Bajaaway Mero Madan Gopal
Choti Choti Gaiya Chotay Chotay Gwaal
Chotoso Mero Madan Gopal
Choti Choti Sakhiyaan Madhuban Baal
Raas Rachaaway Mero Madan Gopal
Choti Choti Gaiya Chotay Chotay Gwaal
Chotoso Mero Madan Gopal
Choti Choti Gaiya Chotay Chotay Gwaal
Chotoso Mero Madan Gopal

~~~

Radhe Govinda Brindavana Chanda

Radhe Radhe Radhe Radhe Govinda
Brindavana Chanda
Anathanatha Deenabandhu Radhe Govinda
Nandakumara Navanita Chora Radhe Govinda
Brindavana Chanda
Anathanatha Deenabandhu Radhe Govinda
Purana Purusha Punya Shloka Radhe Govinda
Brindavana Chanda
Anathanatha Deenabandhu Radhe Govinda
Pandarinata Panduranga Radhe Govinda
Brindavana Chanda,
Anathanatha Deenabandhu Radhe Govinda
Jai Jai Vittala Jaya Hari Vittala Radhe Govinda
Brindavana Chanda
Anathanatha Deenbandhu Radhe Govinda

~~~

Kabhi Ram Banke Kabhi Shyam Banke

Kabhi Ram Banke Kabhi Shyam Banke
Chale Aana Prabhu Ji Chale Aana
Kabhi Ram Banke Kabhi Shyam Banke
Chale Aana Prabhu Ji Chale Aana

Tum Ram Roop Mein Aana
Sita Saath Leke, Dhanush Haath Leke
Chale Aana Prabhu Ji Chale Aana
Kabhi Ram Banke Kabhi Shyam Banke
Chale Aana Prabhu Ji Chale Aana

Tum Shyam Roop Mein Aana
Radha Saath Leke, Murli Haath Leke
Chale Aana Prabhu Ji Chale Aana
Kabhi Ram Banke Kabhi Shyam Banke
~~~

Chale Aana Prabhu Ji Chale Aana

Tum Shiv Ke Roop Mein Aana
Gouri Saath Leke, Damru Haat Leke
Chale Aana Prabhu Ji Chale Aana
Kabhi Ram Banke Kabhi Shyam Banke
Chale Aana Prabhu Ji Chale Aana

Tum Vishnu Roop Mein Aana
Lakshmi Saath Leke, Chakra Haat Leke
Chale Aana Prabhu Ji Chale Aana
Kabhi Ram Banke Kabhi Shyam Banke
Chale Aana Prabhu Ji Chale Aana
Tum Ganapati Roop Mein Aana
Riddhi Saath Leke, Siddhi Saath Leke
Chale Aana Prabhu Ji Chale Aana
Kabhi Ram Banke Kabhi Shyam Banke
Chale Aana Prabhu Ji Chale Aana

Kabhi Ram Banke Kabhi Shyam Banke
Chale Aana Prabhu Ji Chale Aana
Kabhi Ram Banke Kabhi Shyam Banke
Chale Aana Prabhu Ji Chale Aana

~~~

Hey Muralee Shridhara

Hey Muralee Shridhara, Radhe Krishna Radhe Shyam
Keshava Madhava Yaadava Nandana,
Radhe Krishna Radhe Shyam
Hey Muralee Shridhara, Radhe Krishna Radhe Shyam
Nanda Nandana Radhe Shyam
Navneeta Chora Radhe Shyam
Keshava Madhava Yaadava Nandana,
Radhe Krishna Radhe Shyam
Hey Muralee Shridhara, Radhe Krishna Radhe Shyam
~~~

Bhaktavatsala Radhe Shyam
Bhaagavata Priya Radhe Shyam
Keshava Madhava Yaadava Nandana,
Radhe Krishna Radhe Shyam
Hey Muralee Shridhara, Radhe Krishna Radhe Shyam
Panduranga Radhe Shyam – Pandarinaatha Radhe Shyam
Keshava Madhava Yaadava Nandana,
Radhe Krishna Radhe Shyam
Hey Muralee Shridhara, Radhe Krishna Radhe Shyam

~~~

Hari Sundara Nanda Mukunda

Hari Sundara Nanda Mukunda Hari Narayana Hari Om
Hari Keshava Hari Govinda Hari Narayana Hari Om
Vanmali Muralidhari Govardhan Girivardhari
Nit Nit Kar Makhan Chori Gopi Mann Haari
Aao Re Gao Re Gokul Ke Pyaare
Aao Re Kanha Re Gokul Ke Pyaare
Aao Re Naacho Re Raas Rachao Re
Gao Re Naacho Re Raas Rachao Re
Hari Sundara Nanda Mukunda Hari Narayana Hari Om
Hari Keshava Hari Govinda Hari Narayana Hari Om

~~~

Main Nahin Makhan Khayo

Maiyaa Mori, Main Nahi Makhan Khayo
Bhor Bhayo Gaiyan Ke Paache, Madhuvan Mohi
Pathayo Chaar Prahar Vanshivat Bhatakyo,
Saanj Pare Ghar Aayo

Main Baalak Bahiyan Ko Choto, Chinko Kidi Vidhi Payo
Gwaal Baal Sab Bair Pare Hain, Barbas Mukh Laptayo

Tu Janani Man Kii Bhati Mori, Inke Kahe Patiyaayo
Jiya Tete Kachu Bhed Upjihai, Jaani Parayo Jaayo

Yaha Le Apani Lakuti Kambaliyaa, Bahutahi Naach Nachaayo.

Jiya Tete Kachu Bhed Upjihai, Jaani Parayo Jaayo
Surdas Tab Bihashi Yashoda Lai Ur Kanth Lagaayo

~~~

Jai Jai Radha Raman

Jai Jai Radha Raman Hari Bol
Jai Jai Radha Raman Hari Bol
Man Tera Bole Radhe Krishna
Tan Tera Bole Radhe Krishna
Jivya Tera Bole Radhe Krishna
Mukhase Nickle Radhe Krishna

Panke Tera Bole Radhe Krishna
Alke Tera Bole Radhe Krishna
Aake Tera Bole Radhe Krishna
Saase Tera Bole Radhe Krishna

Dharkan Bole Radhe Krishna
Darpan Bole Radhe Krishna
Antar Bole Radhe Krishna
Rom Rom Bole Radhe Krishna

Vrindaban Me Radhe Krishna
Bansa Lele Radhe Krishna
Goverdhan Me Radhe Krishna
Madhuban Ban Me Radhe Krishna

~~~

Vrindavan Ka Krishna Kanhaiya

Vrindavan Ka Krishna Kanhaiya,
Sab Ki Ankhon Ka Tara
Mann Hi Mann Kyun Jale Radhika,
Mohan Toh Hai Sab Ka Pyara
Vrindavan Ka Krishna Kanhaiya,
Sab Ki Ankhon Ka Tara
Jamuna Tat Par Nand Ka Lala,
Jab Jab Ras Rachaye Re
Tan Man Doley Kanha Aisi Bansi Madhur Bajaye Re
Sudh Budh Khoye Khaoi Gopiyan Jane Kaisa Jadu Dara
Vrindavan Ka Krishna Kanhaiya
Rang Salauna Aisa Jaise Chhai Ho Ghat Savan Ki
Airi Main To Hui Deevani Man Mohan Man Bhavan Ki
Tere Karan Dekh Sanvare Chhod Diya Maine Jag Sara
Vrindavan Ka Krishna Kanhaiya
Sab Ki Ankhon Ka Tara

~~~

Bhaja Govinda Jai Gopala

Bhaja Govinda Jai Gopala
Bhaja Murali Manohar Nandalaala
Bhaja Govinda Jai Gopala

Madhur Manohar Saawaray
Shri Hari Nanda Kishoor
Naina Darshan Baawaray
Deejay Charanan Tour

Man Vairaagee Naam Ka Tere
Natwar Deen Dayaalaa
Bhaja Govinda Jai Gopala
Bhaja Murali Manohar Nandalaala
Bhaja Govinda Jai Gopala
~~~

Naam Teraa Bhav Taaran Haaraa
Dukh Bhanjan Sukh Kaaree
Jisne Bhi Hirdai May Dhaaraa
Unkee Bipdaa Taaree

Hai Hitkaaree Saajan Mere
Kasht Mitaanay Waalaa
Bhaja Govinda Jai Gopala
Bhaja Murali Manohar Nandalaala
Bhaja Govinda Jai Gopala

Sab Gat Antar Jhoat Tumharee
Tu Sab Khel Khelaaway
Teraa Darshan Shyam Murari
Koyee Virlaa Paavaay
Janam Janam Ka Saathi Tu Hi
Tu Jag Kaa Rakhwala
Bhaja Govinda Jai Gopala
Bhaja Murali Manohar Nandalaala
Bhaja Govinda Jai Gopala

~~~

Nand Ke Anand Bhayo

Hey Anand Umang Bhayo, Jai Ho Nand Lal Ki
Nand Ke Anand Bhayo, Jai Kanhaiya Lal Ki
Braj Mein Anand Bhayo, Jai Yashoda Lal Ki
Haathi Ghoda Paal Ki, Jai Kanhiya Lal Ki
Jai Ho Nand Lal Ki, Jai Yashoda Lal Ki
Gokul Mein Anand Bhayo, Jai Kanhaiya Lal Ki
Hey Anand Umang Bhayo, Jai Ho Nand Lal Ki
Gokul Ke Anand Bhayo, Jai Kanhaiya Lal Ki
Jai Yashoda Lal Ki, Jai Ho Nand Lal Ki
Hathi Ghoda Paal Ki, Jai Kanhaiya Lal Ki
Jai Ho Nand Lal Ki, Jai Yashoda Lal Ki
Hathi Ghoda Paal Ki, Jai Kanhaiya Lal Ki
Koti Brahmaand Ke, Adhipati Laal Ki
~~~

**Hathi Ghoda Paal Ki, Jai Kanhaiya Laal Ki
Gaune Chaarane Aaye, Jai Ho Pashupaal Ki
Nand Ke Anand Bhayo, Jai Kanhaiya Lal Ki
Punam Ki Chand Jaise, Shobha Hai Baal Ki
Hathi Ghoda Paal Ki, Jai Kanhaiya Laal Ki
Hey Anand Umang Bhayo Jai Ho Nand Laal Ki
Gokul Mein Anand Bhayo, Jai Kanhaiya Laal Ki
Bhakto Ke Anand Kand, Jai Yashoda Laal Ki
Hathi Ghoda Paal Ki, Jai Kanhaiya Laal Ki**

**Hey Jai Yashoda Laal Ki, Jai Ho Gopal Ki
Gokul Mein Anand Bhayo, Jai Kanhaiya Laal Ki
Anand Se Bolo Sab, Jai Ho Braj Laal Ki
Hathi Ghoda Paal Ki, Jai Kanhaiya Laal Ki
Jai Ho Braj Laal Ki, Paawan Pratipaal Ki
Hey Nand Ke Anand Bhayo, Jai Ho Nand Laal Ki**

~~~

Shyam Teri Bansi

**Shyam Teri Bansi Pukare Radha Naam
Log Kare Meera Ko Yun Hi Badnaam
Savre Ki Bansi Ko Bajne Se Kam
Radha Ka Bhi Shyam Vo To Meera Ka Bhi Shyam**

**O... Jamna Ki Lahren Bansi Batki Chaiyaan
Kiska Nahin Hai Kaho Krishna Kanhaiya
Shyam Ka Divana To Sara Brijdham
Log Karen Meera Ko Yunhi Badnaam Shyam.**

**O... Kon Jane Bansuriya Kisko Bulaye
Jiske Man Bhaye Vo Usike Gun Gaye
Kon Nahin Bansi Ki Dhun Ka Gulam
Radha Ka Bhi Shyam Vo To Meera Ka Bhi Shyam**

~~~

O Palanhaare

O Paalanhaare, Nirgun Aur Nyaare
Tumre Bin Hamra Kaunon Naahin
Humri Uljhan Suljhaao Bhagwan
Tumre Bin Hamra Kaunon Naahin
Tumhe Humka Ho Sambhaale
Tumhe Hamre Rakhwaale
Tumre Bin Hamra Kaunon Naahin

Chanda Mein Tumhe To Bhare Ho Chaandni
Sooraj Mein Ujaala Tumhe Se
Yeh Gagan Hai Magan, Tumhe To Diye Ho Isse Taare
Bhagwan, Yeh Jeevan Tumhe Na Sanwaaroge
To Kya Koi Sanwaare
O Paalanhaare, Nirgun Aur Nyaare
Tumre Bin Hamra Kaunon Naahin

Jo Suno To Kahe Prabhuji Hamri Hai Binti
Dukhi Jan Ko Dheeraj Do
Haare Nahin Voh Kabhi Dukh Se
Tum Nirbal Ko Raksha Do
Reh Paaye Nirbal Sukh Se
Bhakti Ko Shakti Do
Jag Ke Jo Swami Ho, Itni To Araj Suno
Hai Path Mein Andhiyaare
Dedo Vardaan Mein Ujiyaare
O Paalanhaare, Nirgun Aur Nyaare
Tumre Bin Hamra Kaunon Naahin
Humri Uljhan Suljhaao Bhagwan
Tumre Bin Hamra Kaunon Naahin

~~~
~~~

Kanha Kanha Aan Padi Main

Kanha, Kanha Aan Padi Main Tere Dwar
Mohe Chakar Samjh Nihar

Tu Jise Chahe Aisi Nahi Main
Ha Teri Radha Jaisi Nahi Main
Phir Bhi Hoon Jaisi Waisi Nahi Main
Krishna Mohe Dekh To Le Ek Bar

Bund Hi Bund Main Pyar Ki Chunkar
Pyasi Rahi Par Layi Hu Girdhar
Tut Hi Jaye Aas Ki Gagar Mohana
Aisi Kakariya Nahi Mar
Mati Ka Roya Swarn Bana Lo
Tan Ko Mere Charno Se Laga Lo
Murli Samjh Hatho Me Utha Lo
Sochona Kachu Ab Hey Krishan Murar

~~~

Mithe Ras Se Bharori

Mithe Ras Se Bharori, Raadha Raani Laage
Raadha Raani Laage
Mane Kaaro Kaaro, Yamunaji-No Paani Laage

Yamunaji To Kaadi Kaadi, Raadha Gori Gori
Vrindavan Mein Dhoom Machave, Barsane Ki Chori
Vraj Dhaam Raadhajuki, Vraj Dhaani Laage,
Vraj Dhaani Laage
Mane Pyaaro Pyaaro, Yamunaji-No Paani Laage
Mithe Ras Se Bharori, Raadha Raani Laage,
Raadha Raani Laage
Mane Kaaro Kaaro, Yamunaji-No Paani Laage
Kaanha Nit Murali Me Tere, Sumire Baaram Baar
~~~

Kotin Roop Dhare Man Mohan, Kahu Na Paave Paar
Roop Rang Ki Chabili, Pata Raani Laage, Pata Raani Laage
Mane Pyaaro Pyaaro, Yamunaji-No Paani Laage
Mithe Ras Se Bharori, Raadha Raani Laage
Raadha Raani Laage

Mane Kaaro Kaaro, Yamunaji-No Paani Laage
Na Bhaave Maney Maakhan Misri, Ab Na Koi Mithai
Maari Jeebhariya Ne Bhaave Ab To Raadha Naama Malai
Vrasa Bhanu Ki Lali To, Guna Dhaani Laage
Guna Dhaani Laage
Mane Pyaaro Pyaaro, Yamunaji-No Paani Laage
Mithe Ras Se Bharori, Raadha Raani Laage
Raadha Raani Laage
Mane Kaaro Kaaro, Yamunaji-No Paani Laage

Raadha Raadha Naam Ratat Hai, Jo Nar Aatho Yaam
Jinki Baadha Dur Karat Hai, Raadha Raadha Naam
Raadha Naam Me Saphal, Zindagaani Laage
Zindagani Laage
Mane Pyaaro Pyaaro, Yamunaji-No Paani Laage
Mithe Ras Se Bharori, Raadha Raani Laage
Raadha Raani Laage
Mane Kaaro Kaaro, Yamunaji-No Paani Laage
Mithe Ras Se Bharori, Raadha Raani Laage
Raadha Raani Laage
Mane Pyaaro Pyaaro, Yamunaji-No Paani Laage

~~~

Yashomati Maiyaa Se

Yashomati Maiyaa Se Bole Nandalaala
Raadha Kyon Gori Main Kyon Kaala
Yashomati Maiyaa Se, Bole Nandalaala
Raadha Kyon Gori, Main Kyon Kaala
~~~

Boli Muskaati Maiya, Lalan Ko Bataaya
Kaali Andhiyari Aadhi, Raat Men Tu Aaya
Laadala Kanhaiya Meraa,
Ho.. Laadala Kanhaiya Meraa,
Kaali Kamali Vaala Isi Lie Kaala
Yashomati Maiya Se Bole Nandalaala
Raadha Kyon Gori Main Kyon Kaala

Boli Muskaati Maiya, Sun Mere Pyaare
Gori Gori Raadhika Ke, Nain Kajaraare
Kaale Nainon Vaali Ne Ho..
Kaale Nainon Vaali Ne,
Aisa Jaadu Daala Isi Lie Kaala

Yashomati Maiya Se Bole Nandalaala
Raadha Kyon Gori Main Kyon Kaala

~~~

Hey Govinda

Hey Govind Hey Gopal, Hey Dya Needhan
Hey Govind Hey Gopal, Hey Dya Needhan
Hey Govind Hey Gopal Hey Govind Hey Gopal
Hey Dya Needhan
Hey Govind Hey Gopal Hey Govind Hey Gopal
Hey Daya Needhan

Paran Naath Anath Sake, Paran Naath Anath Sake
Paran Naath Anath Sake, Deen Darad Niihal
Hey Govind Hey Gopal Hey Govind Hey Gopal
Hey Daya Needhan

Hey Samarath Agamye Puran
Hey Samarath Agamye Puran
Hey Samarath Agamye Puran Moh Maya Dhar
Hey Govind Hey Gopal Hey Govind Hey Gopal
Hey Daya Needhan
~~~

Aand Kup Maha Bhayan Aand Kup Maha Bhayan
Aand Kup Maha Bhayan Nanak Par Uttar
Hey Govind Hey Gopal, Hey Govind Hey Gopal
Hey Dya Needhan

Hey Govind Hey Gopal Hey Govind Hey Gopal
Hey Daya Needhan.

~~~

JAI MADAVA MADAN MURARI

Jai Madhav Madan Murari Jai Madhav Madan Murari
Jai Madhav Madan Murari
Jai Madhav Madan Murari
Jai Keshav Kalimalhari Jai Keshav Kalimalhari
Jai Keshav Kalimalhari
Jai Madhav Madan Murari Jai Madhav Madan Murari

Sundar Kundal Nayan Vishala
Sundar Kundal Nayan Vishala
Sundar Kundal Nayan Vishala
Gale Sohe Vaijantimala, Gale Sohe Vaijantimala
Ya Chav Ki Balihari, Ya Chav Ki Balihari
Jai Madhav Madan Murari Jai Madhav Madan murari

Kabhun Loot Loot Bagi Khayo
Kabhun Madhuvan Ras Rachayo
Kabhun Madhuvan Ras Rachayo
Nachat Vipin Bihari Nachat Vipin Bihari
Jai Madhav Madan Murari Jai Madhav Madan Murari.

Karuna Kar Dropadi Pukari Karuna Kar Dropadi Pukari
Pat Me Lipat Gaye Banwari Pat Me Lipat Gaye Banwari
Nirakh Rahe Narnari Nirakh Rahe Narnari
Jai Madhav Madan Murari, Jai Madhav Madan Murari

~~~

Shree Radhey Govinda

Shree Radhey Govinda, Man Bhaj Le
Hari Ka Pyara Naam Hai
Gopala Hari Ka Pyara Naam Hai,
Nandlala Hari Ka Pyara Naam Hai

Mor Mukut Sir Dalban Mala Kesar Tilak Lagayre
Vrindaban Ki Kunj Galin Mein Sabko Naach Nachaye
Shree Radhey Govinda

Giridhar Nagar Kehti Meera Sur Ko Shyamal Bhaya
Tukaram Aur Naam dev Ne Vitthal Vitthal Gaya
Shree Radhey Govinda
Narsi Ne Kartaal Baja Ke Sanwariya Ko Rijhaya
Shabari apne Hanthon Se Prabhu Ko Ber Khilaya
Shree Radhey Govinda

Radha Shakti Bina Na Koi Shyamal Darshan Paaye
Aaradhan Kar Radhey Radhey Kanha Bhage Aaye
Shree Radhey Govinda

Simran Ka Ras Jisko Aaya Wo Hi Jaane Man Mein
Nirakaar Sakaar Hot re Bhagaton Ke Aangan Mein
Shree Radhey Govinda

Shyam Salona Kunj Bihari Natwar Leela Dhari
Antarwasi Hare Avinasi Lage Sharan Tihari
Shree Radhey Govinda

~~~
~~~

Banwari Re

Banwari Re Jine Ka Sahara Tera Naam Re
Mujhe Duniya Walon Se Kya Kaam Re

Jhoothi Duniya Jhoote Bandhan Jhoothi Hai Ye Maaya
Jhootha Saans Ka Aana Jaana Jhoothi Hai Yeh Kaaya
O Yahan Sancho Tero Naam Re

Rang Mein Tere Rang Gayi Giridhar
Chhod Diya Jag Saara
Ban Gayi Tere Prem Ki Jogan Leke Man Ektaara
O Mujhe Pyara Tera Dhaam Re

Darshan Tera Jis Din Paaun Har Chinta Mit Jaaye
Jeevan Mera In Charnon Mein Aas Ki Jyot Jalaye
O Meri Bah Pakad Lo Shyam Re

~~~

Jai Radha Madhav

Jai Radha Madhav Jai Kunj Bihari
Jai Radha Madhav Jai Kunj Bihari

Jai Gopi Jan Wallabh Jai Gopi Jan Wallabh
Jai Gopi Jan Wallabh Jai Gopi Jan Wallabh
Jai Gopi Jan Wallabh Jai Giridhar Hari

Jai Radha Madhav Jai Kunj Bihari
Jai Radha Madhav Jai Kunj Bihari

Yashoda Nandan Braj Jan Ranjan
Yashoda Nandan Braj Jan Ranjan
Jamuna Teer Ban Chari

Jai Radha Madhav Jai Kunj Bihari
Jai Radha Madhav Jai Kunj Bihari
~~~

Hare Krishna Hare Krishna Krishna Krishna Hare Hare
Hare Krishna Hare Krishna Krishna Krishna Hare Hare
Hare Rama Hare Rama Rama Rama Hare Hare
Hare Rama Hare Rama Rama Rama Hare Hare

~~~

YASHODA KA LAAL YE TO KRISHNA KANHAIYA

Yashoda Ka Laal Ye To Krishna Kanhaiya

Jag Ka Paalanhaar Kanha Bansi Ka Bajaiya
Jai Jai Krishna
Teri Suratiya Man Mein Samayi
Aan Milo Ab Krishna Kanhayi
Tere Daras Ki Lagan Ki Lagayi
Ab To Daras Do Krishna Kanhayi
Teri Muraliya Jab Jab Baaje
Koyal Bhi Gaaye Mayura Nache
Pat Pitambar Tan Par Saaje
Mor Mukut Makarakrit Raaje
Aao Dharam Ka Alakh Jagao
Bhakton Ka Santaap Mitaye
Is Jag Mein Prabhu Prem Badhao
Geeta Ka Hari Vachan Nibhao
Yada Yada Hi Dharmasya
Tadatmananm Srijamyaham
Paritranaya Sadhunaam Vinasayacha Dushkrita
Dharma Sansthapanarth

~~~

Krishna Jinka Naam

Krishna Jinka Naam Hai, Gokul Jinka Dhaam Hai
Aise Shri Bhagwan Ko
Aise Shri Bhagwan Ko
Barambar Pranam Hai,
Barambar Pranam Hai
Yashoda Jinki Maiya Hai,
Nandji Ba Bhaiya Hai
Aise Shri Gopal Ko,
Aise Shri Gopal Ko
Barambar Pranam Hai,
Barambar Pranam Hai

Loot Loot Dadhi Makhan Khayo
Loot Loot Dadhi Makhan Khayo
Gwal Baal Sang Dhenu Charayo
Aise Leela Dham Ko
Aise Leela Dham Ko,
Aise Leela Dham ko
Barambar Pranam Hai,
Barambar Pranam hai

Dhrupad Suta Ko Laaj Bachayo,
Rahashgaj Ko Fand Chhudayo
Aise Kripa Dhaam Ko,
Aise Kripa Dhaam Ko
Barambar Pranam Hai,
Barambar Pranam Hai

~~~

Banke Bihari Krishna Murari Meri Bari Kaha Chhupe

Banke Bihari Krishna Murari Meri Bari Kaha Chhupe
Banke Bihari Krishna Murari Meri Bari Kaha Chhupe
~~~

Dharshan Deejo Sharan Me Lijo
Dharshan Deejo Sharan Me Lijo
Hum Balihari Kaha Chhupe

Banke Bihari Krishna Murari Meri Bari Kaha Chhupe
Banke Bihari Krishna Murari Meri Bari Kaha Chhupe
Aankh Micholi Hamein Na Bhaye
Jag Maya Ke Jaal Bichhaye
Raas Racha Kar Bansi Baja Kar
Dhenu Charakar Preet Lagakar
Natwar Nagar Nishthur Chhaliya
Leela Dhari Kaha Chhupe

Banke Bihari Krishna Murari Meri Bari Kaha Chhupe
Banke Bihari Krishna Murari Meri Bari Kaha Chhupe
Dharshan Deejo Sharan Me Lijo
Dharshan Deejo Sharan Me Lijo
Hum Balihari Kaha Chhupe

Banke Bihari Krishna Murari Meri Bari kaha Chhupe
Banke Bihari Krishna Murari Meri Bari Kaha Chhupe

Sarv Vyapak Tum Avinashi
Jal Thal Gagan Gabighat Vashi
Yog Suna Kar Rath Ko Chala Kar

Kaha Kho Gaye Hamako Lubha Kar
Govind Govind Meera Gaye
Gadkadhari Kaha Chhupe

Banke Bihari Krishna Murari Meri Bari Kaha Chhupe
Banke Bihari Krishna Murari Meri Bari Kaha Chhupe

Dharshan Deejo Sharan Me Lijo
Dharshan Deejo Sharan Me Lijo
Hum Balihari Kaha Chhupe

Banke Bihari Krishna Murari Meri Bari Kaha Chhupe
Banke Bbihari Krishna Murari Meri Bari Kaha Chhupe

~~~
~~~

RAMA BHAJANS

Seeya Ram Mai Sab Jag Jane

Seeya Ram Mai Sab Jag Jane,

Kar Ho Pranam Jori Jogi Pani
Japa He Naam Jana Aar An Bhare
Mita Heko Ke Sankat Hoye Sukare
Naam Leto Bhav Sindu Sukaaye
Karo Vichar Sujan Mana Maaye

Aankh Mari Ughde Tya Sitaram Dekhu,
Dhanya Maru Jeevan Krupa Ani Lekhu,
Ram Krishna Ram Krishna Rasna Uchare,
Hari No Anand Mare Antare Aave.
Ramayan Geeta Mari Anatar Aankho,
Hari A E Didhi Chey Mane Udvani Pankho,
Ram Na Vichoro Mari Adhalak Nalu,
Gavu Mare Nishdin Raan Nu J Ganu.

Prabhu Na Bhakto Mare Saga Re Sambandhi,
Chuti Granthi Tuti Mari Maya Ni Bandhi,
Suddh Bhakti Vadhe Mari Poornima Jevi,
Prabhu Santo Aashih Sada Dejo Avi.

Jene Shri Ram Charan Ras Chakhiyo,
Ane Sansar Ne Mithya Kari Nakhiyo,
Alas Ne Jane Chey Sukdev Jogi,
Kaik Jane Chey Pelo Narsaiyo Bhogi

Tera Ram Ji Karenge Beda Paar

Tera Ram Ji Karenge Beda Paar
Udasi Man Kahe Ko Ddare

Naiya Teri Ram Hawale
Lehar Lehar Hari Aap Sambhale
Hari Aap Hi Uthave Tera Bhar
Udasi Man Kahe Ko Dare

Kabu Mein Majhdhar Usi Ke
Hanthon Mein Patwaar Usi Ke
Teri Haar Bhi Rahi Hai Teri baat
Udsi Man Kahe Ko Dare

Sahaj Kinara Mil Jaayega
Param Sahara Mil jaayega
Dori saup Ke Du dekh Le Ek baar
Udasi man kahe ko dare

~~~

Mujhe Apani Sharan Mein Le Lo Raam

Mujhe Apani Sharan Mein Le Lo Raam, Le Lo Raam

Lochan Man Mein Jagah Na Ho To
Jugal CharaN Mein Le Lo Raam, Le Lo Raam
Mujhe Apani Sharan Mein Le Lo Raam

Jiivan Deke Jaal Bichhaayaa
Rach Ke Maayaa Naach Nachayaa
Chintaa Meri Tabhi Rukegi
Jab Chintan Mein Le Lo Raam, Le Lo Raam
Mujhe Apani Sharan Mein Le Lo Raam

Tu Ne Laakhon Paapi Taare
Meri Baari Baazi Haare, Baazi Haare
~~~

Mere Paas Na Punya Ki Puunji
Padapuujan Mein Le Lo Raam, Le Lo Raam
Mujhe Apani Sharan Mein Le Lo Raam

Raam Hey Raam, Raam Hey Raam
Dar Dar Bhatakuun Ghar Ghar Atakuun
Kahaan Kahaan Apanaa Sar Patakuun
Is Jiivan Mein Milo Na Tum To, Raam He Raam
Is Jiivan Mein Milo Na Tum To
Mujhe Maran Mein Le Lo Raam, Le Lo Raam
Mujhe Apani Sharan Mein Le Lo Raam

~~~

Prem Mudita Mana Se Kaho

Prem Mudita Mana Se Kaho, Rama Rama Ram,
Shree Rama Rama Ram, Shree Rama Rama Ram

Paap Kate, Dukha Mite, Leke Rama Naam
Bhava Samudra, Sukhada Naav, Ek Rama Naam

Prem Mudita Mana Se Kaho Rama Rama Ram
Shree Rama Rama Ram
Shree Rama Rama Ram

Param Shanti, Sukha Nidhaana, Divya Rama Naam
Niraadhaara Ko Aadhar, Ek Rama Naam

Prem Mudita Mana Se Kaho Rama Rama Ram,
Shree Rama Rama Ram
Shree Rama Rama Ram

Parama Gopya, Parama Divya, Mantra Rama Naam
Shanta Hrudaya, Sadaa Vasata, Ek Rama Naam

Prem Mudita Mana Se Kaho Rama Rama Ram,
Shree Rama Rama Ram
~~~

Shree Rama Rama Ram

Maata Pita, Bandhu Sakha, Sab Hi Rama Naam
Bhakta Janara, Jeevan Dhana, Ek Rama Naam

Prem Mudita Mana Se Kaho Rama Rama Ram,
Shree Rama Rama Ram
Shree Rama Rama Ram

~~~

Chali Naav Ganga Ki Dharaa

Chali Naav Ganga Ki Dharaa
Siya Ram Lakhan Ko Paar Utara
Prabhu Dene Lage Naav Utrai Kevat Kahe Nahi Raghurai

Paar Kiya Maine Tumko
Ab Tu Mohe Paar Kare
Nainan Me Siyaram Basoji Mere
Janak Nandini Jagad Vandini Raghunayak Ghanashyam
Kanak Mandap Tale Ratan Simhasan Jugal Murti Abhiram
Sarayu Ke Tir Ayodhya Nagari Citrakut Nij Dham
Tulsidas Prabhu Ki Chhabi Nirakhat Lajat Koti Shatkam

~~~

Paayoji Maine, Raam Raṭana Dhana Paayo

Paayoji Maine, Raam Raṭana Dhana Paayo
Paayoji Maine
Bastu Amolika, Di Mere Satguru
Bastu Amolika, Di Mere Satguru
Kirpaa Karo Apanaayo
Paayoji Maine Kirpaa Kar Apanaayo

Paayoji Maine Raam Raṭana Dhana Paayo

Janam Janam Ki, Punji Paaye
Jaga Mein Sabhee Khovaayo
Paayoji Maine, Jaga Mein Sabhee Khovaayo
Paayoji Maine Raam Raṭana Dhana Paayo

Kharchai Nahin Kuteh, Chora Na Luteh
Dina Dina Baḍhata Savaayo
Paayoji Maine, Dina Dina Baḍhata Savaayo
Paayoji Maine Raam Raṭana Dhana Paayo

Sat Ki Naava Khevatiyaa Satguru
Bhavasaagara Tara Aayo
Paayoji Maine, Bhavasaagara Tara Aayo
Paayoji Maine Raam Raṭana Dhana Paayo

Meeraa Ke Prabhu Giridhara Naagara
Harakha Harakha Jasa Gaayo
Paayoji Maine, Harakha Harakha Jasa Gaayo
Paayoji Maine Raam Raṭana Dhana Paayo

~~~

Mere Man Mein Hain Ram

Mere Man Mein Hain Ram Mere Tan Mein Hain Ram
Mere Naino Ki Nagariya Mein Ram Hain
Mere Rom Rom Ke Hain Ram Hi Ramaiya
Sanson Ke Swami Mere Naiya Ke Khivaiya
Kan Kan Mein Hain Ram Tribhuwan Mein Hain Ram
Neele Nabh Ki Atariya Mein Ram Hain

Janam Janam Ka Jinse Hai Naata
Man Jinke Pal Chhin Gun Gaata
Gun Dhun Mein Hain Ram Run Jhun Mein Hain Ram
Saare Jaga Ki Dagariya Mein Ram Hain

Jahankahin Dekhu Wahin Ram Ki Hai Maaya
~~~

Sab Hi Ke Saath Shree Ram Ji Ki Saaya
Sumiran Mein Hain Ram Darshan Mein Hain Ram
Mere Man Ki Muraliya Mein Ram Hain

~~~

Janam Safal Hoga Re Bande

Janam Safal Hoga Re Bande, Mann Mein Ram Basale
Janam Safal Hoga Re Bande, Mann Mein Ram Basale
Bolo Ram Jai Jai Ram Bolo Ram
Janam safal hoga bande man mein ram basale,
Bolo Ram Jai Jai Ram Bolo Ram

He Ram Naam Ke Moti Ko Saanso Ki Maala Bana Le,
Ram Patit Paawan Karunakar Aur Sadaa Sukh Dataa
Bolo Ram Jai Jai Ram Bolo Ram
Ram Patit Paawan Karunakar Aur Sadaa Sukh Dataa
Saras Suhavan Ati Manbhaavan Ram Se Preet Lagale,
Man Mein Ram Basale
Bolo Ram Jai Jai Ram Bolo Ram

Moh Maya Hai Jhuta Bandhan Tyag Use Tu Prani,
Ram Ki Jyot Jalaa Kar Apna Bhag Jagaa Le,
Man Mein Ram Basale,
Bolo Ram Jai Jai Ram Bolo Ram

Ram Bhajan Mein Doob Kay Apni Nirmal Kar Le Kaya,
Ram Naam Se Preet Lagaa Kay Jeevan Paar Laga Le,
Man Mein Ram Basale,
Bolo Ram Jai Jai Ram Bolo Ram

~~~

Raghupati Raghav Raja Ram

Raghupati Raghav Raja Ram
Patita Pavan Sitaram

Sitaram, Sitaram,
Bhaj Pyare Mana Sitaram
Raghupati Raghav Raja Ram
Patita Pavan Sitaram

Ishwar Allah Tero Nam,
Sabako Sanmati De Bhagawan
Raghupati Raghav Raja Ram
Patita Pavan Sitaram

Mukhmen Tulsi Ghatamen Ram,
Jab Bolo Tab Sitaram
Raghupati Raghav Raja Ram
Patita Pavan Sitaram

Hathose Karo Gharka Kam,
Mukhase Bolo Sitaram
Raghupati Raghav Raja Ram
Patita Pavan Sitaram

Kaushalyaka Vhala Ram,
Dashrathji ka Pyara Ram
Raghupati Raghav Raja Ram
Patita Pavan Sitaram
Bansivala Hay Ghanshyam,
Dhanushya Dhari Sitaram
Raghupati Raghav Raja Ram
Patita Pavan Sitaram

~~~

Shree Ramacandra Kripalu

Shri Ramacandra Kripalu Bhaju Mana
Harana Bhava Bhaya Darunam
Navakanja-Locana Kanja-Mukha
Kara-Kanja Pada-Kanjarunam
~~~

Kandarpa Aganita Amita Chavi
Navalina Niraj Sundaram
Patapita Manahu Tarita Ruchi Suchi
Naumi Janaka-Sutavaram

Bhaju Dinabhandu Dinesha danava
Daitya-Vansha Nikandanam
Raghunanda Anandakanda, Kaushala
Chanda Dasharatha-Nandanam

Sira Mmukuta Kundala Tilaka Caru
Udaru Anga Vibhushanam;
Ajanu Bhuja Sharacapa Dhara,
Sangrama-Jita Khara-Dhushanam

Iti Vadati Tulasidasa Shakara
Shesha Munimana Ranjanam
Mama Hridaya-Kanja Nivasa Kuru
Kamadi Khaladala Ganjanam

~~~

Bhaye Pragat Kripala Dindayala

Bhaye Pragat Kripala Dindayala, Kaushalya Hitkari
Harshit Mahtari Muni Man Haari, Adbhut Rup Vichari

Lochan Abhirama Tanu Ghanshyama,
Nij Aayudh Bhuj Chaari
Bhushan Vanmala Nayan Bisala, Sobhasindhu Kharari
Kah Dui Kar Jori Astuti Tori, Kehi Vidhi Karao Ananta
Maya Gun Gyana Tit Amaana, Ved Puran Bhananta
Karuna Sukh Sagar Sab Gun Aagar,
Jehi Gaavahi Sruti Santa
So Mam Hit Laagi Jan Anuraagi Bhayao Pragat Srikanta
Brahmand Nikaya Nirmit Maya, Rom Rom Prati Ved kahe
Mam Ur So Basi Yah Uphasi,
Sunat Dhir Mati Thir Na Rahe
~~~

Upja Jab Gyana Prabhu Muskana, Charit Bahut Bidhi Kinh Chahe
Kahi Katha Suhai Maatu Bujhai,
Jehi Prakar Sut Prem Lahe
Maata Puni Boli So Mati Doli, Tajahu Taat Yah Roopa
Kije Sisu Lila Ati Priysila, Yah Sukh Param Anoopa
Suni Bachan Sujana Rodan Thana,
Hoyi Balak Surbhoopa
Yah Charit Je Gaavahi Haripad Paawahi,
Te Na Parahi Bhawkoopa

~~~

Mangal Bhavan Amangal Haree

Mangal Bhavan Amangal Haari
Drabahu Su Dasharath Achar Bihari
Raam Siya Raam Siya Raam Jai Jai Raam
Raam Siya Raam Siya Raam Jai Jai Raam

Ho Hoi Hai Wohi Jo Raam Rachi Raakha
Ko Kari Tarak Badhave Saakha
Raam Siya Raam Siya Raam Jai Jai Raam
Ho Dheeraj Dharam Mitra Aru Naari

Aapad Kaal Parakhiye Chaari
Raam Siya Raam Siya Raam Jai Jai Raam

Ho Jehike Jehi Par Satya Sanehu
So Tehi Milay Na Kachhu Sandehu

Ho Jaaki Rahi Bhawana Jaisi
Prabhu Murati Dekhi Tin Taisi

Ho Raghukul Reet Sada Chali Aayi
Praan Jaaye Par Vachan Na Jaayi
Raam Siya Raam Siya Raam Jai Jai Raam, Raam
Raam Siya Raam Siya Raam Jai Jai Raam
~~~

Ho Hari Anant Hari Katha Ananta
Kahahi Sunahi Bahuvidhi Sab Santa
Raam Siya Raam Siya Raam Jai Jai Raam, Raam
Raam Siya Raam Siya Raam Jai Jai Raam
Raam Siya Raam Siya Raam Jai Jai Raam.

~~~

Thumak Chalat Ramchandra

Thumaka Chalat Raamachandra Baajat Paijaniyaan

Kilaki Kilaki Uthat Dhaay Girata Bhuumi Latapataay
Dhaaya Maat God Let Dasharathakii Raniyaan

Anchala Raja Anga Jhaari Vividh Bhaanti So Dulaari
Tana Mana Dhana Vaari Vaari Kahata Mridu Bachaniyaan
Vidrumase Arun Adhara Bolata Mukha Madhura Madhura
Subhaga Naasi Kaamen Chaaru Latakata Latakaniyaan

Tulasiidaas Ati Aananda Dekhake Mukhaaravinda
Raghuvara Chhabike Samaana Raghuvara Chhabi Baniyaan

~~~

Rom Rom Mein Basane Wale Raam

Hey Rom Rom Mein Basane Wale Ram
Jagata Ke Swami, He Antaryami
Main Tujhse Kya Mangu

Aas Ka Bandhan Tod Chuki Hun
Tujh Par Sabakuchh Chhod Chuki Hun
Nath Mere Main Kyo Kuchh Sochu
Tu Jane Tera Kam

Tere Charan Ki Dhool Jo Paye
Wo Kankar Heera Ho Jaye
Bhag Mere Jo Maine Paya
In Charanon Mein Dham

Bhed Tera Koi Kya Pahachane
Jo Tujh Sa Ho, Wo Tujhe Jane
Tere Kiye Ko Hum Kya Dewe
Bhale Bure Ka Nam
Jagata Ke Swami, He Antaryami

Hey Rom Rom Mein Basane Wale Ram
Jagata Ke Swami, He Antaryami
Main Tujhse Kya Mangu

~~~

Hey Ram, Hey Ram, Hey Ram

Hey Ram, Hey Ram, Hey Ram, Hey Ram,
Jag Mein Sacho Tero Naam.
Hey Ram...

Tu Hi Mata, Tu Hi Pita Hai;
Tu Hi Hai Radha Ka Shyam.

Tu Antaryami, Saba Ka Swami;
Tere Charno Me Charo Dham.

Tu Hi Bigare, Tu Hi Savare,
Es Jag Ke Ssare Kaam.

Tu Hi Jagdatta, Vishava Vidhata;
Tu Hi Subah Ho, Tu Hi Sham.

Hey Ram, Hey Ram, Hey Ram, Hey Ram,
Jag Me Sacho Tero Naam.

~~~

SHIVA BHAJANS

Chhote Chhote Shivji

Chhote Chhote Shivji, Chhote Chhote Ram
Chhoto So Mero Madan Gopal

Kya Rahe Shivji, Kya Rahe Ram
Kya Rahe Mero Madan Gopal
Kailash Rahe Shivji, Ayodhya Rahe Ram
Birajmein Rahe Mero Madan Gopal
Chhote Chhote Shivji, Chhote Chhote Ram
Chhoto So Mero Madan Gopal

Kya Khaaye Shivji, Kya Khaaye Ram
Kya Khaaye Mero Madan Gopal
Dhatoora Khaaye Shivji, Laddoo Khaaye Ram
Mitho Mitho Makhan Khaaye Madan Gopal
Chhote Chhote Shivji, Chhote Chhote Ram
Chhoto So Mero Madan Gopal

Kya Piye Shivji, Kya Piye Ram
Kya Piye Mero Madan Gopal
Bhang Piye Shivji, Doodh Piye Ram
Mithi Mithi Chhaas Piye Madan Gopal
Chhote Chhote Shivji, Chhote Chhote Ram
Chhoto So Mero Madan Gopal

Kya Kare Shivji, Kyan Kare Ram,
Kya Kare Mero Madan Gopal,
Dhyaan Dhare Shivji, Raaj Kare Ram,
Raas Rachaave Mero Madan Gopal,

Chhote Chhote Shivji, Chhote Chhote Ram,
Chhoto So Mero Madan Gopal

~~~

Hey Shiv Shankar Hey Karunakar

Hey Shivsankar Hey Karunakar Suniye Araz Humari
Bhav Saagar Se Paar Utaaro Aaye Sharan Tihari
Chandra Lalaat Bhabhut Ramaye Kati Ambar Dhari
Kar Mein Dmaru Gale Bhujanga Nandi Thade Dware
Hey Gangadhr Daras Dikha Do Hey Bhole Bhandari
Janam Maran Ke Tum Ho Swami Hey Shankar Avinashi
Kan Kan Mein Hai Roop Tumhara Hery Bhole Kailashi
Charan Sharan Mein Aaya Jogi Rakhiyo Laaj humari

~~~

Om Namah Shivaya

Om Namah Shivay, Om Namah Shivay
Har Har Bhole Namah Shivay

Rameshwara Shiva Rameshwara
Hara Hara Bhole Namah Shivay
Om Namah Shivay, Om Namah Shivay,
Har Har Bhole Namah Shivay

Ganga Dhara Shiva Ganga Dhara
Hara Hara Bhole Namah Shivaya
Om Namah Shivay, Om Namah Shivay
Har Har Bhole Namah Shivay

Jatadhara Shiva Jatadhara
Hara Hara Bhole Namah Shivay
Om Namah Shivay, Om Namah Shivay
Har Har Bhole Namah Shivay
Someshwar Shiva Someshwar
Hara Hara Bhole Namah Shivay
Om Namah Shivay, Om Namah Shivay
Har Har Bhole Namah Shivay

Vishweshvara Shiva Vishweshvara
Hara Hara Bhole Namah Shivay
Om Namah Shivay, Om Namah Shivay
Har Har Bhole Namah Shivay

Koteshwara Shiva Koteshwara
Hara Hara Bhole Namah Shivay
Om Namah Shivay, Om Namah Shivay
Har Har Bhole Namah Shivay

~~~

Shiva Shambho

Shiva Shambho Shambho, Shiva Shambho Mahadeva
Hara Hara Hara Hara Mahadeva
Shiva Shambho Mahadeva

Gangadhara Hara Shambho, Gauri Manohar Shambho
Shiva Om (3) Namah Shiva
Shiva Shambho Shambho, Shiva Shambho Mahadeva
Hara Hara Hara Hara Mahadeva
Shiva Shambho Mahadeva
~~~

Nandi Vahana Shambho, Natana Manohar Shambho
Shiva Om (3) Namah Shiva
Shiva Shambho Shambho, Shiva Shambho Mahadeva
Hara Hara Hara Hara Mahadeva,
Shiva Shambho Mahadeva

Halahar Dhar Shambho, Anath Natha Shambho
Vishweshwar Har Shambho, Gauri Manohar Shambho
Shiva Shambho Shambho, Shiva Shambho Mahadeva
Hara Hara Hara Hara Mahadeva,
Shiva Shambho Mahadeva

Bolo Naatha Uma Pathey

~~~

Kailash Vasi Dewata

Jai Vishwanath Om Namah Shivaye

Kailash Vasi Dewata Deenanath Hai Vishwanath Hai
Vaamang Sohe Ambika Deenanath Hai Vishwanath hain
Jayati Jaya Ambe Bhawani Jayati Jaya Shiv Pashupati

Shiv Bhaal Sohe Chandrama Sohe Jata Bhagirathi
Prabhu Neelkanth Digambara Shobha Kul Chhavi Raj Ki
Naareesh Jan Gan Keerti Ka Deenath Hai Vishwanath
Vaamang Sohe ...

Shiv Se Hi Sohe Jeev Van Sohe Sakal Ye Vasundhara
Parvat Salil Sagar Nadi Mein Vyapt Shiv Parmeshwara
Shrishti Mein Jinse Bhavyata Deenanath Hai
Vishwanath Vaamang Sohe ...

Prabhu Ashutosh Tridosh Har Kalyaan Karte Sarvada
Damru Ke Dim Dim Taal Par Karte Hai Taandav Shiv Sada
~~~

Bholi Hai Jinki Udaarata Deenanath Hain Vishwanath Hain
Vaamang Sohe ...

Mathura Ayodhya Haridwar Dwarka Avantika Karthi
Puri Saat Hain Moksha Daayini Sabse Badh Kar Hai Kasha

~~~

JAHAN SHIV JI VICHARAN KARTE HAIN

JAI VISHWANATH OM NAMAH SHIVAYE

Jahan Shiv Ji Vicharan Karte Hain
Us Bhoomi Ko Kashi Kehet Hain
Ye Moksha Dayini Kashi Ye Patitpawini Kashi Hai
Hum Kasi Ke Pawan Raj Kan Ko
Nij Apne Sheesh Pe Rakhte Hai

Anandvan Rudravas Ye Shiv Kashi Varanasi
Maha Shmashaan Hai Tapasthali Mukta Bhumi Varanasi
Tripurari Ki Nagari Hai Yeh
Shiv Shambhoo Ki Hai Yeh Pari
Jagvipada Hari Nagari Ganga Tat Bhari Nagari
Jahan Paap Sabhi Ke Mitate Hain
Us Bhoomi Ko Kashi Kehte Hain
Ye Moksha Dayini ....

Shiv Trishool Pe Thehri Hui Hai Param Pawini Yeh Kashi
Param Bhakti Ki Khaan Hai Ye Jan Man Bhaawan Ye Kashi
Sakal Dewata Angin Roop Se Nitya Hi Poojan Karte
Jyotirling Vishweshwar Ji Ka Nit Darshan Karte Rehte
Jahan Vishwanath Ji Baste Hain
Us Bhoomi Ko Kashi Kehte Hain
Ye Mokshadayini ...

~~~

Aaya Shivratri Tyohaar

Aaya Shivratri Tyohaar Chalo Re Shiv Vandan Kare
Vandan Kare Abhinandan Kare
Aaj Hai Gauri Shiv Ka Milan Shivratri Parv Manao Sabhi
Shree Gauri Shankar Ka Darshan Karne
Shivalaya Aao Sabhi
Aao Kar De Shiv Shingaar Chalo Re ...

Shiv Shiv Japta Manwa Humara Dhyan Mein Shiv Sakaar
Baraat Aayi Shiv Shankar Ki Bhoot Pret Nach Karte
Jaikaar
Shiv Dulha Bane Kartaar Chalo Re Shiv Poojan Kare

Thali Mein Chandan Phoolon Ka Haar Haathon Mein
Le Lo Ganga Jali
Abhishek Shankar Ji Ka Karo Pushpanjali Karo Deepanjali
Vrat Kar Lo Tyag Ahaar Chalo Ri Shiv ...

Shiv Ji Ko Pooje Vishnu Aur Brahma
Shiv Ka Hai Ye Sansaar
Shiv Ke Bina Nahi Shrishti Ki Raachana Bhakton Karo
Maan Se Jaijai Kaar
Taar Denge Taaranhaar Chalo Re Shiv...

~~~

Jaya Bhola Bhandari

Jaya Bhola Bhandari Shivhar
Jai Kailash Pati Shivshankar
Sab Jag Ke Hitkari

Nis Din Tera Dhyan Karen Hum Simre Mantra Tumhara
Hey Shiv Shankar Mantra Jagao Hove Ghat Ujiyara
Namami Shankar Namami Shankar
Kripa Karo Tripurari

Shankh Naad Se Shabd Jaga Kar Swar Sangeet Banaya
~~~

Yug Yug Se Ye Shrishti Naache Aisa Damaru Bajaya
Teri Yaad Bhula Ke Jag Mein Dukh Paave Sansaari

Teeno Taap Haran Kar Deta Yeh Trishul Tumhara
Tera Naam Jape Se Jag Mein Milta Mukti Dwara
Mahadev Parbrahma Vidhata Aayen Sharan Tihari

~~~

Awo Baitho Japo Hari Naam

Awo Baitho Japo Hari Naam Shivaji Ki Mandir Mein
Shivaji Ki Mandir, Shivaji Ki Mandir,
Shivaji Ki Mandir Mein

Sona Kay Adumurti Bane Hai,
Sita Aur Shri Raam Shivaji...
Awo Baitho Japo Hari Naam Shivaji Ki Mandir Mein
Shivaji Ki Mandir, Shivaji Ki Mandir,
Shivaji Ki Mandir Mein

Tulsidas Bhajo Bhagawana,
Lakshman Aur Hanuman Shivaji...
Awo Baitho Japo Hari Naam Shivaji Ki Mandir Mein
Shivaji Ki Mandir, Shivaji Ki Mandir,
Shivaji Ki Mandir Mein

Sona Kay Adumurti Bane Hai,
Sita Aur Shri Raam, Shivaji...
Awo Baitho Japo Hari Naam Shivaji Ki Mandir Mein
Shivaji Ki Mandir, Shivaji Ki Mandir,
Shivaji Ki Mandir Mein

Tulsidas Bajo Bhagawana,
Lakshman Aur Hanuman Shivaji...
Awo Baitho Japo Hari Naam Shivaji Ki Mandir Mein
Shivaji Ki Mandir, Shivaji Ki Mandir,
Shivaji Ki Mandir Mein

~~~

HAR GANGA JATAADHARA GAURI SHANKARA

Har Ganga Jataadhara Gauri Shankara
Girijaa Mana Ramanaa
Har Mrityum Jaya Mahaadeva Maheshvara
Mangala Shubha Charanaa
Nandi Vaahanaa Naaga Bhushanaa
Nirupama Guna Sadanaa
Natana Mano Hara Neela Kantha Hari
Neeraja Dala Nayanaa..Aaa Neeraja Dala Nayanaa..Aaa

~~~
~~~

HANUMAAN BHAJANS

CHALE HANUMAAN

Chale Hanuman Yaha Aye,
Shree Ramji Ki Dhoon Machaye

Dhoon Machaye, Aysi Dhoon Machaye
Chale Hanuman Yah Aye..

Sitaram Naam Dhoon Aysi Machaye
Sunker Aye Raghurai Shre Ramji
Chale Hanuman Yah Aye..

Gangaji Aye Jamnaji Aye
Triveni Sangam Aye Ahree Ramji Ki Dhoon Machaye
Chale Hanuman Yah Aye..
Bhakta Janoka Ghar Pawan Karne
Avo aAvo Ne Raghurai Shree Ramji Ki Dhoon Machaye
Chale Hanuman Yah Aye..

Das Janoki Yahi Vinanti
Charan Kamal Balihari Shree Ramji Ki Dhoon Machaye
Chale Hanuman Yah Aye...

~~~
~~~

Jay Jay Jay Hanumana Gosai

Vegi Haro, Hanumana Mahaprabhu
Jo Kachu Sankata Hoye Hamaro
Kauna Sa Sankata Mora Gariba Ko
Jo Tuma Se Nahi Jata Hai Taro
Jay Jay Jay Hanumana Gosai
Kripa Karo, Maharaja

Tana Me Tumhare Shakti Viraje Mana Bhakti Se Bhina
Jo Jana Tumhari Sharana Me Aye Dukha Darada Harlina
Mahavira Prabhu Hama Dukhiyana Ke
Tuma Ho gariba Nivaja, Hanumata

Rama Lakhana Vaidehi Tum Par Sada Rahe Harshaye
Hriday Chirake Rama Siya Ka Darshana Diya Karaye
Do Kara Jora Araja H̃anumanta
Kahiyo Prabhu Se Aja H̃anumata

~~~

Mangal Murti Maaruti Nandan

Mangal Murti Maaruti Nandan,
Sakal Amangal Mool Nikandan
Pavan Tanay Santan Hitkaari
Hriday Viraajat Avadh Bihaari
Mangal Murti Maaruti Nandan
Sakal Amangal Mool Nikandan

Maat Pita Guru Ganpati Shaarad
Shivaa Samet Shambhu Shuk Naarad
Mangal Murti Maaruti Nandan
Sakal Amangal Mool Nikandan
~~~

Charan Kamal Bandau Sab Kaahu
Dehu Raampad Nehu Nibhaahu
Mangal Murti Maaruti Nandan
Sakal Amangal Mool Nikandan

Jai Jai Jai Hanuman Gowsai
Kripa Karo Gurudev Ki Naai
Mangal Murti Maaruti Nandan
Sakal Amangal Mool Nikandan

Bandau Raam Lakhan Baidhehi
Yeh Tulsi Ke Param Sanehi
Mangal Murti Maaruti Nandan
Sakal Amangal Mool Nikandan

~~~

BOLE BOLE HANUMAAN

Bolo Bajrang Bali Ki Jai, Bol Pavanputra Hanumaan Ki Jai
Bole Bole Hanuman Bolo Bhakto Siya Ram

Shri Ram Ke Charno Mein Bante Bigade Kaam
Bole Bole Hanuman Bolo Bhakto Siya Ram
Shri Ram Ke Charno Mein Bante Bigade Kaam

Uski Shobha Hai Vishnu Mein
Uski Shobha Hai Mohan Si
Tulsi Ne Jab Sheesh Jhukaya
Dhanus Bani Kanha Ki Banshi
Ram Hi Maya Ram Hi Jaane, Kan Kan Me Shri Ram
Bole Bole Hanuman Bolo Bhakto Siya Ram
Shri Ram Ke Charno Me Bante Bigade Kaam
Bole Bole Hanuman Bolo Bhakton Siya Ram

Lipat Lipat Ke Ram Charno Mein
Aankho Mein Ganga Jal Bhar Le
Shri Ram To Chhama Sheel Hai
Paapo Ko Swikar Tu Karle
~~~

Shri Ram Ke Charan Kamal Jaise Baikuthi Dham
Bole Bole Hanuman Bolo Bhakto Siya Ram
Shri Ram Ke Charno Me Bante Bigade Kaam
Bole Bole Hanuman Bolo Bhakto Siya Ram

Bol Bol Tu Ram Ramaiya
Jeevan Phir Na Milega Bhaiya
Duniya To Bhram Jaal Hai Murakh
Ram Hi Paar Lagaye Naiyya
Raghav Ke Charno Me, Payega Tu Vishraam
Bole Bole Hanuman Bolo Bhakto Siya Ram
Shri Ram Ke Charno Me Bante Bigade Kaam
Bole Bole Hanuman Bolo Bhakto Siya Ram

Bol Bajrang Bali Ki Jai, Bol Pawan Putra Hanuman Ki Jai
Bole Bole Hanuman Bolo Bhakto Siya Ram
Shri Ram Ke Charno Mein Bante Bigade Kaam

Bole Bole Hanuman Bolo Bhakto Siya Ram
Bol Bajrang Bali Ki Jai, Bol Pawan Putra Hanuman Ki Jai

~~~

Hey Dukh Bhanjan

Hey Dukh Bhanjan Maruti Nandan,
Sun Lo Meri Pukar Pawansut Vinti Baarambaar

Ast Siddhi Naw Nidhi Ke Data
Dukhiyon Ke Tum Bhagya Vidhata

Siya Ram Ke Kaj Sawaren Mera Kar Uddhar
Pawansut Vinati Barambar
Hey Dukh Bhanjan Maruti Nandan,
Sun Lo Meri Pukar Pawansut Vinati Baarambaar

Pawansut Vinati Barambar
Aprampar Hai Shakti Tumhari
Tum Par Reejhe Awadh Bihari
~~~

Bhakti Bhav Se Dhyaoo Tohe
Kar Dukhho Se Par Pawansut Vinati Baarambaar
Hey Dukh Bhanjan Maruti Nandan,
Sun Lo Meri Pukar Pawansut Vinati Baarambaar
Pawansut Vinati Barambar

Japu Nirantar Naam Tihaara
Ab Nahi Chodun Tera Dwar
Ram Bhakt Mohe Sharan Me Lije
Bhav Saagar Se Taar
Pawansut Vinati Baarambaar

Hey Dukh Bhanjan Maruti Nandan Sun Lo Meri Pukar
Pawansut Vinati Baarambaar

~~~

Veera Hanumana

Veera Hanumana, Ati Balwana, Ram Nama Rasiya Re
Hei Hei Hei Hei Prabhu Mana Basiya Re
Ho Ho Ho Ho Prabhu Manabasiya Re

Ram Lakshman Jaanki, Jai Bolo Hanuman Ki
Ram Lakshman Jaanki, Jai Bolo Hanuman Ki

Veera Hanumana, Ati Balwana, Ram Nama Rasiya Re
Hei Hei Hei Hei Prabhu Mana Basiya Re
Ho Ho Ho Ho Prabhu Manabasiya Re

Sita Ram Jai Sita Ram, Bhaja Pyare Tu Sita Rama
Sita Ram Jai Sita Ram, Bhaja Pyare Tu Sita Rama
Veera Hanumana, Ati Balwana, Ram Nama Rasiya Re
Hei Hei Hei Hei Prabhu Mana Basiya Re
Ho Ho Ho Ho Prabhu Manabasiya Re

Raghupati Raghava Raja Ram, Patita Pavan Sita Ram
Raghupati Raghava Raja Ram, Patita Pavan Sita Ram
Veera Hanumana, Ati Balwana, Ram Nama Rasiya Re
~~~

Hei Hei Hei Hei Prabhu Mana Basiya Re
Ho Ho Ho Ho Prabhu Mana Basiya Re

Jai Jai Jai Hanuman Gosai, Krupa Karo Guru Deva Kinayi
Jai Jai Jai Hanuman Gosai, Krupa Karo Guru Deva Kinayi
Veera Hanumana, Ati Balwana, Ram Nama Rasiya Re

~~~
~~~

SELECTED BHAJANS

Guru Ji Ki Charno Mein
Dedicated To Shri Prakash Gossai

Guru Ji Ki Charno Mein Sheesh Ko Jhukayoo
Janam Janam Ka Bhaag Pal Paawoo
Guru Ji Ki Charno

Laage Moha Maya Na, Kab Hoon Jagat Ke
Daiya Sindhu Guriji Ki, Charnan Dhaanoo
Guru Ji Ki Charno

Bhatak Taa Rahaa Hoon Mein, Yug Yug Se Swami
Mile Gyaan Aate, Hari Darsha Paawoon
Uru Ji Ki Charno

Kaam Krodh Moha Lobha, Shatru Hain Baree
Guru Ghyaan Khand Se, Maare Bhagawoon
Guru Ji Ki Charno.

Jesse Ved Kahetaa Hain Ajanma Anadee
Usse Dekh Kar Man Ki Duvidha Mitaawoon
Guru Ji Ki Charno

~~~
~~~

Malik Tere Charnon Ki

Malik Ttere Charnon Ki, Agar Dhool Hi Miljaye
Sach Kehta Hun Meri, Takdeer Hi BadaljayeCharano
Me Tere Data, Nit Ber Sat Hai Rehemat
Ik Boondh Jo Miljaye, Jeevan Ki Badal Jaaye Re
Nazronse Jisne Na, Mujhe Tu Na Sazaa Dena
Nazronse Jis Jaaye, Do Sach Me Pahucha Jaaye
Guru Devo Mere Pyaare, Bas Itni Dayaa Karuna
Darbaar Me Jab Aawo, Tera Darshan Ho Jaaye Re

~~~

Bhagvan Meri Naiyaa

Bhagavaan Meri Naiyaa Uspar Lagaa Denaa
Abtak To Nibhaayaa Hai Aagebhi Nibhaa Lenaa
Bhagavaan Meri Naiyaa...

Dal Bal Ke Saath Maayaa Ghere Jo Muze Aakar
To Dekhate Na Rehena Zald Aake Bachaa Lenaa,
Bhagavaan Meri Naiyaa...
Sambhav Hai Zanzatome Main Tumako Bhul Jaun
Par Naath Kabhi Tumabhi Muzkona Bhula Denaa,
Bhagavaan Meri Naiyaa...

Tum Dev Main Pujari Tum Ishta Main Upaasak
Yah Baat Agar Sach Hain Sach Kar Ke Dikhaa Denaa
Bhagavaan Meri Naiyaa...

~~~

Vaishnav Jan To

Vaishnav jan to tene kahiye
Jay peerh paraaye janneyray
Par dukkhey upkar karey teeyey
Man abhiman na anney ray

KASHI SATSANGH

Sakal lokma sahuney bandhey,
Ninda na karye kainee ray
Baach kaachh, man nischal raakhey
Dhan-dhan jananee tainee ray

Samdrishi nay trishna tyagee
Par-stree jaynay mat ray
Vivihva thaki asatya na bolay
Pardhan nav jhaley haath ray

Moh maaya vyaayey nahin jeynay
Dridth vairagya jana manma ray
Ram-nam-shoom taalee laagee
Sakal teerth seyna tanma ray

Vanloohee nay kapat rahit chhay
Kaam, krodh nivarya ray
Bhane narsinhyo tainoo darshan karta kul
Ekotair Taarya Re

Speak only as godlike of the man who feels another's pain
Who shares another's sorrow and pride does disdain
Who regards himself lowliest of the low
Speaks not a word of evil against anyone
Blessed is the mother who gave birth to such a son
Who looks upon everyone as his equal
Lust he has renounced
Who honors women like he honors his mother
Whose tongue knows not the taste of falsehood
Nor covets another's worldly goods
Who longs not for worldly wealth or fame
For he treads the path of renunciation
Ever on his lips is Ram's holy name
All places of pilgrimage are within him
He has conquered greed, is free of deceit, lust and anger
Through him Narsinh has godly vision
And his generation to come will attain salvation.

~~~
~~~

Ai Malik Tere Bande Hum

Ai malik tere bande ham
Aise hon hamare karam
Neki par chalen, Aur badi se talen
Taki hanste huye nikale dam
Ai malik tere bande ham

Jab zulmon ka ho samana
Tab tu hi hamen thamana
Wo burai karen, ham bhalai bharen
Nahin badale ki ho kamana
Badh uthe pyar ka har kadam
Aur mite bair ka ye bharam
Neki par chalen . . .

Ye andhera ghana chha raha
Tera insan ghabara raha
Ho raha bekhabar, kuchh na ata nazar
Sukh ka suraj chhipa ja raha
Hai teri roshani men wo dam
Jo amavas ko kar de poonam
Neki par chalen . . .

Bada kamzor hai adami
Abhi lakhon hain ismen kamin
Par tu jo khada, hai dayalu bada
Teri kripa se dharti thami
Diya tune hamen jab janam
Tu hi jhelega ham sabke gam
Neki par chalen . . .

~~~

Choti Choti Gaiyan

Choti choti gaiyan, chote chote gwaal
Choto so mero madana gopal
Aage aage gaiyan, peeche peeche gwaal
~~~

Beecha mein mero madana gopal
Kaare kaare gaiyan , gore gore gwaal
Shyama varana mero madana gopal
Ghaas khaye gaiyaa, doodh piye gwaal
Maakhan khaave mero madan gopal
Choti choti lakhotee, chote chote haath
Bansi bajaave mero madan gopal
Choti choti sakhiya madhuvanmaa
Raas rachaave mero madan gopal

~~~

He Prabhu Anand Data

He prabhu anand data, gyan hamko dijiye
Shighra sare durgunoko door hamase kijiye
He prabhu anand data
Lijiye hamko sharanmen, ham sadachari bane
Shanti chahak dharm rakshak, veer vratadhari bane
He prabhu anand data
Ninda kabhibhi ham kisiki, bhul kabhi na kare
Satya bole juth tyage, mil aapasmen rahe
He prabhu anand data
Premase ham guru janonki, nitya hi sewa kare
Divya jiwan ho hamara, tere yash gaya kare
He prabhu anand data

~~~

Sabse Unchi Prem Sagaai

Sabse unchi prem sagaai
Sabse unchi prem sagaai

Duryodhana ko meva tyagyo
Saag vidur ghar khai
Sabse unchi...

Juthe phal sabri ke khaaye
Bahu vidi swada batayi

Sabse unchi prem ....

Prem ke bas arjun rath hakyo
Bhool gaye thakurai
Sabse unchi prem ...

Aisi preet barhi vrindavana
Gopin naach nachaai
Sabse unchi ....

Sur kroor is laayak nahi
Kah lag karehu badhai
Sabse unchi ....

~~~

Prabhu Ji Tum Chandan Hum Paani

Prabhu ji tum chandan hum paani
Jaki ang ang baas samayi

Prabhu ji tum moti hum dhaga
Jaise sonehu milat suhaga

Prabhu ji tum deepak hum baati
Jaki jyot bare din raati

Prabhu ji tum ghanban hum mora
Jaise chitvat chand chakora

Prabhu ji tum swami hum dasa
Aisi bhakti kare Raidasa

~~~

Mera Jeevan Teri Sharan

Mera jeevan teri sharan
Saare raag virag hue ab
Moh saare tyag hue ab
Ek yahi mera bandhan

Avirat raha bhatakta ab tak
Bhatkun aur abhi main kab tak
Paalun keval tujhko hi maa
Ek yehi meri hai lagan

Tere charnon pe ho arpan
Mere jeevan ke gun avagun
Saari vyathayen door karo maa
Ho kusumit mera vandan

~~~

Prabhu Hum Pe Kripa

Prabhu hum pe kripa karna, Prabhu hum pe daya karna
Baikunth to yahi hai, hirday mein raha karna.

Goonjenge raag bankar, veena ki taar banke
Pragatoge nath mere, hriday mein pyar banke
Har ragini ki dhun par, swar bankar utha karna

Nachenge mor bankar, hey Shyam tere dware
Ghanshyam chhaye rahna, bankar ke megh kaare
Amrit ki dhar bankar, pyaason pe daya karna

Tere viyog mein hum, din raat hain udasi
Apni sharan mein le lo, hey Nath Braj ke waasi
Tum so hum shabd bankar, prano mein rama karna

~~~

Data Ek Raam

Data ek ram bhikhari saari duniya
Raam ek devata pujari saari duniya

Dware pe uski jaake koi bhi pukarta
Param kripa de apni bhav se ubarta
Aise deenanath pe balihari saari duniya
Do din ka jeevan prani kar le vichar tu
Pyare prabhu ko apne man mein vichar tu
Bina hari naam ke dukhiyari saari duniya

Naam ka prakaash jab antar jagayega
Pyare shreeram ka tu darshan payega
Jyoti se uski hai ujiyari sari duniya

~~~

Aisa Pyar Baha De Maiya

Ya Devi Sarvabhuteshu daya rupen sansthita
Namastasyaiya namahtasyaiya namo namah

Durga durgati door kar mangal kar sab kaaj
Man mandir ujjwal kar kripa karke aaj

Aisa pyar baha de maiya
Charanon se lag jaaun main
Sab andhkar mita de maiya
Daras tera lakh paun main

Jag mein aakar jag ko maiya
Ab tak na pehchan saka
Kyu aaya hoon kahan hai jaana
Ye bhi na main jaan saka
Tu hai agam agochar maiya
Kaho kaise lakh paaun main
Karo kripa Jagdamb bhawani
Main balak naadan hoon
~~~

Nahi aaradhan jap tap jaanu
Main avaguna ki khan hoon
De aisa vardaan hey maiya
Sumiran tera gaun main

Main balak tu maiya meri
Nis din teri oat hai
Teri kirpa hi mein teri
Bhitar jo bhi khot hai
Sharan laga lo mujhko maiya
Tujhpe bali bali jaaun main

~~~

Na Yeh Tera

Na ye tera na ye mera, mandir hai bhagwan ka
Paani uska bhumi usi ki, sab kuchh usi mahan ka

Hum sab khel khilone uske khel raha kartaar re
Uski jyoti sab mein damke sab mein uska pyar re
Man mandir mein darshan kar le un pranon ke pran ka
Pani uska bhumi usi ki ..

Teerath jaaye mandir jaaye angin roop manaye re
Deen roop mein ram samne dekh ke nayan phiraye re
Man ki aankhen khul jayen to kya krna hume gyan ka
Pani uska bhumi usi ki ..

Kaun hai uncha kaun hai neecha sab hain ek saman re
Prem ki jyot jaga hirdaya mein
Sab mein prabhu pehchan re

Saral hridaya ko sharan mein rakhe hari bhole nadaan ka
Pani uska bhumi usi ki ....

~~~

Jo Tum Toda Piya

Jo tum todo piya main nahi todun
Toson preet tod krishna kaun sang jodun

Tum bhaye truvar main bhai pankhiya
Tum bhaye sarowar main teri machiya
Tum bhaye girivar main bhayi chaya
Tum bhaye chanda main bhayi chakora

Tum bhaye moti prabhu hum bhaye dhaga
Tum bhaye sona hum bhaye suhaga
Meera kahe prabhu braj ke vasi
Tum mere thakur main teri dasi

~~~

Tumhi Ho Mata

Tumhi ho mata, pita tumhi ho
Tumhi ho Bandhu, sakha tumhi ho

Tumhi ho sathi, tumhi sahare
Koyee na apna siva tumhare
Tumhi ho naiya tumhi khavaiya
Tumhi ho bandhu sakha tumhi ho

Jo khil sake na woh phool ham hain
Tumhare charano ki ghool ham hain
Daya ki drishti sada hi rakhna
Tumhi ho bandhu sakha tumhi ho

Tumhi ho mata, pita tumhi ho
Tumhi ho bandhu, sakha tumhi ho

~~~

Jyot Se Jyot Jalate Chalo

Jyot se jyot jalate chalo prem ki ganga bahate chalo
Rah mein aaye jo deen dukhi sabko gale se lagate chalo
Jis ka na koi sangi sathi ishwar hai rakhwala
Jo nirdhan hai, jo nirbal hai, woh hai prabhu ka pyara
Pyar ke moti lutate chalo

Aasha tooti mamta roothi chhod gaya hai kinara
Band karo mat dwaar daya ka de do kuchh to sahara
Deep daya ka jalate chalo

Chhayi hai chau ore andhera bhatak gayi hain dishayen
Maanav ban baitha hai daanav kisko byatha sunaye
Dharti ko swarg banate chalo

~~~

Sita Ke Ram Radha Ke Shyam

Sita ke ram radha ke shyam
Meera ke giridhar nagar sur ke ghanshyam

Mehlon ka sukh siya ne ram ka sath nibhaya
Laxmi ne dhar roop siya ka jag ka paap mitaya
Bana diya tha is dharti ko ram bhakti ka dham

Radha ne shree shyam sundar sang aisa raas rachaya
Teeno lok mein shyam aur radha ka roop samaya
Koti koti bhakton ke mukh par radhe shyam ka naam

~~~

Govind Jai Jai

Govind jai jai gopal jai jai
Radha raman hari govind jai jai

Brahma ki jai jai vishnu ki jai jai
Uma pati shiv shankar ki jai jai

Radha ki jai jai rukmini ki jai jai
Mor mukut bansi wale ki jai jai

Ganga ki jai jai yamuna ki jai jai
Saraswati triveni ki jai jai

Ram ji ki jai jai shyam ji ki jai jai
Dashrath kunwar charon bhaiyon ki jai jai

Krishna ki jai jai laxmi ki jai jai
Krishna baldev dono bhaiyon ki jai jai

~~~

Rang De Chunaryan

Rang de chunariya
Shyam piya meri rang de chunariya

Aisi rang de ki rang nahi chhute
Dhobiya dhove chahe ye saari umariya
Shyam piya...

Lal na rangau main to hari na rangau
Apne hi rang mein rang de chunariya
Shyam piya ...

Bina rangaye main to ghar nahi jaungi
Beet hi jaaye chahe ye saari umariya
~~~

Meera ke prabhu giridhar naagar
Jal se patla kaun hai, kaun bhumi se bhari
Kaun agan se tez hai aur kaun kaajal se kaali

Jal se patla gyan hai aur paap bhumi se bhari
Krodh agan se tez hai aur kalank kaajal se kaali
Hari charnan mein, shyam charnan mein,
Prabhu charnan mein
Jaoon balihariya
Shyam piya ...

~~~

ITNA TO KARNA SWAMI

Itna to karna swami jab pran tan se nikale
Gobind naam lekar tab pran tan se nikale

Pitambari kashi ho chhavi man mein ye basi ho
Honthon pe kuchh hansi ho jab pran tan se nikale

Us waqt jaldi aana nahi shyam bhool jaana
Radhe ko saath laana jab pran tan se nikale

Ek bhakt ki hai arzi khudgarj ki hai garzi
Aage tumhari marzi jab pran tan se nikale
Hari Naam Ka Pyala

Hari naam ka pyaalaa hare Krishna ki haalaa
Aisi haalaa pi pi karke chalaa chale matwaalaa

Radha jaisi baalaa aur vrindavan ka gwaalaa
Aisaa gwaalaa murli manohar japo Krishna ki maalaa

Hare Krishna kaa jap ho aur Hare Krishna ki maalaa
Dev jyoti se hriday suddha ho nikle man ki jwaalaa

Krishna ki dhun main tan ho,
Aur hare Krishna main man ho
~~~

Aise tan man ke mandir main Krishna dale haalaa
Hare Krishna main bal hain, Krishna jal aur thal hai
Aise jal thal nabh se pi lo Narayan ki haalaa

~~~

Jag Mein Hai Sundar Do Naam

Jag mein sundar hain do naam
Chahe Krishna kaho ya Ram
Bolo Ram Ram Ram
Bolo Shyam Shyam Shyam

Makhan brij mein ek churaave
Ek ber bhilni ke khaave
Prembhav se bhare anokhe
Donon ke hain kaam
Bolo Ram, Ram, Ram
Bolo Shyam, Shyam, Shyam

Ek kams paapi ko maare
Ek dusht Ravan samhare
Donon deen ke dukh harat hain
Donon bal ke dhaam
Ek radhika ke sang raaje
Ek janaki sang biraaje
Chaahe Sita-Ram kaho
Ya bolo Radhe-Shyam

Ek hriday mein prem badhaave,
Ek taap santap mitaave,
Donon sukh ke sagar hain,
Aur donon pooran kaam,
Chaahe Krishna kaho ya Ram
Jag mein sundar hain do naam
Chaahe Krishna kaho ya Ram
Bolo Ram, Ram, Ram
Bolo Shyam, Shyam, Shyam

~~~

Aisi Laagi Lagan

**Hai aankh wo jo Shyam ka darshan kiya kare
Hai sheesh woh prabhu charnon mein jo vandan kiya kare
Bekar woh mukh hai jo lage vyarth baaton mein
Mukh woh hai jo hari naam ka sumiran kiya kare**

**Heere moti se nahi hai shobha hanthon ki
Hain haath woh bhagwaan ka pujan kiya kare
Mar kar bhi amar hai us jeev ka is jag mein
Prabhu prem mein balidan jo jeevan kiya kare**

**Aisi lagi lagan meera ho gayi magan
Woh to gali gali hari gun gaane lagi
Mehalon mein pali ban ke jogan chali
Meera rani deewani kahane lagi**

**Koi roke nahi koi toke nahi
Meera Govind Gopal gaane lagi
Baithi santon ke sang rangi mohan ke rang
Meera premi preetam ko manane lagi
Woh to gali gali hari gun gaane lagi**

**Rana ne vish diya mano amrit piya
Mano sagar mein sarita samane lagi
Dukh lakhon sahe mukh se Govind kahe
Meera Govind Gopal gaane lagi
Woh to gali gali hari gun gaane lagi**

~~~

Badi Der Bhayi Naandlala

**Badi der bhayi nandlala teri raah take brijbaala
Gwal baal sab poochh rahe hain kahan hai muraliwala**

Koi na jaaye kunjgalin mein tujh bin kaliyan chunane ko
~~~

Taras rahe hai jamuna ke tat, dhun murali ki sunane ko
Ab to daras dikha ja mohan kyu duvidha mein dala

Sankat mei hai aaj wo dharti jis par tune janam liya
Poora kar de aaj vachan wo geeta mein jo tune diya
Koi nahi hai tujh bin mohan bharat ka rakhwala

~~~

Radhike Tune Bansari Churayi

Radhike tune bansuri churayi
Radhike tune bansuri churayi
Bansuri churayi kya tere man me aayi
Bansuri churayi kya tere man me aayi
Kahe ko rar machai, machai re
Radhike tune bansuri churayi
Radhike tune bansuri churayi

Dedungi kahe, qasame khaye
Dedungi kahe, qasame khaye
Kaha chhupayi, par na bataye
Kaha chhupayi, par na bataye
Natkhat dard ki taye re taye
Radhike tune bansuri churayi
Radhike tune bansuri churayi

Na teri bairan, na teri sautana aa aa sautan
Na teri bairan, na teri sautan
Meri muraliya, mohe sabka man
Meri muraliya, mohe sabka man
Kare teri kaun burayi
Radhike tune bansuri churayi
Radhike tune bansuri churayi.

~~~

Tora Man Darpan Kehlaaye

Tora man darpan kehlaaye
Tora man darpan kehlaaye
Bhale bure saare karmo ko
Dekhe aur dikhaaye
Tora man darpan kehlaaye

Man hi devta
Man hi ishwar
Man se bada na koye
Man ujiyara jab jab phaile
Jag ujiyara hoye
Is ujle darpan par praani
Dhool na jamne paaye
Tora man darpan kehlaaye

Sukh ki kaliyaan
Dukh ke kaante
Man sab ka aadhar
Man se koi baat chhupe na
Man ke nain hazaar

Jag se chaahe bhaag le koi
Man se bhaag na paaye
Tora man darpan kehlaaye

~~~

Yeh To Sach Hai Ki Bhagwan Hai

Yeh to sach hai ki bhagwan hai
Hai magar phir bhi anjaan hai
Dharti pe roop maa baap ka
Us vidhaata ki pehchaan hai

Janmdaata hai jo, naam jinse mila
Thamkar jinki ungli hai bachpan chala
~~~

Kaandhe par baithke, jinke dekha jahaan
Gyan jinse mila, kya bura kya bhala
Itne upkaar hain kya kahen
Yeh bataana na aasaan hai
Dharti pe roop maa baap ka
Us vidhaata ki pehchaan hai
Janam deti hai jo, maa jise jag kahe
Apni santaan mein, pran jiske rahe
Loriyan hothon par, sapne bunti nazar
Neend jo vaar de, hanske har dukh sahe
Mamta ke roop mein hai prabhu
Aapse paaya vardaan hai
Dharti pe roop maa baap ka
Us vidhaata ki pehchaan hai
Aapke khwab hum, aaj hokar jawaan
Us param shakti se karte hain prarthna
Unki chhaya rahe, rehti duniya talak
Ek pal reh sake hum na jinke bina
Aap dono salaamat rahe
Sabke dil mein yeh armaan hai
Dharti pe roop maa baap ka
Us vidhaata ki pehchaan hai
Yeh to sach hai ki bhagwan hai

~~~
~~~

MOTHER

Yeh Bandhan Toh

Ho ho ho ho ho
Ho oh oh oh oh
Ho ho oh oh ho
Suraj kab door gagan se
Chanda kab door kiran se
Khushboo kab door pawan se
Kab door bahaar chaman se
Ye bandhan toh pyaar ka bandhan hai
Janmon ka sangam hai
Ye bandhan toh pyaar ka bandhan hai
Janmon ka sangam hai

Suraj kab door gagan se
Chanda kab door kiran se
Khushboo kab door pawan se
Kab door bahaar chaman se
Ye bandhan toh pyaar ka bandhan hai
Janmon ka sangam hai

Tum hi mere jeevan ho
Tumhe dekh dekh jee loongi
Tum hi mere jeevan ho
Tumhe dekh dekh jee loongi
Main to tumhaare khaatir
Duniya ka zaher pee loongi

Tere paavan charnon mein
Aakaash jhuka denge hum
Teri raah mein jo sholay ho
To khud ko becha denge hum
Ye bandhan toh pyaar ka bandhan hai
Janmon ka sangam hai

Ye bandhan toh pyaar ka bandhan hai
Janmon ka sangam hai

Mamta ke mandir ki hai tu
Sab se pyaari murat
Mamta ke mandir ki hai tu
Sab se pyaari murat
Bhagwaan nazar aata hai
Jab dekhe teri surat
Jab jab duniya mein aaye
Tera hi aanchal paaye
Janmon ki deevaaron par
Hum pyaar apna likh jaaye
Ye bandhan toh pyaar ka bandhan hai
Janmon ka sangam hai
Ye bandhan toh pyaar ka bandhan hai
Janmon ka sangam hai

Suraj kab door gagan se
Chanda kab door kiran se
Khushboo kab door pawan se
Kab door bahaar chaman se
Ye bandhan toh pyaar ka bandhan hai
Janmon ka sangam hai
Ho ho ho ho ho
Ho oh oh oh oh
Hp ho oh oh ho.

~~~

Maiya Yashoda

Maiyya yashoda...
Yeh tera kanhaiya...
Maiyya yashoda, yeh tera kanhaiya,
Panghat pe meri, pakde hai baiyan,
Tang mujhe karta hai, sang mere ladta hai,
Ramji ki kripa se, main bachi,
Ramji ki kripa se, main bachi,
Ramji ki kripa se...
Gokul ki galiyon mein, jamuna kinaare,
Woh more kankariya, chhup chhup ke maare,
Natkhat adayen, soorat hai bholi,
~~~

Holi mein meri bhigaye woh choli,
Baiyan na chhode...
Kalaiyan marode...
Baiyan na chhode, kalaiyan marode,
Paiyan padun phir bhi, peechha na chhode,
Meethi meethi baaton mein, mujhko phansaye, hai.
Ramji ki kripa se, main bachi,
Ramji ki kripa se, main bachi,
Ramji ki kripa se...

Jab jab bajaye, mohan muraliya,
Chhan chhan chhanakti hai, meri payaliya,
Nainon se jab woh kare chhedkhani,
Dil thaame reh jaye, prem deewani,
Sudh-budh gawai...
Neende udayee...
Sudh-budh gawai, neende udayee,
Jo karne baithi thi, woh kar na payee,
Badi mushkil se dil ko sambhaala, hai.
Ramji ki kripa se, main bachi,
Ramji ki kripa se, main bachi,
Ramji ki kripa se...

Gokul ka kanha, har dil mein samaaya,
Main bhagyashaali, unhe maine paaya,
Maana ke sabke, hain yeh kanhaiya,
Kehlayenge par, tumhare hi maiyya,
Pyara piya hai...
Tumne diya hai...
Pyara piya hai, tumne diya hai,
Mamta ke aanchal mein, humko liya hai,
Charano mein teri o maa humko rehna hai,
Ramji ki kripa se,
Haan ji haan,
Ramji ki kripa se...

~~~
~~~

ACHHI ACCHI PYARI PYARI

Achhi achhi pyari pyari, Bholi bhali maa
O maa O maa
Achhi achhi pyari pyari, Bholi bhali ma
O maa O maa

Duniya bhar ki khushiya, Humko dene wali
O maa O maa
Achhi achhi pyari pyari, Bholi bhali ma
O maa O maa, O maa O maa

Tune jag jag ke raato mein
Hume mithi neend
Sulaya hai
Teri mamta ke saye
Ne hume
Sardi garmi se bachaya hai
Har haal mein yeh
Ghar swarg lage
Yeh to maa teri maya hai
O maa O maa, O maa O maa
Achhi achhi pyari pyari, Bholi bhali ma
O maa O maa

Data jo kabhi galati pe hume
Humse dukh jyada
Tumko hua
Hum aansu baha ke
Chhup ho gaye
Lekin maa tera man roya
Aisi mamta ki murat ki
Jivan bhar karte rahe puja
O maa O maa, O maa O maa
Achhi achhi pyari pyari, Bholi bhali ma
Duniya bhar ki khushiya
Humko dene wali
O maa O maa
O maa O maa O maa

O maa O maa
O maa O maa O maa.

~~~

Mere Raaja Mere Laal

Mere raaja, mere laal, tujhko dhundu main kahaan
Mere raaja, mere laal, tujhko dhundu main kahaan
Roye mamta, tadpe maa, tujhko dhundu main kahaan
Mere raaja, mere laal, tujhko dhundu main kahaan
Tu kya jaane tere kal se,
Chale jaane pe kya beeti mere pyaare
Tu kya jaane tere kal se,
Chale jaane pe kya beeti mere pyaare
Teri maata O teri behna,
Tere ghum mein ro ro mar jaayenge saare
Aaja waapas aaja
Mere raaja, mere laal, tujhko dhundu main kahaan
Mere raaja, mere laal, tujhko dhundu main kahaan
Iss jag mein kya hai mera, ik sapna tu mera woh bhi tuta
Iss jag mein kya hai mera, ik sapna tu mera woh bhi tuta
Ruthi kismat, ruthi duniya,
Meri akhiyo ke taare tu kyun rutha
Aaja waapas aaja
Mere raaja, mere laal, tujhko dhundu main kahaan
Mere raaja, mere laal, tujhko dhundu main kahaan
Roye mamta, tadpe maa, tujhko dhundu main kahaan
Mere raaja, mere laal, tujhko dhundu main kahaan
Tujhko dhundu main kahaan.

~~~

Tu Kitni Achchhi Hai

Tu kitni achchhi hai, tu kitni bholi hai
Pyaari pyaari hai O maa aa aa O maa
O maa aa aa O maa

Tu kitni achchhi hai, tu kitni bholi hai
Pyaari pyaari hai O maa aa aa O maa
O maa aa aa O maa
Ke yeh jo duniya hai, yeh ban hai kaanto ka
Tu phulwaari hai O maa aa aa O maa
O maa aa aa O maa
Dukhan laagi hai maa teri akhiya
Dukhan laagi hai maa teri akhiya
Mere liye jaagi hai tu saari saari ratiya
O meri nindiya pe apni nindiya bhi tune waari hai
O maa aa aa O maa
O maa aa aa O maa
Tu kitni achchhi hai, tu kitni bholi hai
Pyaari pyaari hai O maa aa aa O maa
O maa aa aa O maa
Apna nahi tujhe sukh dukh koyi
Apna nahi tujhe sukh dukh koyi
Main muskaaya tu muskaayi, main roya tu royi
Mere hasane pe, mere rone pe tu balihaari hai
O maa aa aa O maa
O maa aa aa O maa
Maa bachcho ki jaan hoti hai
Maa bachcho ki jaan hoti hai
Woh hote hai kismatwale jinake maa hoti hai
Kitni sundar hai, kitni shital hai
Nyaari nyaari hai O maa aa aa O maa
O maa aa aa O maa

Tu kitni achchhi hai, tu kitni bholi hai
Pyaari pyaari hai O maa aa aa O maa
O maa aa aa O maa.

~~~

Maa Mujhe Apne Anchal Mein

Maa mujhe apne anchal mein
Chhipa ley, gale se laga ley
Ki aur mera koyi nahi
Maa mujhe apne anchal mein
~~~

Chhipa ley, gale se laga ley
Ki aur mera koyi nahi
Phir na sataunga kabhi pas bula ley
Gale se laga ley ki aur mera koyi nahi
Ki aur mera koyi nahi
Bhul meri chhoti si bhul jao mata
Bhul meri chhoti si bhul jao mata
Aise koyi apno se ruth nahi jata
Ruth gaya hu mai to mujhko mana ley
Gale se laga ley ki aur mera koyi nahi
Ki aur mera koyi nahi

Na to yaha aandiya na koi jyot hai
Na to yaha aandiya na koi jyot hai
Na to yaha jivan hai na koi maut hai
Tune kiya hai mujhko kiske hawale
Gale se laga ley ki aur mera koyi nahi
Maa mujhe apne anchal mein
Chipa ley, gale se laga ley
Ki aur mera koyi nahi

Phir na sataunga kabhi pas bula ley
Gale se laga ley ki aur mera koyi nahi
Ki aur mera koyi nahi.

~~~

Maine Maa Ko Dekha Hai

Maine maa ko dekha hai
Dekha hai maa ko dekha hai
Maa kaa pyar nahi dekha
Maine maa ko dekha hai
Maa kaa pyar nahi dekha
Maine phool toh dekhe hain
Dekhe hain phool toh dekhe hain
Phoolon kaa har nahi dekha
Maine maa ko dekha hai
Maa kaa pyar nahi dekha
Maine maa ko dekha hai
~~~

Vaise toh ghar main
Maa ki tasveer hai
Vaise toh ghar main
Maa ki tasveer hai
Lekin meri kab aisi takdir hai
Kabhi jo ghabraun gale se lag jaon
Agar naa neend aaye to lori woh gaye
Meri mann jiska pyasa hai
Pyasa hai jiska pyasa hai
Woh lad dular nahi dekha
Maine maa ko dekha hai
Maa kaa pyar nahi dekha
Maine maa ko dekha hai

Vaise toh meri maa
Kaa dil koi sakt nahi
Vaise toh meri maa
Kaa dil koi sakt nahi
Par uske pas jara bhi wakt nahi
Hai uska nam bada
Hai usako kam bada
Woh devi mamta ki
Hai leader janta ki
Maa ke photo ke bina
Bina ji photo ke bina
Koi akhbar nahi dekha
Maine maa ko dekha hai
Maa kaa pyar nahi dekha
Maine maa ko dekha hai

Pyari pyari hai
Woh bholi aisi hai
Pyari pyari hai
Woh bholi aisi hai
Pan aaya se poochha
Ki baby kaisi hai
Meri maa sachi hai
Badi hi achhi hai
Yeh uska dosh nahi
Use kuchh host nahi

Maa ne duniya dekhi hai
Dekhi hai duniya dekhi hai
Ghar sansar nahi dekha
Maine maa ko dekha hai
Maa kaa pyar nahi dekha
Maine phool toh dekhe
Hain dekhe hain
Phool toh dekhe hain
Phoolon kaa har nahi dekha
Maine mann ko dekha hai.

~~~

I Hope You Dance

Dedicated to My Mother

I hope you never lose your sense of wonder,
You get your fill to eat but always keep that hunger,
May you never take one single breath for granted,
GOD forbid love ever leave you empty handed,
I hope you still feel small when you stand beside the ocean,
Whenever one door closes I hope one more opens,
Promise me that you'll give faith a fighting chance,
And when you get the choice to sit it out or dance.
I hope you dance....I hope you dance.

I hope you never fear those mountains in the distance,
Never settle for the path of least resistance
Livin' might mean takin' chances but they're worth takin',
Lovin' might be a mistake but it's worth makin',
Don't let some hell bent heart leave you bitter,
When you come close to sellin' out reconsider,
Give the heavens above more than just a passing glance,
And when you get the choice to sit it out or dance.

I hope you dance....I hope you dance.
I hope you dance....I hope you dance.
~~~

Time is a wheel in constant motion always rolling us along,
Tell me who wants to look back on their years and
Wonder where those years have gone.

I hope you still feel small when you stand beside the ocean,
Whenever one door closes I hope one more opens,
Promise me that you'll give faith a fighting chance,
And when you get the choice to sit it out or dance.

Dance....I hope you dance.
I hope you dance....I hope you dance.
I hope you dance....I hope you dance.

Time is a wheel in constant motion always rolling us along
Tell me who wants to look back on their years and
wonder where those years have gone.

~~~
~~~

RAKSHA BANDHAN

Behana Ne Bhai Ki Kalai Se

Behana ne bhai ki kalai se
Behana ne bhai ki kalai se
Pyaar bandha hai
Pyaar ke do taar se,
Sansaar bandha hai

Resham ki dori se
Resham ki dori se
Resham ki dori se,
Sansaar bandha hai

Sundarata me jo kanhaiya hai
Mamata me yashoda maiya hai
Wo aur nahi dujaa koi
Wo to mera raja bhaiya hai

Behana ne bhai ki kalai se
Behana ne bhai ki kalai se
Pyaar bandha hai
Pyaar ke do taar se,
Sansaar bandha hai

Meraa phul hai tu, talvar hai tu
Meri laaj ka paharedar hai tu
Mai akeli kahan is duniya me
Mera saraa sansar hai tu

Behana ne bhai ki kalai se
Behana ne bhai ki kalai se
Pyaar baandhaa hai
Pyaar ke do taar se,
Sansar bandha hai

Hame dur bhale kismat kar de
Apane man se na juda karana
Sawan ke pawan din bhaiya

Bahana ko yaad kiya karana

Behana ne bhai ki kalai se
Behana ne bhai ki kalai se
Pyaar bandha hai
Pyaar ke do taar se,
Sansar bandha hai
Resham ki dori se
Resham ki dori se
Resham ki dori se,
Sansar bandha hai
Behana ne bhai ki kalai se
Pyaar bandha hai.

~~~

MereE Bhaiyaa Mere Chanda

Mere bhaiyaa mere chandaa, mere anamol ratan
Tere badale mai zamaane ki, koi chiz na lun
Mere bhaiyaa mere chandaa, mere anamol ratan
Tere badale mai zamaane ki, koi chiz na lun

Teri saanso ki kasam khaake, havaa chalati hai
Tere chahare ki khalak paake, bahaar aati hai
Ek pal bhi meri nazaro se tu jo ojhal ho
Har taraf meri nazar tujhako pukaar aati hai
Mere bhaiyaa mere chandaa, mere anamol ratan
Tere badale mai zamaane ki, koi chiz na lun
Mere bhaiyaa mere chandaa, mere anamol ratan
Tere badale mai zamaane ki, koi chiz na lun

Tere chahare ki mahakati hui ladiyo ke lie
Anaginat phul ummido ke chune hai maine
Vo bhi din aae ki un kvaabo ke taabir mile
Tere khatir jo hasi khvaab bune hai maine
Mere bhaiyaa mere chandaa, mere anamol ratan
Tere badale mai zamaane ki, koi chiz na lun

Mere bhaiyaa mere chandaa, mere anamol ratan
~~~

Tere badale mai zamaane ki, koi chiz na lun
Mere bhaiyaa.

~~~

Hum Behano Ke Lie Mere Bhaiya

Hum bahano ke lie mere bhaiya
Aata hai ek din saal me, aata hai ek din saal me
Aaj ke din mai jahaan bhi rahun
Chale aana waha har haal me, chale aana waha har haal me
Hum bahano ke lie mere bhaiya
Aata hai ek din saal me, aata hai ek din saal me

Kitane din aur kitani raine, is aangan me rehana hai maine
Kitane din aur kitani raine, is aangan me rehana hai maine
Paradesi hoti hai bahane, Baabul jaane bhej de meri
Doli kab sasuraal me, Chale aana waha har haal me

Hum bahano ke lie mere bhaiya
Aata hai ek din saal me, aata hai ek din saal me

Me hu bholi bairi zamana
Bhaiya meri laaj bachana
Me hu bholi bairi zamana
Bhaiya meri laaj bachana
Es rakhi ki rit nibhana
Esa na ho mai tadapu ese
Bulbul jaise jaal me
Chale aana waha har haal me
Hum bahano ke lie mere bhaiya
Aata hai ek din saal me, aata hai ek din saal me.

~~~

Bhaiya Mere Raakhi Ke Bandhan Ko Nibhana

Bhaiya mere raakhi ke bandhan ko nibhana
Bhaiya mere chhoti bahan ko na bhulana
Dekho ye nata nibhana, nibhana
Bhaiya mere raakhi ke bandhan ko nibhana
Bhaiya mere chhoti bahan ko na bhulana
Bhaiya mere...

Ye din ye tyohar khushi ka, pawan jaise nir nadi ka
Bhaai ke ujale maathe pe, bahan lagaye mangal tika
Jhume ye sawan suhaana, suhaana
Bhaiya mere raakhi ke bandhan ko nibhana
Bhaiya mere chhoti bahan ko na bhulana
Bhaiya mere...

Baandh ke hamane resham dori, tum se wo ummid hai jodi
Naazuk hai jo daant ke jaise, par jivan bhar jaae na todi
Jaane ye sara zamaana, zamaana
Bhaiya mere raakhi ke bandhan ko nibhana
Bhaiya mere chhoti bahan ko na bhulana
Bhaiya mere...

Shayad wo sawan bhi aaye, jo bahana ka rang na laye
Bahan paraae desh basi ho,
agar wo tum tak pahunch na paaye
Yaad ka dipak jalaana, jalaana
Bhaiya mere raakhi ke bandhan ko nibhana
Bhaiya mere chhoti bahan ko na bhulana
Bhaiya mere...

~~~

Phoolo Ka Tarron Ka

Hmm hmm hey hey, hey hoo hoo hoo
Phoolon ka taaron ka, sab ka kehna hai
Ek hazaron mein, meri behna hai
~~~

Sari umar hame, sang rehna hai
Phoolon ka taaron ka, sab ka kehna hai
Ek hazaron mein, meri behna hai
Sari umar hame, sang rehna hai
Phoolon ka taaron ka, sab ka kehna hai

Jabse meri aankhon, se ho gayi tu door
Tabse sare jeevan ke, sapne hain choor
Jabse meri aankhon, se ho gayi tu door
He he tabse sare jeevan, ke sapne hain choor
Aankhon mein neend, na dil mein chaina hai
Ek hazaron mein, meri behna hai
Sari umar hame, sang rehna hai,
Phoolon ka taaron ka, sab ka kehna hai
Hey hey hey hoo hoo hoo

Dekho hum tum dono, hain ek dali ke phool
Maein na bhoola tu kaise, mujhko gai bhool
Haan dekho hum tum dono, hain ek dali ke phool
Maein na bhoola tu, kaise mujhko gai bhool
Aa mere paas aa, keh jo kehna hai
Ek hazaron mein, meri behna hai
Sari umar hame, sang rehna hai
Phoolon ka taaron ka, sab ka kehna hai

Jivan ke dukho se, yun darate nahi hai
Aise bachake sach se, guzarate nahi hai
Haan jivan ke dukho se, yun darate nahi hai
Aise bachake sach se, guzarate nahi hai
Sukh ki hai chaah to, dukh bhi sahanaa hai
Ek hazaron mein, meri behna hai
Sari umar hame, sang rehna hai
Phoolon ka taaron ka, sab ka kehna hai
Ek hazaron mein, meri behna hai

Hey la la lala la la la la la
Ek hazaron mein
Ho la la lala la la la
Lala la la la la la.

~~~
~~~

FRIENDSHIP

Janey Valo Jara

Janey valo jara, mud ke dekho mujhe
Ek insan hu mai tumharee tarah
Jisne sabko racha, apne hee rup sey
Usakee pahchan hu mai tumharee tarah
Janey valo jara...
Iss anokhe jagat kee mai takdir hu
Mai vidhata ke hatho kee tasvir hu, ek tasvir hu
Iss jahan ke liye, dharatee man ke liye
Shiv kaa varadan hu, mai tumharee tarah
Janey valo jara...
Mann ke andar chhipaye milan kee lagan
Apne suraj sey hu ek bichhadee kiran, ek bichhadee kiran
Phir raha hu bhatakata, mai yaha sey vaha
Aur pareshan hu, mai tumharee tarah
Janey valo jara...
Mere pas aao chhodo yah sara bharam
Jo mera dukh vahee hai tumhara bhee gum, hai tumhara bhee gum
Dekhata hu tumhe janata hu tumhe
Lakh anjan hu mai tumharee tarah
Janey valo jara...

~~~
~~~

Koyi Jab Raah Naa Paye

Koyi jab raah naa paye, mere sang aaye
Ke pag pag dip jalaye
Meri dosti mera pyaar
Meri dosti mera pyaar
Koyi jab raah naa paye, mere sang aaye
Ke pag pag dip jalaye
Meri dosti mera pyaar
Meri dosti mera pyaar

Jivan kaa yahi hain dastur
Pyar bina akela majbur
Dosti ko mane toh sab dukh dur
Dosti ko mane toh sab dukh dur
Koyi kahin thhokar khaye, mere sang aaye
Ke pag pag dip jalaye
Meri dosti mera pyar
Meri dosti mera pyaar

Dono ke hain rup hajar, par meri sune jo sansar
Dosti hain bhayi toh, bahana hain pyaar
Dosti hain bhayi toh, bahana hain pyaar
Koyi mat nain churaye
Mere sang aaye
Ke pag pag dip jalaye
Meri dosti mera pyaar
Meri dosti mera pyaar
Pyar kaa hain pyaar hi nam
Kahi mira kahi ghanashyam
Dosti kaa yaro nahi koyi dham
Dosti kaa yaro nahi koyi dham
Koyi kahi dur naa jaye, mere sang aaye
Ke pag pag dip jalaye
Meri dosti mera pyaar
Meri dosti mera pyaar
Koyi jab raah naa

~~~
~~~

Yeh Dosti Hum Nahin Todenge

Yeh dosti hum nahin todenge
Todenge dam magar
Tera saath na chhodenge
Yeh dosti hum nahin todenge
Todenge dam magar
Tera saath na chhodenge
Ae meri jeet teri jeet
Teri haar meri haar
Sun ae mere yaar
Tera gam mera gam
Meri jaan teri jaan
Aisa apna pyaar
Jaan pe bhi khelenge
Tere liye le lenge
Jaan pe bhi khelenge
Tere liye le lenge
Sab se dushmani
Yeh dosti hum nahin todenge
Todenge dam magar
Tera saath na chhodenge

Logon ko aate hain do
Nazar hum magar
Dekho do nahin
Are ho judaa ya khafa
Ae khuda hai dua
Aisa ho nahin
Khaana peena saath hai
Marna jeena saath hai
Khaana peena saath hai
Marna jeena saath hai
Saari zindagi
Yeh dosti hum nahin todenge
Todenge dam magar
Tera saath na chhodenge

~~~
~~~

HOLI

Holi Aayi Re

Holi aayi re kanhaai, Holi aayi re
Holi aayi re kanhaai
Rag chhalake suna, de zara bansuri
Holi aayi re aayi
Re holi aayi re

Barase gulaal rang more aangnava
Apane hi rang me rang de mohe sajanva
Ho dekho nache mora manwa
Tore kaaran gharase aai tore kaaran ho
Tore kaaran gharase aai
Hun nikalake suna de zara bansuri
Holi aayi re kanhaai
Rag chhalake suna de zara bansuri
Holi aayi re aayi re holi aayi re

Chhute na rang aisi rang de chunariyaa
Dhoba ye dhoye chaahe saari umariyaa
Ho man ko rang dega saawariya
Chhute na rang aisi rang de chunariyaa ji,
Rang de chunariyaa
Dhoba ye dhoye chaahe saari umariyaa
Mohe bhaaye na harjaai mohe bhaaye na
Mohe bhaaye na harjaai mohe bhaaye na
Rang halake suna de zara bansuri
Holi aayi re kanhaai
Rang chhalake suna
De zara bansuri
Holi aayi re kanhaai
Rang chhalake suna
De zara bansrri.

~~~
~~~

Rang Barase

Rang barase bhige, chunarawali rang barase
Are kaine maari pichakaari
Tori bhigi angiyaa
O rangrasiya rangrasiya
Rang barase
Rang barase bhige chunarawali rang barase
O rang barase bhige chunarawali rang barase
Ha rang barase bhige chunarawali rang barase
Sone ki thaali mein jonaa parosa
Are sone ki thaali mein
Haan sone ki thaali, mein jonaa parosa
Are khaae gori kaa, yaar balam tarase
Rang barase holi hai!
O rang barase bhige, Chunarawali rang barase

Laungaa ilaayachi kaa
Are laungaa ilaayachi kaa bhai
Haan laungaa ilaayachi kaa

Haan... are laungaa ilaayachi kaa bidaa lagaya
Laungaa ilaayachi kaa bidaa lagaya
Are laungaa ilaayachi kaa
Haan laungaa ilaayachi kaa bidaa lagaya
Are chaabe gori kaa yaar, balam tarase rang barase
Holi hai!

O rang barase bhige, Chunarawali rang barase
O rang barase bhige, Chunarawali rang barase
O rang barase bhige, Chunarawali rang barase

Are belaa chameli kaa... sej bichhaya
Are belaa chameli kaa... sej bichhaya
Belaa chameli kaa... sej bichhaya
Belaa chameli kaa... sej bichhaya
Are belaa chameli kaa...
Haan belaa chameli, kaa sej bichhaya

Soe gori kaa yaar, balam tarase rang barase

Holi hai!
O rang barase bhige chunarawali rang barase
O rang barase bhige chunarawali rang barase
O rang barase bhige chunarawali rang barase
O rang barase bhige chunarawali rang barase
O rang barase bhige chunarawali rang barase
O rang barase bhige chunarawali rang barase haai.

~~~

Holi Ke Din

Holi ke din dil khil jaate hain
Rangon mein rang mil jaate hain
Holi ke din dil khil jaate hain
Rangon mein rang mil jaate hain
Gile shikawe bhul ke doston
Dushman bhi gale mil jaate hain
Holi ke din dil khil jaate hain
Rangon mein rang mil jaate hai
Holi ke din dil khil jaate hain
Rangon mein rang mil jaate hai
Holi hain
Gori tere rang jaisaa
Thodasa main rang bana lu
Aa tere gulabi gaalon se
Thoda sa gulaal chura lu
Jare ja deewane tu
Holi ke bahane tu
Jare ja deewane tu
Holi ke bahane tu
Chhed na mujhe besaram
Puchh le zamane se aise hi
Bahane se liye aur
Diye dil jaate hain
Holi ke din dil khil jaate hain
Rango mein rang mil jaate hain.

~~~

WEDDING

PREM RATAN DHAN PAYO

Sukh dukh jhoothe
Dhan bhi jhootha
Jhoothi moh-maaya
Saccha mann ka wo kona jahaan
Prem ratan paayo
Prem ratan paayo
Ni ni sa sa re re sa sa

Payo payo laayo chaayo
Aayo gaayo payo

Saiyan tu kamaal ka, baatein bhi kamaal ki
Saiyan tu kamaal ka, baatein bhi kamaal ki
Laaga rang jo tera, hui main kamaal ki

Payo re payo re payo re payo re payo
Payo re payo re payo re payo re payo re
Prem ratan dhan payo payo
Prem ratan dhan payo payo
Rut milan ki laayo
Prem ratan
Prem ratan dhan payo maine payo
Prem ratan dhan payo

Kya main dikha doon, yaa main chupa loon
Jo dhan hai mann mein, yeh bhi na jaanu
Bajne lagi kyun, sargam si tann mein
Khushiya si hai aangan mein
Chehre pe aaye meri
Rangatein gulaal ki
Laaga rang jo tera, hui main kamaal ki

Payo re payo re payo re payo re payo
Payo re payo re payo re payo re payo re
Prem ratan dhan payo payo
Prem ratan dhan payo payo

Mann gagan par chayo
Prem ratan
Prem ratan dhan payo maine payo
Prem ratan dhan payo

Mujhko the ghere jitne andhere, ho gaye door sabhi
Sab sapno ki, sab rishton ki paa li hai keemat bhi
Prem ko main samjhi
Kisi ne na ki meri, tune jo sambhaal ki
Laaga rang jo tera, hui main kamaal ki
Payo re payo re payo re payo re payo
Payo re payo re payo re payo re payo re
Prem ratan dhan payo payo
Prem ratan dhan payo payo
Aaj mann bhar aayo
Prem ratan
Prem ratan dhan payo maine payo
Prem ratan dhan payo
Chaayo aayo laayo paayo paayo

~~~

Mahalo Kaa Raaja

Mahalo kaa raajaa milaa
Ke raani beti raaj karegi
Khushi khushi kar do bidaa
Tumhaari beti raaj karegi
Mahalo kaa raajaa milaa
Ke raani beti raaj karegi

Galiyo galiyo dhum machegi
Galiyo galiyo dhum machegi
Kaandhe kaandhe doli chalegi
Doli me dolegaa jiyaa
Doli me dolegaa jiyaa
Ke raani beti raaj karegi
Khushi khushi kar do bidaa
Tumhaari beti raaj karegi
~~~

Jis ghar jaae swarg banaa de
Jis ghar jaae swarg banaa de
Dono kul ki laaj nibhaa de
Yahi baabul ji denge duaa
Yahi baabul ji denge duaa
Ke raani beti raaj karegi
Khushi khushi kar do bidaa
Tumhaari beti raaj karegi

Beti to hai dhan hi paraayaa
Beti to hai dhan hi paraayaa
Paas apane koi kab rakh paayaa
Bhaari karanaa naa apanaa jiyaa
Bhaari karanaa naa apanaa jiyaa
Tumhaari beti raaj karegi
Mahalo kaa raajaa milaa
Ke raani beti raaj karegi
Khushi khushi kar do bidaa
Tumhaari beti raaj karegi
Mahalo kaa raajaa milaa.

~~~

Bahaaro Phool

Bahaaro phul barsaao
Mera mehboob aaya hai
Mera mehboob aaya hai
Hawao raagini gaao
Mera mehboob aaya hai
Mera mehboob aaya hai

O laali phul ki mehandi
Laga in gore haatho me
Utar aa ai ghata kajal
Laga in pyaari aankho me
Sitaaro maang bhar jaao
Mera mehboob aaya hai
Mera mehboob aaya hai
~~~

Nazaaro har taraf ab
Taan do ik nur ki chaadar
Badaa sharmilaa dilabar hai
Chala jaaye na sharma kar
Zaraa tum dil ko bahalaao
Mera mehboob aaya hai
Mera mehboob aaya hai

Sajaai hai javaan kaliyo
Ne ab ye sej ulfat ki
Inhe maalum tha aayegi
Ik din rut muhabbat ki
Fizaao rag bikharaao
Mera mehboob aaya hai
Mera mehboob aaya hai

~~~

Behana O Behana

Behna O behna teri
Doli mai sajaunga
Behna O behna teri
Doli mai sajaunga
Teri jayegee barat
Hogi ankho me barsat
Hans hanske mai dukhada
Bidayi kaa chhupaunga
Behna O behna teri
Doli mai sajaunga
Meri gudiya jaisi behna
Meri gudiya jaisi behna
Too toh hai is ghar kaa gehana
Ja ke too sasural me
Apni sita jaisi ban ke rehna behna O behna
Teri doli mai sajaunga
Jiwan me too sab khushi pana
Jiwan me too sab khushi pana
Sada sukhi sasural me rehna
Sukh ke us jiwan me hamko
~~~

Bhul naa jana pyari behna
Behna O behna teri
Doli mai sajaunga

Teri jayegee barat
Hogi ankho me barsat
Hans hanske mai dukhada
Bidayi kaa chhupaunga
Behna O behna teri
Doli mai sajaunga.

~~~

Meri Pyari Bahaniya

Meri pyari bahaniya, banegi dulhaniya
Meri pyari bahaniya banegi dulhaniya
Sajake aayenge duulhe raja O
Bhaiya raja bajayega baja
Bhaiya raja bajayega baja
Meri pyari bahaniya
Banegi dulhaniya

Solah singar meri bahina karegi
Solah singar meri bahina karegi
Tika chadhega aur haldi lagegi
Bahana ke honthon
Pe jhulegi nathaniya
Aur jhumenge dulhe raja
Bhaiya raja bajayega baja
Bhaiya raja bajayega baja
Meri pyari bahaniya banegi dulhaniya

Sej pe baithegi woh
Doli pe chalegi
Sej pe baithegi woh
Doli pe chalegi
Dharati pe bahana rani
Panv naa dharegi
Palakon ki palaki mein
~~~

Bahana ko bitha ke
Le jayenge duulhe raja
Bhaiya raja bajayega baja
Bhaiya raja bajayega baja
Meri pyari bahaniya, banegi dulhaniya

Sajana ke ghar chali
Jayegi jo bahana
Sajana ke ghar chali
Jayegi jo bahana
Honth hansenge
Mere roenge yeh naina
Rakhiya ke roj rani
Bahana ko bulauunga
Rakhiya ke roj rani
Bahana ko bulauunga
Le ke aayenge dulhe raja
Bhaiya raja bajayega baja
Bhaiya raja bajayega baja
Meri pyari bahaniya, banegi dulhaniya
Sajake aayenge duulhe raja o
Bhaiya raja bajayega baja
Bhaiya raja bajayega baja
Meri pyari bahaniya
Banegi dulhaniya.

~~~

Didi Tera Devar

Didi tera devar deewana
Didi tera devar deewana
Hai ram, kudiyon ko daale daana
Hai ram, kudiyon ko daale daana
Dhandha hai yeh uska puraana
Dhandha hai yeh uska puraana
Hai ram, kudiyon ko daale daana
Hai ram, kudiyon ko daale daana

Main boli ke laana tu imli ka daana
~~~

Magar woh chuaare le aaya deewana
Main boli ke machle hai dil mera haaye
Woh kharbuja laaya jo neembu mangaaye
Pagla hai koi usko bataana
Pagla hai koi usko bataana
Hai ram, kudiyon ko daale daana
Hai ram, kudiyon ko daale daana
Didi tera devar deewana
Hai ram, kudiyon ko daale daana

Main boli ke laana tu mitti pahaadi
Magar woh bataashe le aaya anaadi
Main boli thi la do mujhe tu khataayi
Woh baazar se le ke aaya mithaai
Mushkil hai yoon mujhko phasaana
Mushkil hai yoon mujhko phasaana
Hai ram, kudiyon ko daale daana
Hai ram, kudiyon ko daale daana
Didi tera devar deewana
Hai ram, kudiyon ko daale daana

Bhabhi teri behna ko maana
Bhabhi teri behna ko maana
Hai ram, kudiyon ka hai zamaana
Hai ram, kudiyon ka hai zamaana
Rabba mere mujhko bachaana
Rabba mere mujhko bachaana
Hai ram, kudiyon ka hai zamaana
Hai ram, kudiyon ka hai zamaana
Hukum aapka tha jo maine na maana
Khatavaar hoon main na aaya nibhaana
Sazaa jo bhi dogi woh manzoor hogi
Aji meri mushkil tabhi door hogi
Bandaa hai yeh khudse begaana
Bandaa hai yeh khudse begaana
Hai ram, kudiyon ka hai zamaana
Hai ram, kudiyon ka hai zamaana.

~~~
~~~

Babul Jo Tumne

Babul jo tumne sikhaaya
Jo tum se paaya
Sajan ghar le chali
Sajan ghar le chali
Sajan ghar main chali
Yaadon ke lekar saaye
Chali ghar paraaye
Tumhari laadli
Huum huum
Kaise bhool paaongi main baba
Suni jo tumse kahaaniyan
Chhod chali aangan mein maiya
Bachpan ki nishaaniyan
Sun meri pyari behna
Sajaye rehna
Yeh babul ki gali
Huum huum
Huum huum huum huum
Ban gaya pardes ghar janam ka
Mili hai duniya mujhe nayi
Naam jo piya se maine joda
Naye rishton se bandh gayi
Mere sasur ji pita hain
Pati devta hain
Devar chhavi krishna ki
Sajan ghar main chali
Sajan ghar main chali
Huum huum huum
Huum huum huum

~~~
~~~

Teri Rabb Ne Bana Di Jodi

Teri rabb ne bana di jodi
Teri rabb ne
Teri rabb ne bana di jodi
Tu haan kar ya naa kar yaara
Oh yaara ye jogi ka bole ik tara haay

Teri rabb ne bana di jodi
Teri rabb ne
Teri rabb ne bana di jodi
Tu haan kar ya naa kar yaara
Oh yaara ye jogi ka bole ik tara haay

Kya bole tera ik tara kya bole
Kya bole tera ik tara mujhe kya
Laina ha jogi, jogi meri shaadi
Marzi se hogi ho

Teri rabb ne bana di jodi
Teri raab ne
Teri rabb ne bana di jodi
Tu haan kar ya naa kar yaara
Oh yaara ye jogi ka bole ik tara haay
Kya karne hain ghode haathi
Kya karne hain barati
Naino ki is doli mein chal
Mujhe bithale saathi

Aisi ladki kaha milti hai
Gudiya ki tarah hilti hai
Din raat tadapte bhanvere
Tab ek kali khilti hai
Oh hatt jao mujhe jaane do
Hatt jao, hatt jao mujhe jaane do
Na khankao khan khan kangana
Oh kangna mujhe nahi banana tera sajana haay

Teri raab ne bana di jodi

Teri rabb ne
Teri rabb ne bana di jodi
Tu haan kar ya naa kar yaara
Oh yaara ye jogi ka bole ik tara haay
Teri rabb ne bana di jodi
Teri rabb ne
Teri rabb ne bana di jodi
Teri rabb ne
Teri rabb ne bana di jodi
Teri rabb ne
Teri rabb ne bana di jodi
Teri rabb ne, haay..

~~~
~~~

BIRTHDAY

O Nanhe Se Farishte

O nanhe se farishte
Tujh se ye kaisa nata
Kaise ye dil ke rishte
O Nanhe se farishte
Happy birthday to you, happy birthday to you
Happy birthday to you

Tujhe dekhane ko tarase
Kyo har ghadi nigaahe
Tujhe dekhane ko tarase
Kyo har ghadi nigaahe
Bechain si rahati hai
Tere liye ye baahe
Mujhe khud pataa nahi hai
Mujhe tujhase pyaar kyu hai
O Nanhe se farishte

Happy birthday to you, happy birthday to you
Happy birthday to you

Naazuk saa phul hai tu
Kisi aur ke chaman kaa
Naazuk saa phul hai tu
Kisi aur ke chaman kaa
Khushabu se teri mahake
Kyo baag mere man kaa
Meri zindagi me chhaai
Tujhase bahaar kyu hai
O Nanhe se farishte
Happy birthday to you, happy birthday to you
Happy birthday to you

Tu kuchh nahi hai mera
Phir bhi ye tadap kaisi
Tujhe dekhate hi khun me

Uthati hai ik lahar si
Har vakt mujhako rahataa
Tera intazaar kyu hai
O nanhe se farishte
Tujh se ye kaisa nata
Kaise ye dil ke rishte
O nanhe se farishte
Happy birthday to you, happy birthday to you
Happy birthday to you

~~~

Baar Baar Din Yeh Aaye

Happy birthday to you, happy birthday to you
Happy birthday to you
Sunita happy birthday to you

Baar baar din yeh aaye, baar baar dil yeh gaaye
Baar baar din yeh aaye, baar baar dil yeh gaaye
Tu jiye hazaro saal
Yeh meri hai aarzu
Happy birthday to you, happy birthday to you
Happy birthday to you
Sunita happy birthday to you
Baar baar din yeh aaye, baar baar dil yeh gaaye
Tu jiye hazaro saal
Yeh meri hai aarzu
Happy birthday to you, happy birthday to you
Happy birthday to you
Sunita happy birthday to you

Beqaraar hoke daaman, thaam lun main kis ka
Beqaraar hoke daaman, thaam lun main kis ka
Kya misaal dun main teri, naam lun main kis ka
Nahin nahin aisaa hasin koi nahin hai
Jis pe yeh nazar ruk jaaye bemisaal jo kahalaaye
Tu jiye hazaro saal
Yeh meri hai aarazu
Happy birthday to you, happy birthday to you
~~~

Happy birthday to you
Sunita happy birthday to you

Auron ki tarah kuchh main bhi tohfaa aaj laataa
Main teri hasin mahafil mein phool le ke aataa
Jee ne kahaa use kyaa hai phoolon ki zarurat
Jo bahaar khud kahalaaye har kali kaa dil dhadakaaye
Tu jiye hazaro saal
Yeh meri hai aarzu
Happy birthday to you happy birthday to you
Happy birthday to you
Sunita happy birthday to you
Phoolo ne chaman se tujhako hai salaam bhejaa
Phoolo ne chaman se tujhako hai salaam bhejaa
Taaro ne gagan se tujhako ye paiyaam bhejaa
Duaa hai khudaa kare ai shokh tujhako
Chaand ki umar lag jaaye aaye to qayaamat aaye
Tu jiye hazaro saal
Yeh meri hai aarzu
Happy birthday to you, happy birthday to you
Happy birthday to you
Sunita happy birthday to you
Baar baar din yeh aaye
Baar baar dil yeh gaaye, baar baar din yeh aaye
Baar baar dil yeh gaaye, baar baar din yeh aaye
Tu jiye hazaro saal
Yeh meri hai aarzu
Happy birthday to you, happy birthday to you
Happy birthday to you
Sunita happy birthday to you

~~~

Mere Ghar Aayi

Mere ghar aayi, mere ghar aayi
Ek nanhi pari, ek nanhi pari
Chaandani ke hasin
Rath pe sawaar
~~~

Mere ghar aayi hoo, mere ghar aayi
Ek nanhi pari, ek nanhi pari

Uski baaton mein shahad jaisi mithaas
Uski saason mein itar ki mahakaas
Honth kaise ke bhige-bhige gulaab
Gaal jaise ke bahake-bahake anaar
Mere ghar aai hoo, mere ghar aayi
Ek nanhi pari, ek nanhi pari

Us ke aane se mere aangan me
Khil uthhe fool gunagunaayi bahaar
Dekh kar us ko ji nahin bharataa
Chaahe dekhoo use hajaaro baar
Chaahe dekhoo use hajaaro baar
Mere ghar aai hoo, mere ghar aayi
Ek nanhi pari, ek nanhi pari

Maine poochhaa use ke kaun hain too
Has ke boli ke main hoo teraa pyaar
Mai tere dil mein thi humeshaa se
Ghar mein aayi hoo aaj pahali baar
Mere ghar aai hoo, mere ghar aayi
Ek nanhi pari, ek nanhi pari
Chaandani ke hasin, rath pe sawaar
Mere ghar aayi, mere ghar aayi
Ek nanhi pari, ek nanhi pari
Ek nanhi pari

~~~

Humbhi Agar Bachche Hote

Happy birthday to you
Hum bhi agar bachche hote, hum bhi agar bachche hote
Naam hamara hota gabalu babalu
Khaane ko milate laddu
Aur duniyaa kahati
~~~

Happy birthday to you, happy birthday to you
Koi laataa gudiyaa motar rel
To koi laataa phiraki lattu
Koi chaabi kaa tattu
Aur duniyaa kahati
Happy birthday to you, happy birthday to you

Kitani pyaari hoti hai ye bholi si umar
Na naukari ki chintaa na roti ki phikar
Nanhe munne hote
Ham to dete sau hukum
Pichhe pichhe papa
Mummy banake naukar
Chocolate biscuit toffee
Khaate aur pite duddu
Aur duniyaa kahati
Happy birthday to you

Ham bhi agar bachche hote, ham bhi agar bachche hote
Naam hamara hota gabalu babalu
Khaane ko milate laddu
Aur duniyaa kahati
Happy birthday to you, happy birthday to you

Kaise kaise nakhare karate gharawaalo se ham
Pal me hansate pal me rote karate naak me dam
Akkad bakkad lukka
Chhupi kabhi chhuaa chhu
Karate din bhar hallaa
Gullaa dagaa aur udham
Aur kabhi zid par ad
Jaate jaise adiyal tattu
Aur duniyaa kahati
Happy birthday to you

Ham bhi agar bachche hote, ham bhi agar bachche hote
Naam hamara hota gabalu babalu
Khaane ko milate laddu
Aur duniyaa kahati
Happy birthday to you, happy birthday to you

Ab to ye hai haal ke jab se bitaa bachapan
Maan se jhagadaa baap se takkar biwi se anaban
Kolhu ke ham bail bane
Hai dhobi ke gadhe
Duniyaa bhar ke dande
Sar pe khaaye danaadan
Bachapan apanaa hota to
Na karate dhenchu dhenchu
Aur duniyaa kahati
Happy birthday to you, happy birthday to you
Ham bhi agar bachche hote, ham bhi agar bachche hote
Naam hamara hota gabalu babalu
Khaane ko milate laddu
Aur duniyaa kahati
Happy birthday to you, happy birthday to you

~~~

Tare Tare Kitne Neel Gagan

Tare tare kitne neel gagan pe tare
Tare tare kitne neel gagan ke tare
Tare tare kitne neel gagan pe tare
Teri uamr ho uthane saal
Jitane neel gagan pe tare
Tare tare kitne neel gagan pe tare
Tare tare kitne neel gagan ke tare

Phool hai kitane pyare
Phoolo se pyara tu hai
Happy bairthday to you, happy bairthday to you
Log hai kitne nyare
Logo se nyara tu hai
Happy bairthday to you
Aaja gale lag ja
Mere dil ke sahare
Tare tare kitne neel gagan pe tare
Tare tare kitne neel gagan ke tare
~~~

Tum hi mere daddi
Aur tum hi mere meet
Daddy you are very sweet
Uncle you are very sweet
Mammy se sikha hai
Maine ye naya geetDaddy you are very sweet
Aaja gale lag ja papa
Mere pyare pyare
Tare tare kitne neel gagan pe tare
Tare tare kitne neel gagan ke tare
Saal ke raja ye din
Mubarak mere laal ji
Jiye tu hazaro saal Jiye tu hazaro saal
Tujhe kuch ho jaye To kya ho mera haal
Jiye tu hazaro saal
Aaja gale lag ja
Mere raaj dulare
Tare tare kitne neel Gagan pe tare
Tare tare kitne neel Gagan ke tare
Teri uamr ho utane saal
Jitane neel gagan pe tare
Tare tare kitne neel Gagan pe tare
Tare tare kitne neel Gagan ke tare
Tare tare kitne neel Gagan pe tare

~~~

Oh Mama Dear Mama

Apna sab ko rup dikhau
Jab ishwar ke man me aaya
Tab naa usne tujhko banaya
Tujhme apna rup sajaya
Aaj tera maa janamdin aaya
Happy birthday O mamma dear mamma
Happy birthday to you
O mamma dear mamma
Happy birthday to you
La lala lala la lala la la
~~~

Jiwan ke jitne pal hamne
God me teri gujare
Jiwan ke jitne pal hamne
God me teri gujare
Baho pal jiwan hamko
Lagte hai sabse pyare
O mamma dear mamma
O mamma pyari mamma
Happy birthday to you
O mamma dear mamma
Happy birthday to you

Pyar ko tu anurog samjhke
Sab kuch hampe lutaye
Pyar ko tu anurog samjhke
Sab kuch hampe lutaye
Lakho hi upkar kare
Upkar kabhi jataye
O mamma dear mamma
O mamma pyari mamma
Happy birthday to you
O mamma dear mamma
Happy birthday to you

Ham hai tere pyar ki kaliya
Tu mamata ki dali
Ham hai tere pyar ki kaliya
Tu mamata ki dali
Janam diwas ho tujhko mubarak
Hamko janam dene wali
O mamma dear mamma
O mamma pyari mamma
Happy birthday to you
O mamma dear mamma
Happy birthday to you
O mamma dear mamma
Happy birthday to you

~~~
~~~

BEREAVEMENT

Pinjre Ke Panchhi Re Tera Dard Na Jane Koi

Pinjare ke panchhi re
Tera darad na jaane koi
Bahar se to khamosh rahe tu
Bhitar bhitar roye re

Keh na sake tu apni, apni kahani
Teri bhi panchhi kya zindagani re
Vidhi ne katha likhi
Aansu mein kalam duboye

Chupke chupke rone wale
Rakhna chhupa ke dil ke chhale re
Yeh patthar ka des hai pagle
Koi na tera hoye

~~~
~~~

Koi Laakh Kare Chaturai

Koi lakh kare chaturayi karam ka lekh mite na re bhai
Zara samjho re iski sacchayi re

Is duniya mein bhagya ke aage chale na kisi ka upaaye
Kagad ho to sab koyi banche karam na bancha jaaye
Ek din isi kismat ke kaaran ban ko gayen thein raghurai re
Kahen manwa dheeraj khota kahen tu nahat roye
Apna socha kabhi nahi hota bhagya kare so hoye
Chahe ho raja chahe bhikari thokar sabhi ne yahan khayi

~~~

Maili Chadar Odh Ke Kaise

Maili chaadar odhke kaise
Dwaar tumhaare aaoon
Hey paavan parameshwara mere
Man hi man sharmaaoon

Tune mujhko jag me bhejaa
Nirmal dekar kaayaa
Aakar is sansaar maine
Isko daag lagaaya
Janam janam ki maili chaadar
Kaise daag chudaaoon

Nirmal vaani paakar tujhse
Naam na teraa gaayaa
Nain moondhkar he parameshwar
Kabhi naa tujhko dhyaayaa
Man veena ki taaren tooti
Ab kyaa geeth sunaaoon

In pairon se chal kar tere
Mandir kabhi na aayaa
Jahaan jahaan ho poojaa teri
~~~

Kabhi naa sees jhukaayaa
Hey harihar main haar ke aayaa
Ab kyaa haar chadhaaoon

~~~

Toot Gai Hai Mala Moti Bikhar Chale

Toot gayi hai mala moti bikhar chale
Do din rah ke saath jaane kidhar chale

Milan ki duniya chhod chalen ye aaj birah mein apne
Khoye khoye naino mein hai ujade ujade sapne
Yaad ki gathari liye jhukaye nazar chale
Do din reh ke saath ...

Ab to jag mein jiyenge aansu pite pite
Jaisi inpe beeti waisi aur kisi pe na beete
Koi mat puchho inse ki yeh kis dagar chale
Do din reh ke saath....

~~~

Mukhda Dekh Le Prani

Mukhada dekh le prani zara darpan mein
Dekh le kitna punya hai kitna paap tere jeevan mein

Kabhi to pal bhar soch le prani kya hai teri karam kahani
Pata laga le pade hai kitne daag tere daaman mein

Khud ko dhokha de mat bande achhe na hot kapat ke dhandhe
Sada na chalta kisi ka naatak duniya ke aangan mein

~~~
~~~

Kabhi Dhoop To Kabhi Chhaon

Sukh dukh dono rehte jisme jeevan hai woh gaon
Kabhi dhoop to kabhi chhaon
Upar wala paasa pheke niche chalte daaon
Kabhi dhoop kabhi chaaon

Bhale bhi din aate jagat mein bure bhi din aate
Karve mithe phal karam ke yahan sabhi paate
Kabhi sidhe kabhi ulte padte ajab samaya ke paanv

Kya khushiyan kya gam yeh sab milte bari bari
Malik ki marzi pe chalti yeh duniya saari
Dhyan se khena jag nadiya mein bande apni naav

~~~

Dekh Tere Sansar Ki Haalat Kya Ho Gayi Bhagwan

Dekh tere sansaar ki haalat kya ho gayi bhagwaan
Kitna badal gaya insaan
Suraj na badla chand na badla na badla re aasmaan
Kitna badal gaya insaan

Aaya samaya bedhanga aaj aadmi bana lafanga
Kahin pe jhagda kahin pe danga
Naach raha nar ho kar nanga
Chhal aur kapat ke haanthon apna bech raha imaan

Ram ke bhakt rahim ke bande
Rachate aaj phareb ke dhandhe
Kitne yeh makkar yeh andhe dekh liyen inke bhi dhandhe
Inhi ki kaali kartuton se hua yeh mulk masaan

Jo hum aapas mein na jhagadte
Bane huye kyu khel bigadte
~~~

Kahe lakhon ghar ye ujadate kyun
Yeh bachhe ma se bichhadate
Phoot phoot ke kyun rote pyare bapu ke pran
Kitna badal gaya insaan...

~~~

Tere Dwar Khada Bhagwan

Tere dware khada bhagwaan
Bhagat bhar de re jholi
Tera hoga bada kalyaan
Ki jug jug teri rahegi shaan
Bhagat bhar de re jholi

Dol uthi hai sari dharti dekh re dola gagan hai saara
Bhikh maangane aaya hai tere ghar jagat ka paalanhaara re
Main aaj tera mehmaan kar le re mujhse zara pehchaan
Bhagat bhar de re jholi

Aaj luta de tu sarbas apna maan le kehna mera
Mit jayega pal mein tera janam janam ka phera
Tu chhod sakal abhimaan amar kar le re tu apna daan
Bhagat bhar de re jholi

~~~

Bachane Wala Hai Bhagwan

Shraddha rakho jagat ke logon apne deenanath pe
Labh hani jeevan aur mrityu sab kuchh uske haanth mein

Marne wala hai bhagwaan bachane wala hai bhagwaan
Bal bhi baanka na hota uska jiska rakshak daya nidhan

Tyag do re bhai phal ki asha swarth bina preet jodo
Kal kya hoga uski chinta jagatpita par chhodo
Kya honi hai kya anhoni sabka usko gyan

Jal thal agan aakaash pawan par kewal uski satta
Uski marji ke bina hil na sake ek patta
Usi ka socha yahan pe hota uski shakti mahan

~~~

Bhagwaan Meri Naiya

Bhagwaan meri naiya us paar laga dena
Ab tak to nibhaya hai aage bhi nibha dena

Dal bal ke saath maaya ghere jo mujhko aakar
Tum dekhte na rehna jhat aake bacha lena

Sambhav hai jhanjhato mein main tumko bhool jaun
Par nath kahin tum bhi mujhko na bhula dena

Tum dev main pujari tum isht main upasak
Yah baat agar sach hai sach kar ke dikha dena

~~~

Doosron Ka Dukhra Door Karne Wale

Doosaron ka dukhada door karne wale
Tere dukh door karenge ram
Kiye ja tu jag mein bhalayi ka kaam
Tere dukh door karenge ram

Kat-ta hai path yeh dharma ka
Marag sambhal ke chalna prani
Pag pag pare hai yahan re to tote
Kadam kadam par kurbani
Magar tu danwadol na hona teri sab peer harenge ram
doosaron ka dukhada ....

Kya tune paaya kya tune khoya kya tera labh hai kya haani
Iska hisab karega wo ishwar tu kyu phikar kare prani
Tu bas apna kaam kiye ja tera bhandaar bharenge ram

Doosaron ka dukhada ....

Ponchh le tu apne aansu
Tamam tere dukh door karenge ram

~~~

Humne Jag Ki Ajab Tasveer Dekhi

Humne jag ki ajab tasveer dekhi
Ek hasta hai dus rote hain
Yeh prabhu ki adbhut zageer dekhi
Ek hasta hai dus rote hain

Humne haste mukhade char mile
Dukhiyare chehre hazar mile
Yahan sukh se sau guni peer dekhi
Do ek sukhi yahan lakhon mein
Aansu hain karoron aankhon mein
Humne gin gin har taqdeer dekhi

Kuchh bol prabhu yeh kya maaya
Tera bhed samajh mein na aaya
Humne dekhe mahal re kutir dekhi

~~~

ATH SHREE VISHNU SHAHASTRANAAM STOTRAM

Yasya smaranmatrena janma sansaar bandhanaat
Vimuchyate namastasmai vishnave prabhavishnave
Namah samasta bhutanaam aadi bhutaya bhubhrite
Anek roop roopaya vishnave prabhavishnave

Shrutva dharmansheshena paavanani cha sarvashah
Yudhishthirah shantanavam punarevabhyabhashat
Kimekam devatam loke kim vapyekam parayanam
Stuvantah kam kamarchantah prapnurmyumanvahshubham
Ko dharmah sarva dharmanam bhavato parmo matah
kim japanmuchhyate janturjanma sansaarbandhanaat

Bhishma Uvaach

Jagatprabhum deva devam anantam purushottamam
Stuvan naam shahastrena purush satatosthita

Tameva charchayannityam bhaktya purush avyayam
Dhyayanstuvannamasyanscha yajamanastameva cha
Anadinidhanam vishnum sarva lok maheshwaram
Lokadhyaksham stuvannityam sarvadukhatigobhavet
Brahmanyam sarvadharmagyam lokanaamkirtivardhanam
Loknatham mahadbhutam sarvabhut bhavodbhavam

Esh me sarvadharmanaamdharmoadhikatamo matah
Yadbhaktya pundareekaksham stavairchainnarah sada

Paramam yo mahattezah paramam yo mahattapah
Parmam yo mahadbramha paramam yah parayanam

Pavitranaam pavitram yo mangalanaam cha mangalam
Daivatam devatanaam cha bhutanaam avyayoa pita

Yatah sarvani bhutani bhavanti aadiyugagame
Yasmincha pralayam yanti punarev yugachhaye

Tasya lokpradhanasya jagannathasya bhupate
Vishnornaam shahastram me shrinupaap bhayapaham

Taani naamani gaudhani vikhyatani mahatmanah
Tishibhih parigitani tani vakshyami bhutaye

~~~

Shree Vishnushahastranaam

Om Visham Vishnu Vashatkaro
Bhut bhavyabhavatprabhuh
Bhutkrit bhutbhrit bhavo bhutatma bhutabhavanah
~~~

Putanaam parmatmacha muktanaam parmagatih
Avyayo purushah shakshi kshetragyo akshar ev cha

Yogoy yog vidanneta pradhanpurusheshwarah
Narshinghvapuh sreemaan keshavah purushhottamam

Sarvah sarvah shivah stharurabhutadirnidhiavyayah
Sambhavo bhavano bharta prabhavah prabhurishwarah

Swayambhu sambhuraditya pushkaraksho mahaswanah
Anadinidhano dhata vidhata dhaturutaamah

Aprameyo hrishikeshah padmanabhahoamaraprabhuh
Vishwakarma manustwashta sthavishtah sthaviro dhurva

Agrahyah shashwatah krishno lohitakshayah Pratardanah
Prabhutstrikakubdham pavitram mangalam param

Ishanah prandah prano Jyesthah shreshathah Prajapatih
Hiranyagarbho bhugarbho maadhavo madhusudanah

Ishwari vikramo dhanvi medhavi vikramah kramah
Anuttamo duradharsh kritagyah kritiraatmavaan

Sureshah sharanam sharma vishwaretah prajabhavah
Ahah samvastaro vyalah pratyayh sarvadarshanah
Ajah sarveshwarah sidhhah siddhih sarvadirachutah
Vrishakapirmeyatama sarvayogvinishritah

Vasurvasurmanaah satyah sammatma sammitah samah
Amoghah pundareekaksho vishkarma vishakritih

Rudro bahushira babhrurvishwayonih Suchishrawah
Amritah shashwatasthanurwararoho mahatapaah

Sarvagah sarvavidbhanurvishwakseno janardanah
Vedovedvidavyango vedango vedvittkavih

Lokadhyakshah suradhyaksho dharmadhyakshah
kritakritah
Chaturatma chaturvyuhash

Chaturdramshtrashchaturbhujah

Bhrajishnurbhojanam bhokta sahishnurjagadadijah
Anagho vijayo jeta vishwayonih punarvasuh

Upendro vamanah pranshurmoghah shuchirurjitah
Atindrah sangrahah sargo dhritatma niyamo yamah

Vedyo vaidyah sada yogi veeraha madhavo madhuh
Atindriyo mahamayo mahotsaho mahabalah

Mahabuddhirmahaviryo mahashaktirmahadyutih
Anirdeshyavapuh shreemaanmeyatma mahadidhrikah

Maheshwaso mahibharta shreeniwaso satamgatih
Aniruddho suranando govindo govidampatih

Marichirdamano hansah suparno bhujagottamah
Hiranyanabhah sutapa padmnanabhah prajapatih
Amrityuh sarvadrik singhah sandhata sandhimaansthir
Ajo durmarshanah shashta vishrutatma Surariha

Gurur guruttamo dhaam satyah satyaprakramah
Nimisho animishah shragwi vachaspatirudaradhih

Agranirgramanih shreemaanyayo neta samiranah
Shahastra murdha vishwatma shahastraaksha shahastrapaat

Aavartano nivritatma samvritah sampramardanah
Ahah samvartako vahniranilo dharanidharah

Suprasadah prassannatma vishwadhrigivishwabhugvibhuh
Satkarta satkritah sadhurjahnurnarayano narah

Asankhyeyo aprameyatma vishishtah shishtakrichchhuchih
Siddharthah siddhasankalpah siddhidah siddhisaadhanah

Vrishahi vrishabho vishnurvishparva vishodarah
Varadhano vardhamanascha viviktah shrutisagarah

Subhujo durdharo vagmi mahendro vasudo vasuh
Naikarupo brihadrupah shipivishtah prakashanah

Ojastejodyutidharah prakashatma pratapanah riddhah
Spashtakhsaro mantrashchandranshurbhashkardyutih

Amritanshudbhavo bhanuh shashibinduh sureshwarah
Aushadham jagatah satuh satyadharmaparakramah

Bhutbhavyabhavannathah pavanah pavanoanalah
Kamaha kaamkritkaantah kaamah kaampradah prabhuh

Yugadikrityugavarto naikamaayo mahashanah
Adrishyo avyaktarupashcha shahastrajid anantjit

Ishtoavashishtah shishteshtah shikhandi nahusho Vrishah
Krodhahha krodhkritkarta vishwabahurmahidharh

Achutah prathitah pranah prando vasavanujah
Apaam nidhiradhishthanam apramattah pratishthitah

Skandah skanddharo dhuryo vardo vayuvahanah
Vasudevo brihadbhanuradidevah purandarah

Ashokastarana starah shurah saurijaneshwarah
Anukulah shatavartah padmipadmanibhekshanah

Padmanabhoarvindakshah padmagarbhah sharirbhrit
Mahardhiridhho vridhhatma mahaksho garunadhwjah

Atulah sharbho bhimah samyagyo havirharih
Sarvalakshanlakshanyo lakshmivansamitinjayah

Viksharo rohito margo heturdamodarah sahana
Mahidharo mahabhago vegavanmitashanah

Udbhavah kshobhano devah shree garbhah parmeshwarah
Kranam kaaranam karta vikarta gahano guhah

Vyavasayo vyavasthanah sansthanah sthando dhurvah
Parardhi paramspashtushtah pushtah shubhekshanah

Ramo viramo virjo margo neyo nayoanayah
Veerah shaktimatamshreshtho dharmo
Dharmaviduttamah

Vaikunthah purushah pranah prandah pranavah prithuh
Hiranya garbhah shtrughno vyapto vayuradhokshjah

Ritu sudarshanah kaalah parameshthi parigrahah
Ugrah smvatsaro daksho vishramo vishwadakshinah

Vistarah sthawarasthanuh pramaanam beejamavyayam
Arthoanartho mahakosho mahabhogo mahadhanah

Anirvinnah sthavishthoabhurdharmayupo mahamakhah
Nakshtranemi nakshtri kshamah kshamah sameehanah

Yagya ijyo mahejyashch kratuh satram sataam gatih
Sarvadarshi vimuktatma sarvagyo gyanamuttamam

Suvratah sumukhah sukhshmah sugoshah sukhadah suhrit
Manoharo jitakrodho veerbahurvidaranah

Swapanah swavaso vyapi naikatma naikkarmakrit
Vatsaro vatsalo vatsi ratnagarbho dhaneshwarah

Dharmagubdharmakriddharmi sadsattksharamksharam
Avigyata shhastranshurvidhata krit lakshanah

Gabhastinemih satvasthah singho bhutmaheshwarah
Adidevi mahadevo devesho devabhridguruh

Uttaro gopatirgopta gyangamya puratanah
Sharirbhutbhridbhokta kapindro bhuri dkhshinah

Somapoamritapah somah prujit purushattamah
Veenayo jayo satyasandho dasharha satvatam patim

Jeevo vinayitasakhshi mukundoamitvikramah
Ambhinidhiranantatma maho dadhishayaoantakah

Ajo maharhah swabhavyo jitamitrah pramodanah
Aanando nandano nanadah satyadharma trivikramah

Maharshi kapilacharyah kritagyo medinipatih
Tripadstridashadhyaksho mahashringah kritantakritah

Mahavaraho govindah sushenah kanakangadi
Guhyo gabhiro gahano guptaschakragadadharah

Vedhah swangoajitah krishno dridh sankarsanoachutah
Varuno vaaruno vrikshah pushkaraksho mahamana

Bhagwaan bhagahanandi vanmali halayudhah
Aadityo jyotiraadityah sahishnurgatisattamah

Sudhanava khandparshudaruno dravidpradah
Divispriksarvadrigvyaso vachaspatiryonijah

Trisama saamagah saam nirvaanam bheshajam bhishak
Sanyaaskrichhhamah shanto nishtha shanti parayanam

Subhangah shantidah shrashta kumudah kuvaleshayah
Gohito gopatirgopta vrishabhaksho vishapriyah

Anivarti nivrittatma sankshepta kshemakrichhhivah
Shreevatsavakshah shreevaasah shreepatih
Shreematamvarah

Shreedah shreeshah shreeniwasah shreenidhih
Shreevibhavanah
Shreedharah shreekarah shreyah
Shreemaanlokatrayashrayah

Swakshah swangah shatanando nandijyotirganeshwarah
Vijitatma vidheyatma satkirtichhhinnashanshayah

Udirnah sarvataschakshurnishah shaswatsthirah
Bhushayo bhushano bhutirvishokah shokanaashanah

Archishmaanarchito kumbho vishuddhatma
Vishodhanah
Anirudhhoapratirathah pradyumnoamitvikramah

Kaalneminiha veerah shauri shurjaneshwarah
Trilokatma trilokesha kesawah keshiha harih

Kaamdev kaampaal kanti kantah kritagamah
Anirdeshyavapurvishnurveeroananto dhananjayah

Brahmanyo brahmakridbrahma brahma
Brahmavivardhanah
Brahmavidbrahmano brahmi brahmagyo
Brahmanahpriyah

Mahakramo mahakarma mahateja mahoragah
Mahakraturmahayajwa mahayagyo mahahavih

Stavyah stavyapriyah stotram stuti stota ranapriyah
Purnah purayita punayah punyakirtiranamayah

Manojavasteerthkaro vasureta vasupradah
Vasuprado vasudevo vasurvasumna havih

Sadgatih satkriti satta sadbhuti satparayanah
Surseno yadushreshtha sannivasah suyamunah
Bhutavaso Vasudevah sarvasunilayoanalah
Darpaha darpado dripto durdharoathaparajitah

Vishwamurti maha murtirdiptamurtirmurtimaan
Anekmurtiravyaktah shatamurtih shatananah

Eko naikah savah kah kim yatatpadmanuttamam
Lokabandhurloknatho maadhavo bhaktvattsalah

Suvarnavarno hemango varangaschangangadi
Veeraha vishamah shunyo dhritashirchalaschalah

Amani manado manyo lokaswami trilokdhrik
Sumedha medhajo dhanyah satyamedha dharadharah

Tejovrisho dyutidharah sarvashashtrabhritamvarah
Pragraho nigraho vyagro naikashringo gadagrajah

Chaturmurtischachaturbahuschachaturvyuhachaturgatih
Chaturatma chaturbhavaschaturvedavidekpaat

Samavarto anivritatma durjayo duratikramah
Durlabho durgamo durgo duravaso durariha

Shubhango lokasarangah sutantutantuvardhanah
Indrakarma mahakarma kritkarma kritagamah

Udbhavah sundarah sundo ratnanabhah sulochanah
Arko vajsanah shringi jayantah sarvavijjayi

Suvarnabindurchhobhya sarvabagishwareshawarah
Mahahrido mahagarto mahabhuto mahanidhih

Kumudah kundarah kundah parjanyah paavanoanilah
Amritansho amritvapuh sarvagyah sarvatomukhah

Sulabhah suvratah siddhah shatrujit shatrutapanah
Nyagrodhodumbaroashwasthachandhranishudanah

Shahastrarchi saptazihwah saptaindha saptwahanah
Amurtiranaghoachintyo bhayakrit bhayanashanah

Arunbrihatkrishah sthulo gunbhrinnaguno mahan
Adhritah swadhritah swasyah pragvansho vansh
Vardhanah

Bharbhrit kahito yogi yogishah sarvakaamdah
Aashramah kshamadah kshaamah suparno
Vayuvahanah

Dhanurdharo hanurvedo dando damayita damah
Aprajitah sarvasaho niyanta niyamo yamah

Sarvavan satvikah satvo satvadharma parayanah
Abhipraya priyarhorha priyakrit preetivardhanah

Vihayasagatijyotir suruchirhutbhugvibhuh
Ravirvilochanah suryah savita ravilochanah

Ananto hutbhugbhokta sukhdo nikajograjah
Anirvinnna sadamarshi lokadhishthanamadbhutah

Sanatsnatamah kapilah kapirapyahah
Swastidah swastikridswasti swastibhugswastidakhshinah

Araudrah kundali chakri vikramyurjitshashanah
Sabdatigah sabdasaha shishirah sarwarikarah
Akrurah peshalo dakhsho dakshinah kshminamvarah
Vidwatamo veetbhayah punyasravankeertanah

Uttarano dushkritiha punyo dukhswapna nashanah
Veeraha rakhsanah santo jeevanah paryavasthito

Anantrupo anantsheerjitmanyurbhayapah
Chatustro gambhiratma vidisho vyadishodishah

Anadirbhurbhuvolaxmi suviro ruchirangadah
Janano janmadirbhimo bhimaparakramah

Aadhar nilayo dhata pushpahaasah prajagarah
Urdhavgah satpathacharo prandah panavah pranah

Pramanam pranneelayah pranbhrit pranjeevanh
Tatvam tatwaviidekatma janmamriturjaratigah

Bhurbhuvah swastarustarah savita prapitamah
Yoagyo yagyapatiryajva yagyangoyagyavahanah

Yagyakridyagyabhridyagyi yagyabhugyagyasaadhanah
Yagyantkritagyaghuhyamannamannad ev cha

Aatmayonih swyamjaato vaikhanah saamgaayanah
Devakinandanah shrashta kshitishah paapnaashanah

Shankhbrinnanandki chakri sarangdhanwa gadadharah
Rathangpanirchhhobhyah sarvaprahanayudhah

Sarvpraharnayudhah om namah iti
Itidam keertaniyasya keshwasya mahatmanah
Namnaam shahastrena divyanamsheshena prakirtitam

Ya idam shinuyanityam yaschapi parikirtiyet
Naashubham prapnuyaatkinchitsoamutreh cha manavah

Vedantago brahmanah syatkshatriyo vijayi bhavet
Vaishyo dhan samridhhah syashchhudrah
Sukhamvapnuyaat

Darmarthi prapnuyaddharmamartharthi charthmapnuyaat
Kaamanvaapnuyaatkaami prajaarthi prapnuyatprajaam

Bhaktimaanyah sadotthaya shuchistadgatmaanasah
Shahastram vasudevasya naamnamekaprakirtyet

Yashah prapnoti vipulam gyati pradhanyameva cha
Achalam shreeyamapnoti shreyah prapnotyanuttamam

Na bhaam kwatchidapnoti veeryam tejascha vindati
Bhavatyarogo dyutimaanbalroop gunanvitah

Rogarto muchayate rogadbadhho muchyet bandhanaat
Bhayaanmuchyet bhitastu muchyetaappanna aapdah

Durganyatitaratyashu purushah purushhotaamam
Stuvannamshahastrena nitayam bhaktisamanvitah

Vasudevashrayo maryo vasudevaparayanah
Sarvapaap vishhudhhatma yati brahma sanatam

Na vasudev bhaktanaam ashubham vidyate kwachit
Janmamrityu zaravyadhi bhayam saivopajayate

Imam stavamadhiyanah shraddha bhakti samanvitah
Yujyetaatmasukhkshanti shree dhritismritikirtibhih

Na krodho na cha martasyam na lobho na shubha matih
Bhavanti kritpunyanaam bhaktanaam purushhottame

Dyau sa chandrarkanakshtra kham disho bhurmaho dadhih
Vasudevasya veeryena vidhritani mahatmanah

Sasurasurgandharvam sayakshogaraksham
Jagadwashe wartatedam krishnasya sacharacharam

Indriyani manobudhhih satvam tejo balam dhritih
Vasudevatmakanyahu kshetram kshetragya eva cha

Sarvagamanamacharah prathamam parikalpate
Aacharprabhavo dharmo dharmasya prabhurachyutah

Rishayah pitaro deva mahabhtani dhatavah
Jangamajangamam chedam jagadnarayanodbhavam

Yogo gyanam tatha sankhyam vidyah shilpadi karma cha
Vedah shashtrani vigyanmetatsarvam janardanaat

Eko Vishnurmahadbhutam prithagbhutanyanekashah
Trilokaanyavyapyabhutatmabhungatevishwabhugavyayah

Imam stavam bhagwato vishnovyarsen kirtitam
Pathedya ichheta purushah shreyah praptum sukhani cha

Vishweshwarmajam devam jagatah prabhavapyayam
Bhajanti ye pushkaraksham na tey yanti parabhavam

Om tatsaditi shreemahabharate shatshahastryam
Sanhitayam vaiyasikyamaanushasanike
Parvani bhishma yudhhishthir sanvaade
Shree Vishnordivyashahastranaamstotram

Hari Om Tat Sat Hari Om Tat Sat
Hari Om Tat Sat Hari Om Tat Sat

~~~
~~~

SHANTI PAATH

Brahmaarpanam Brahma Havir

**Brahmaarpanam Brahma Havir
Brahmaagnau Brahmanaa Hutam
Brahmaiva Tena Gantavyam
Brahma Karma Samaadhinaa**

**Aham Vaishvaanaro Bhutvaa
Praanimaam Dehamaashritah
Praanaapaanasamaa Yuktah
Pacaamyannam Caturvidham**

~~~

Kayena Vacha

**Kayena Vacha Mana-Sendriyair Va
Budhyaatmana Va Prakruteh Swabhavath
Karoami Yadyad Sakalam Parasmai
Narayana Yeti Samarpayami**

~~~

Shanta Karam

**Shanta Karam Bhujaga Shayanam,
Padmanabham Suresham.
Vishvadharam Gagana Sadrusham,
Megha Varnam Shubhangam.
Lakshmi Kantam Kamala Nayanam,
Yogibhir Dhyana Gamyam.
Vande Vishnum Bhava Bhaya Haram,
Sarva Lokaia Kanatham.**

~~~
~~~

Mangalam Bhagvaan

Mangalam Bhagvaan Vishnu
Mangalam Garudadhwajah
Mangalam Pundarikakshah
Mangalayatano Harih
Sarvamangala Maangalye
Shive Sarvaarth Saadhike
Sharnye Tryambake Gauri
Naaraayni Namostute

~~~

Om Dyauh Shanti

Om Dyauh Shaantir, Antarikshagung Shaantih
Prthivii Shaantir, Aapah Shaantir
Oshadhayah Shaantih, Vanaspatayah Shaantir
Vishve Devaah Shaantir, Brahma Shaantih
Sarvagung Shaantih, Shaantireva Shaantih Saa Maa, Shaantir-Edhi
Om Shaantih Shaantih Shaantih

Om, May there be Peace in Heaven, May there be Peace in the Sky
May there be Peace in the Earth, May there be Peace in the Water May there be Peace in the Plants
May there be Peace in the Trees, May there be Peace in the Gods
May there be peace in the various Worlds
May there be Peace in Brahman
May there be Peace in All, May there be Peace Indeed within Peace, Giving Me the Peace which Grows within Me
Om, Peace, Peace, Peace.

OM SHANTI OM SHANTI OM SHANTI

~~~